Transitioning to Internal Family Systems Therapy

Transitioning to Internal Family Systems Therapy is a guide to resolving the common areas of confusion and stuckness that professionals often experience when facilitating the transformational potential of the IFS model. Real-life clinical and autobiographical material is used throughout from the author's supervision practice, together with insights from IFS developer Richard C. Schwartz and other lead trainers and professionals. With the use of reflective and practical exercises, therapists and practitioners (those without a foundational therapy training) are encouraged to get to know and attend to their own inner family of parts, especially those who may be struggling to embrace the new modality. Reflective statements by professionals on their own journeys of transition feature as a unique element of the book. Endnotes provide the reader with additional information and direct them to key sources of information on IFS.

Emma E. Redfern is a certified IFS therapist, approved IFS clinical supervisor/consultant, and an experienced IFS Institute program assistant. Working online in private practice in the southwest of England, she is a senior BACP-accredited psychotherapist and supervisor. Emma has experience offering workshops (including on IFS and supervision) and has had several articles published in professional journals. She is the editor of *Internal Family Systems Therapy: Supervision and Consultation*, also published by Routledge.

"IFS is a radically different paradigm from most other psychotherapies. So many new IFS therapists struggle to fully understand the new concepts and fully embrace the new techniques. Emma Redfern is an accomplished IFS therapist who has years of experience helping therapists make this transition. In this book, she has distilled the lessons from that experience into practical tips and exercises. She has also borrowed IFS wisdom from me and many IFS trainers and offers all of this in a very readable and relatable package. If you're struggling at all with becoming an IFS therapist, this book is for you."

Richard Schwartz, PhD, *creator of internal family systems therapy*

"This is a book for all. Emma's inclusive style brings a deeper understanding of IFS to practitioners from a non-counselling background. She guides the reader to a deeper understanding of the methodology, making IFS accessible and real. She answers the 'why' so that you can adapt and take IFS to your own organisations and communities. It's like learning to play music by ear when you have previously only played off the script."

Helen Telford, *certified IFS practitioner and leading independent management consultant working across Australia and New Zealand*

"*Transitioning to Internal Family Systems Therapy* is a welcome addition to the IFS literature, filling a void for therapists and practitioners making this sometimes challenging transition. With refreshing clarity, Redfern demystifies common and predictable dilemmas and potential barriers that those transitioning to IFS will encounter. Practical exercises complement each chapter's text. The reader is encouraged to remember they are training in a new modality from a position of competence and ability, and Redfern reassures that with study and practice, the gaps in knowledge and skill will begin to fill in. Encouragement to embrace IFS practice by experiencing it not only as a provider but also as a client is especially poignant. There are many examples from Redfern's own practice that help to normalize the challenges of this type of transition and offer ongoing compassion to parts of the therapist and practitioner who may get polarized during their journey. This book will be a very compelling companion and an invaluable resource to be returned to many times."

Ann E. Drouilhet, LMFT, LICSW, *AAMFT-approved supervisor and certified IFS therapist and co-lead trainer for IFIO*

Transitioning to Internal Family Systems Therapy

A Companion for Therapists and Practitioners

Emma E. Redfern

Routledge
Taylor & Francis Group

NEW YORK AND LONDON

Designed cover image: © Kathy Nettles Art, Devon, UK

First published 2023
by Routledge
605 Third Avenue, New York, NY 10158

and by Routledge
4 Park Square, Milton Park, Abingdon, Oxon, OX14 4RN

Routledge is an imprint of the Taylor & Francis Group, an informa business

ISBN: 9781032153100 (hbk)
ISBN: 9781032153094 (pbk)
ISBN: 9781003243571 (ebk)

DOI: 10.4324/9781003243571

Typeset in Goudy
by Newgen Publishing UK

Access the Support Material: http://www.routledge.com/9781032153094

Permission Statements

Abbreviations

AAMFT	American Association for Marriage and Family Therapy
BACP	British Association for Counselling and Psychotherapy
BFOI	Bigotry From the Outside In
BIPOC	Black and Indigenous People of Colour
CBT	Cognitive Behavioural Therapy
CSTD	Centre for Supervision and Team Development
DBT	Dialectical Behavioural Therapy
DDP	Dyadic Developmental Psychotherapy
EMDR	Eye Movement Desensitisation and Reprocessing
HCPC	Health and Care Professions Council
IFIO	Intimacy From the Inside Out
IFS	Internal Family Systems
IFSI	IFS Institute
NLP	Neuro-Linguistic Programming
PA	Program Assistant
PCT	Person-Centred Therapy
PTSD	Post-Traumatic Stress Disorder
SSRI	Selective Serotonin Reuptake Inhibitor
TRP	Therapeutic Reconsolidation Process
UCLA	University of California, Los Angeles
UK	United Kingdom

Contents

Support Materials, Exercises, Figures and Tables

Support materials

Introduction eResource: Recognising your current professional self

Chapter 7 eResource: Values

Chapter 11 eResource: Tips for transitioning from graduate to IFS Institute program assistant from Louise O'Mahony

Exercises

Chapter 10

Figures

Tables

Foreword

Last night, as I drove home with my 15-year-old daughter, she asked me what my plans were for this weekend. I told her I would be writing a foreword for a new IFS book. Having read mostly fictional works, and being familiar with prologues, which often involve an account of characters' lives prior to the events of the novel, she asked, "What are you going to write about? Life before IFS?" Reflecting for a moment on the content and purpose of *Transitioning to Internal Family Systems Therapy*, I replied, "Thank you! That's exactly what I'm going to do."

I've been a therapist for as long as I can remember; long before my formal academic training gave me the credibility to charge money for my services. I saw my first "official" therapy client in April of 1999 at the UCLA (University of California, Los Angeles) Psychology Clinic, where I was a first-year doctoral student. My first day on the job was a "baptism by fire," as my client, a high-powered man more than twice my age, walked into our first session moments after having received a serious medical diagnosis. What little formal training I had received flew out the window as I intuitively sensed that the only thing I could (and maybe should) do in that moment was to hold a compassionate space for this man so that he would not be alone in the first few moments of being "in the after" of this terrifying diagnosis. When my client left and I entered the adjacent viewing room, where my supervisor and fellow first-year students (none of whom had yet had their first sessions) were waiting for me, I was greeted with praise for how well I had "done." But, as far as I knew, I hadn't "done" anything.

This session marked the first of thousands in my "pre-IFS" therapy career. Like most mental health professionals, I was exposed to several theoretical orientations and treatment approaches during my formal training years and beyond. I worked in the university counseling centers and psychology clinics at UCLA and Emory University, my undergraduate alma mater, and in 2004

I opened my private practice. I truly enjoyed my work, and my clients seemed to appreciate our time together. However, no matter how much I learned and which approaches I used, I could never escape the nagging feeling that the only consistently valuable element of treatment that I was providing for my clients was exactly what I had offered to my very first client, which was, as I said to so many supervisors with a healthy dose of frustration and despair, "that I'm a really nice person."

As the years went on, my clientele shifted from being predominantly composed of what one of my supervisors called, "the worried well" to involving a much greater proportion of clients who had severe trauma histories and extensive symptom profiles. In 2010, when it became abundantly clear to me that two of my clients would undeniably qualify for a diagnosis of Dissociative Identity Disorder, a part of me let me know, in no uncertain terms, that I had to find a way to work more safely and effectively with these clients' systems. In April of 2011, approximately 12 years to the day that I had my first session, I traveled to the International Trauma Conference in Boston in search of a way to better serve my most traumatized clients. It was there that I spent a life-changing six hours in an introductory IFS workshop with Dick Schwartz, the founder of IFS. I have never looked back.

It would take a full-length book for me to fully describe what IFS has given me – both personally and professionally. To sum it up in a sentence, I know I would not be the therapist I am, the wife I am, the parent I am, nor the teacher I am, without this model. And this is not because IFS infused qualities into me that I lacked, nor made me into someone I am not, but because it helped release the constraints to me being more fully who I am, which includes being "a really nice person." But I no longer say this phrase with despair, because IFS has helped me understand that what I previously understood as "just" being "nice" actually reflected my ability to consistently hold Self-energy for my clients, no matter how they presented and what challenges they faced. It now makes sense to me why my compassionate presence often had proven to be the most valuable element of the treatment I offered, regardless of which techniques I used or which theoretical framework guided my interventions – because my ability to hold Self-energy facilitated my clients accessing their own Self-energy, which we understand in IFS to be the agent of healing. IFS also provided me with a safe and effective method for engaging with the wounded and burdened parts of my clients' internal systems to move them towards healing and wholeness.

To date, as an IFS speaker, educator, and IFSI-approved clinical consultant, I have introduced the IFS model to thousands of clinicians and practitioners across the United States, Canada, and Europe. As my workshops are often their first exposure to the model, I have received hundreds of questions about how to transition to using IFS from other therapy models and how to become a more competent IFS professional. I am very pleased to say that Emma Redfern's book provides substantial insight and guidance on these issues. It also offers numerous opportunities for reflection, self-exploration, and personal and professional growth for aspiring IFS therapists/practitioners and supervisors.

In this book, the author offers therapists and practitioners who wish to unleash the transformative power of IFS in service of their clients and supervisees a guide to the transition process. Emma includes a wealth of information and exercises designed to help the reader become aware of and work with common barriers to transitioning to IFS. I appreciate the book's focus on these widely experienced barriers, which include factors such as not "buying in" to Self or to the IFS model, not fully understanding key IFS concepts and practices, fear, loss, and frustration, and professional isolation and loneliness, as I routinely encounter each of these in work with my consultees. Detailed information on important aspects of the IFS process that often confuse newer IFS therapists, such as contracting, direct access, and working with Self-like parts are given ample attention. In authentic IFS fashion, readers are repeatedly guided to turn inwards to make the "U-turn" that allows us to look within and notice parts of us that need or want attention, consideration, and healing, such that they can relax back and open space for that all-important Self-energy to flow and support the effectiveness of any formal intervention we attempt.

As the IFS model spreads throughout the world, offering the possibility of healing and transformation to the wounded and burdened parts of us all, I believe that this book is a resource that may make it easier for therapists and practitioners to transition not just to competently incorporating the perspective and techniques of this model, but also to increasingly embodying Self. *Transitioning to Internal Family Systems Therapy* is a valuable contribution to the field.

Alexia D. Rothman, PhD, May 2022

Preface

Introducing the book's context and my credentials

This book arises out of my own transitioning, from becoming an IFS therapist, then a certified IFS therapist and now an approved IFS clinical consultant. I began the book during the summer of 2020 amid the global pandemic and submitted the book proposal to the publisher in the late spring of 2021 when the world was still coming out of the worst of the crisis. During this time, I experienced a heightened awareness of my human frailty and sense of "If not now, when?" Within the book's pages are real-life accounts of my work with supervisees – most of whom are white, privileged, and European. This work involves vulnerability, intimacy, connection, and challenge. In capturing the accounts, requesting permission, and dialoguing about their use, I have felt joined in serving the wider IFS community. By supervising therapists and practitioners, I help them experience and become fluent in a new modality. I also attend to helping them (especially those from a non-therapy back-ground) fill in gaps in their knowledge and experiences (for example, around boundaries and contracting or assessing therapist–client fit).

The timing for this book also seems right as training in IFS expands beyond the IFS Institute's own teachings, with PESI and other mental health training organisations trying to meet an increased demand for courses in this transformative modality. The Institute is more openly facing up to the transitioning it wants and needs to do to become a more culturally diverse, equitable and inclusive community.

Successful transitioning involves more than completing IFSI training

Although it may seem obvious, I'll state it anyway: more is needed to truly become skilled as an IFS therapist and practitioner (or professional user of IFS in some other context, pastorally or in education perhaps) than attending a Level 1 training or doing the Online Circle. I sense this is partly why IFSI, as the IFS Institute is known, currently offers multiple Level 2 trainings and a Level 3 training, as well as a certification process. Also, this is where supervisors like me come in. We find ourselves working with those who are early in their IFS journey who come with their questions about the model, with their stuckness and struggles with themselves and their clients. Together, we face the tricky and challenging task of their transitioning. Tricky and challenging, because it may well include an element of deconstruction and reconstruction of their professional and personal identities/systems. Such transitioning includes both embracing and welcoming new ideas and practices as well as questioning and even letting go of often dearly held beliefs and approaches. It involves Self-to-part relationships, inner negotiation, and inner and outer collaboration and teamwork.

In addition, however good any entry-level training is, it cannot cover all that it needs to (particularly for those who have not already attended a therapy training of some kind and want to work therapeutically and ethically as happens in the UK and Europe if not in the US where strict state-based licensing is legally binding). Nor can entry-level training provide enough practical experience of the various aspects of IFS so that all graduates of Level 1 feel competent and confident when working with clients or when using IFS in their chosen field. As I will explain in the book, supervision is crucial in successfully transitioning and, although some of the IFS trainers provide consultation groups, most are already stretched to capacity. American charging also provides barriers for UK and European consultees to have regular, individual attention from IFS trainers, who are predominantly American.

Transition reflection

"I am reminded of André Gide's words that sailors who wish to discover new lands must be willing to lose sight of the shore." (LA)

Also, with only a handful of us in the UK currently endorsed to offer consultation for IFS certification, there are many going without the support they might want. My hope is that this book will go some way towards filling gaps in provision for graduates of Level 1 and for those who are using IFS from their own reading or from non-IFSI trainings. It also contains much to inspire, challenge and inform those who are interested in transitioning to becoming IFS supervisors.

April 2022

Acknowledgments

I wish to acknowledge and appreciate the founder of IFS, Richard C. Schwartz, and the other IFS trainers whose live trainings I have attended whether as student or PA (in alphabetical order): Frank Anderson, Osnat Arbel, Chris Burris, Barb Cargill, Mike Elkin, Paul Ginter, Susan McConnell and Cece Sykes.

Appreciation and thanks to all clients, supervisees and colleagues who have contributed in various ways to this book (in alphabetical order): Lisa Alton, Brian McMillan, Melanie Blaymires, Sarah Burns, Ellen Bush, Carol Cullen, Rosa Chillari, Elisa Dari, Sandra Hailes, Graeme Jardin, Royston Kershaw, Paul Khosla, Louise O'Mahony, Nina Mohammed, Sarah Murphy, Elise Parsons, Alessio Rizzo, Jo Schroeder, Vicki Simpson-Price, Sue Smith, Beata Szweryn, Helen Telford, Sarah Tomley, Romy Wakil and Gayle Williamson. Thanks also to Debra Hayden and Andrew Forrester for their long-term, non-IFS and valuable supervisory support.

Finally, I extend gratitude to Anna Moore, Priya Sharma and Lauren Ellis of Routledge; to highly experienced and skilled IFS psychotherapist and writer Gayle Williamson, without whose informed and expert editing this book would be all the poorer; to copyeditor Jacqueline Dias for her patience and commitment to clarity; and to Emma Steele of Emphasis Creative, Devon, who designed the figures. Thanks, also, to Kathy Nettles for use of her striking original artwork which appears, adapted slightly, on the front cover.

Introduction

Is this book for you?

Perhaps you have recently completed an IFS Level 1 training with the IFS institute (IFSI) or some online training with PESI or Life Architect, for example. You might be a trained therapist or IFS might be your first training in a psychotherapy modality and you are keen to transition to using IFS well and fully in a coaching practice, educational or management setting.

Do you find yourself with unanswered questions about Self? Are you lacking confidence in how to position yourself professionally? Perhaps, as a practitioner in the UK, you feel unsure about what supervision is and how to use it or what might be on offer. Do you feel parts of you are getting in your own way of using this transformational modality in your life and your work? Perhaps, as a supervisor who has trained in IFS, you are curious about what being an IFS supervisor might be like for you.

This book seeks to help address such concerns, and more.

Aims of this book

This book will help you:

- increase access to your Self-energy;
- aid your conscious transitioning;
- address potential barriers to committing to learning IFS well; and
- increase your conscious competence in IFS in whatever ways you offer it.

DOI: 10.4324/9781003243571-1

Increased Self-Energy

A goal of any IFS practice (therapy and supervision, as well as just living it) is increased Self-energy and Self-leadership. One of the book's goals is to help you to be able to face whatever comes your way in your practice as a practitioner, coach, therapist, supervisor, entrepreneur, etc., knowing that your Self-who-has-no-fear, only calm, clarity, confidence, courage and so on, is in the lead. However, for learner parts, worried parts, parts that want answers to help them relax a little and feel less scared or anxious in the face of new clients and new professional experiences, I am offering:

- clinical examples;
- my own take on standard IFS information, which may help you grasp something if you haven't already; and
- signposting to other key sources of information about IFS and the topics covered in this book.

Hopefully you will not only engage with the material but spend time in Self-to-part relationship with your parts so that you may come to collaborate with them and lead them as you embrace life after initial IFS training.

Conscious transitioning

As part of consciously and actively transitioning, you will be facing paradoxes. One such paradox is that IFS therapists and practitioners need to be taught IFS and how to help clients "do IFS" alongside knowing that we, and people in general, already have all that's needed within to lead and heal: Self. Conscious transitioning involves coming to terms with the different "knowings" in a room:

- your knowledge of IFS (and knowledge from prior trainings that may be compatible with IFS) that you, the IFS professional, hold;
- your client's self-knowledge, expertise, and experience;
- parts with valuable information in the moment – your parts and the parts of the person or people with whom you are interacting;
- The internalisations of our trainers (*I can remember Dick saying …*) and supervisors;
- Self's clarity and perspective (your Self and the Self of whoever you are with); and
- knowledge and experience from your family of origin, lineage, people (some in the nature of heirlooms; some in the form of legacy burdens).

Another related challenge of consciously moving to using "a protocol-style therapy" such as IFS is to explore for yourself the challenge of valuing both therapeutic spontaneity (following what the client brings) and technique (having the client follow your lead). Yalom (2001) believes "technique" facilitates when it emerges from the therapist's unique encounter with every patient or client. For therapists with parts who, for example, value a person-centred or meditative approach, then making the decision to use the 6 Fs and taking ownership of the IFS steps of healing – the "technique" as Yalom calls it – might prove challenging in various ways. Discovering how to be relational while also following a protocol *is* challenging. One of the important transitions made by the IFS founder was in his re-evaluation of the nature and significance of the therapeutic relationship in IFS (Schwartz, 2013).

Removing barriers to transitioning

The third aim for the book is in line with the nature of IFS therapy as a *constraint-releasing approach*. This concept goes hand-in-hand with a basic premise of IFS that people can heal and that this healing comes from within, in relationship to Self. Thus, IFS clinicians do not feel the need to resource clients and "add to" or teach them in ways that non-IFS clinicians may do. Instead, in IFS the idea is to remove what gets in the way of health, to ask parts not to block access to Self and so on.

Increasing conscious competence

Fourthly, using this book is intended to increase conscious competence in IFS therapy, IFS supervision/consultation, or using IFS in your chosen non-therapy setting. If you let it, this book will come alongside you to encourage, support, comfort, and challenge. This is in line with IFS in which Self comes alongside our parts, our wounds in an empowering relationship in which parts are met and known, can heal, grow, and become their potential.

Why me?

As a successful and experienced therapist coming to IFS post-qualifying, I too have struggled to transition to a new modality, often feeling alone and frustrated. (If you are a practitioner wanting to transition to using IFS in some way, I am aware that you may feel even more isolated.) This book is written to help you feel less alone and deskilled.

Also, as a seasoned IFS professional offering IFS supervision/consultancy, I have had the privilege and pleasure of supporting many professionals making this transition. As I cannot be with each one of you, this book comes in my place and brings my personal and professional experience on this subject.

Outline of the book

The book is divided into four sections, each of which highlights one or more potential constraint or barrier you may be experiencing which is getting in the way of you successfully moving over to IFS. (Don't forget, these barriers are *not* insurmountable.) The first barrier is not "buying in" to the concept of Self and Self-leadership or to the IFS model. If you want to transition to fully using IFS, then buying into the concept and reality of Self within you and others is a must.

The second potential barrier is not grasping key IFS concepts and practices. This will get in the way as you learn, not least because it is discouraging to never quite get the results your parts are hoping for. Keep persisting. Perspective does come if you keep engaging with the model and your parts.

The third barrier I think of in terms of fear, loss, and frustration. Any process of change is likely to be scary, involve feeling deskilled, unsure as to whether you'll ever "get it" and feeling like who you are is shifting, no longer known, and unstable. Loss is also intrinsic to the process, and frustration is often a companion along the way.

The potential barrier inspiring Part IV is the loneliness that can occur when we move from one professional group or camp to another or when we don't feel we belong anywhere anymore. There might be the urge to go it alone, possibly out of fear of being shamed (having already been shamed in our early years) or through scarcity mentality, for example, "I can't afford an IFS supervisor" and, "The trainings are so booked up I'll just learn it from the book, that'll be fine" (both of which may have some truth for you and be real, practical constraints). In this fourth and last section, I include material encouraging readers to get personal support in supervision (whether group or individual) and to consider what sort of supervision would be a fit.

Engaging with the material

By reading this book, you will absorb new didactic material which will refresh your understanding of IFS, its concepts and practices. In 10 of the 11 chapters, you will read inspiring case material taken from my own practice, used with permission and disguised. I also précis some of what I have learned from studying with the IFS Continuity Program. All chapters apart from Chapter 11 include exercises at the end to help you reflect and find those "answers" within, and to hear from your parts and dialogue with them from Self. In addition, scattered throughout the book are "transition reflections" from others in the IFS community, like you who are in transition in their IFS practices. These are brief reflective statements on their experience of transitioning (used with permission). Your studious parts will find signposting in the Endnotes to key sources of information which are beyond the capacity of this book to feature.

The book begins with a chapter on Self to reflect the centrality of Self in the IFS model. However, I suggest you read the book in whatever order feels most relevant to you at the time. You might want to flick through and read the transition reflections or go straight to the exercises. Take the material at your own pace – for example, you might not be ready to go inside yet. And, if an exercise doesn't work for you, tweak it (the language of "client" may not fit your circumstances, for example) or shelf it to come back to another time.

Those who have already read the book have found benefit from different aspects of it, for example appreciating and learning from the chapter on contracting; another has found comfort in knowing she's not alone in her struggles; another is rising to the challenge and giving direct access a chance. See which sections or exercises work best for you.

As I cannot come alongside each of you in real-life, you might wish to imagine your supervisor, peer supervisor, favourite IFS figurehead, or trainer, etc., reading the instructions to the exercises and holding space for you to engage with them. Alternatively, complete the exercises with someone else and read them to each other; another option might be to record yourself reading the exercises, which you can then listen back to. The exercises are intended to help you get to know yourself and your own system (parts and Self) better.

The first exercise of the book appears online as an eResource, available at http://www.routledge.com/9781032153094. This takes you to the book's product page on the publisher's website.

Limitations to the book

Partial answers

You may notice my use of the active "transitioning" rather than the noun "transition" in the book's title. Although I and the professionals who appear in the book may have "arrived" in some senses, we are all still transitioning. In my 21-year psychotherapy (second) career, I have yet to "resolve" (and may never fully do so) the polarisation within me of parts – one of whom fully embraces the role of being "the one with the answers", and its counterpart who eschews the role of "expert". Yes, there are "answers" to be had from engaging with this book – some will be second-hand from IFS founder and maestro Richard Schwartz, and other IFS lead trainers; some answers will be mine and those of the supervisees whose real-life experiences are included. However, I trust that you will come to embrace your own answers and "awarenesses" as you engage with the material, complete the exercises, and reflect on your own learning, practising, and transitioning. I ask forbearance of parts who may be frustrated by my choice, at times, not to be the expert by providing only partial answers.

You will do much of the work

Although you will find examples of some of the transitioning challenges faced by therapists previously trained in CBT, DBT, EMDR, PCT, Family Systems, etc. if you are looking for a book of explicit step-by-step instructions for moving from one of these modalities to IFS then you will not find that here. The first reason for this is that I am not trained in each of these modalities – my core therapy training is Humanistic Integrative with additional grounding in Voice Dialogue, Art Therapy, Developmental Transformations (a form of Dramatherapy), and Group Analysis, together with full EMDR and Attachment-Focused EMDR trainings. These are some of the modalities about which I have direct experience and this book includes autobiographical material that provides examples of my professional journey pre- and post-IFS "conscious competence" (see Chapter 2). I trust that the book will be relevant to therapists with different core trainings and of interest to those who are IFS-trained and not therapists.

Looking towards the goal

Another reason I have not focused in on multiple individual modalities is because in my view one of the keys to transitioning successfully is to grasp in as much depth and clarity as possible the basics of the *new* model *on its own terms*. If you are translating IFS into CBT and trying to use it with your CBT clients, in my mind this is not making the move to IFS therapy. This book is intended primarily to help readers transition to IFS in their existing practice – either as their main therapist identity or as one of their offerings as a therapist. Although you may find much here of interest and benefit if you wish to become "an IFS-informed CBT practitioner", or "an EMDR therapist who works with parts" etc., there are other sources of material for the journey of integrating IFS into an existing practice. I believe that learning a new modality is best learnt "clean", "pure" or, as I think of it, "plain vanilla", before then tweaking it later (adding in the chocolate chips, chocolate sauce, etc.) if necessary. If you and your system think IFS is worth learning well and are willing to learn it "plain vanilla", then I have written this book for you.

Language triggers, and a spoiler alert

Although language is a wonderful tool, it also has its limitations. Every profession has its jargon and shorthand, and therapy is no different. I use terms that may be unhelpful or off-putting, such as "emotional/psychological pain", "transitioning" and writing about "triggering client parts". Please feel free to translate in your mind, and/or with your pencil such words. We all have parts that "trigger" others and I don't mean to be offensive or hurtful by including examples of specific client parts that novices may struggle with (Chapter 7). Also, I cannot know what will be upsetting in the case material shared so take care as you read. And, early in Chapter 7, I give away a key plot point regarding the early life of the *Hunger Games*' President Snow.

Private practice

Another potential limitation to bear in mind is that I am writing as a therapist working in private practice in the UK mostly with individuals. If you are employed as a therapist, you may not have the freedom to make full use of all that this book contains. Similarly, if you are a teacher, a priest or in business or education, for example, then much of what is written may not scratch where you itch.

Ethical practice

IFS Level 1 is not a stand-alone therapy training, and at the time of writing, non-therapists can take the training. My system welcomes the equity in this and values that IFS is a practice for life as much as a therapy for professional use. However, if this is the only therapy training you do, then there may be noticeable knowledge gaps between you and those for whom it is a post-graduate or post-qualification training. This book may go some way towards helping readers know what they don't know, but it, too, cannot cover everything. For example, it does not contain a detailed exploration of ethical aspects of the work, such as boundaries, dual relationships or self-disclosure by the therapist or practitioner. Much of this can be explored in supervision but that, too, will not make up for the knowledge and holding of a sound therapy training and professional body's expectations by way of an ethical code. This book does not replace IFS therapy, IFS supervision/consultation, and IFS training.

Glossary

I have not made room to include a glossary and refer the reader to any of the core IFS texts.

Bon voyage and welcome aboard

Back to you, the reader. Your parts and your system have achieved so much already. Please send them some appreciation from both of us. Yes, the way forward may be rocky, arduous, and discouraging at times and parts may already be in conflict at the prospect of transitioning to IFS. However, there will also be many transformative moments of calm, clarity, connectedness, and all that your therapist/practitioner and non-professional parts may be hoping for through learning, using and offering IFS. I wish for you a feeling of "coming home" to yourself and your Self as you continue exploring this lifechanging modality and how to use it.

Transition reflection

"As an IFS therapist, I'm like a small plant growing in its own time. I can't pull it and make it grow taller faster. I can notice when it sprouts new growth." (Sandra Hailes, psychotherapist in private practice, level 3 IFS)

To the part(s) who wants to improve as an IFS therapist/practitioner/parent/ teacher/coach/ supervisor/leader etc., my system salutes you. For any parts feeling stuck or overwhelmed, take it gently. I trust you will find some encouragement in these pages. To the parts with fear and confusion, please know that you are not alone and may you feel less alone by allowing yourself and your system to engage with this book. To the lovers of everything IFS, a part hopes you are not disappointed. To the bookworm parts, put on the kettle, break open the biscuits, dig in . . . whoever it is that brought you here, they and you are most welcome.

Part I
Barriers to transitioning
Not buying into Self,
Self-leadership and
the IFS model

1
Self-leadership is the gamechanger in IFS

Introducing the chapter

Buying into, experiencing and understanding the concept of Self and Self's healing and leading (Self-energy and Self-leadership) are the subjects of the whole book, but this chapter and Chapter 2 (Part I) are specifically written with this in mind.

The main foci of this chapter are:

- reflecting on Self and how to communicate about Self in your context(s);
- reminding you about the concept of Self-leadership (IFS is about parts *and* Self); and
- introducing the idea of parts as "consultants" to Self.

Exercises at the end help you reflect on your access to Self, your therapeutic relationships, and any existing IFS competencies.

What is Self?

I remember during my three IFS trainings being fascinated by the concept of Self, and I would take notes that I later typed up as a reminder for myself. In addition to the 8 C qualities of Self – which are, calm, clarity, compassion, confidence, connectedness, courage, creativity and curiosity – here are the initial notes I wrote about Self from my personal experience and from what the different trainers shared:

- In Self (i.e., when there is no fear present), nothing on the inside can harm you.
- Self is what is present when parts have unblended.

DOI: 10.4324/9781003243571-3

- Self is our birthright and everybody has Self.
- Self cannot be damaged or broken (regardless of how "broken" or "damaged" a person feels).
- Self can apologise and be sorry for bad stuff that happened to parts.
- Self has no need for anything to change. Though Self has a light agenda for healing, connection, and harmony, it isn't attached to them.
- Self contains logic, knowledge and reason and has access to the client's brain (clarity and perspective = qualities of Self).
- Self has OK-ness, non-damage, health, and goodness at the core.[1]
- Self is a resource that has no fear, no need and feels no separation from others and from the world.
- Self is available in full strength in everybody, including children, as it does not have to develop. (However, it does need a mature body and brain to manifest fully.)
- The larger Self is unlimited and limitless.
- Self is the ideal inner attachment figure.
- Parts *can* overwhelm Self (like clouds hide the sun) and/or push it out of the body.
- Parts – through no fault of their own – cannot bring healing and transformation as Self does.
- If, when you are working inside, you see yourself as Self, then you are seeing a part not Self (Self sees through your own eyes).
- Self is real (everything else is an illusion or distortion).

In her book, Susan McConnell writes of her personal somatic experience of Self (2020, p. 42), "I feel expansive, relaxed, and alert when I am in Self-energy; and contracted, tense, or cut off when a part is dominant." I imagine you may have experienced Self-energy in others; certainly, I have. In the summer of the first COVID-19 lockdown, I had a hospital appointment for a medical procedure. Like oil and water, hospitals and I don't mix well. I was simultaneously blended with a scared "rabbit caught in car headlights" part and a "let's look after the nurses" part as my veins rushed from the surface of my skin and hid. The first nurse was feeling the pressure of finding a vein, with only one of my arms able to be used for this purpose. She tried a couple of times without success as we joked and chatted, with me averting my gaze. Her colleague also failed at the task; but not to be deterred, there was an expert colleague to call in. I followed her with my gaze as she entered the room, silent and methodical as she sanitised, gloved up and came to sit next to me. Without chitchat, she introduced herself and inside me a voice responded: "This is the one, she'll get it first time." She did; my parts noticed the Self-energy she communicated in her movement, her energy, and in the steady grounding she possessed as she went about her work, and they relaxed.

Of course, non-IFS trainers, therapists and practitioners also access Self in their work and in daily life. I have been fortunate to have had some supervision training with Robin Shohet, a pioneer in the world of supervision. He leads workshops, one of which I attended during the redrafting of this chapter (Shohet, 2021), in which he spoke of parts and Self (using different words and perhaps without realising that it mapped easily onto IFS). He spoke of how a supervisor's biggest asset is themselves and what they bring to a session, including whether they are looking and listening from a critical or fearful ear or eye, or whether they are listening from a place of love – in IFS terms, being Self-led or leading with parts. In the day's discussion, he and participants expanded my understanding of Self's love, which is:

- Not fluffy or "nicey-nicey love";
- tough love;
- honest love;
- connecting love that sits and comes close; and
- love that listens and connects and doesn't fix or see from a problem viewpoint.

IFS therapy without Self is not IFS therapy

Grasping the concept of and experiencing Self, and your system allowing Self to lead, may not come easily. This isn't an instant or "one-and-done" achievement. It is worth persisting and persevering. For those who practise IFS therapy and call what they do IFS, the centrality of Self is non-negotiable. Mary Steege, certified IFS therapist and consultant and presenter on IFS and the Christian tradition, writes (2023, p. 142): "The universal availability of Self is an essential element of an IFS practice." Writing about IFS consultation, she says (2023, p. 145): ". . . at heart lies something that is, well, literally more at the heart: trust in the presence of Self. Trust in Self, both immanent and transcendent,[2] both in us and beyond us – Self, a spiritual presence by whatever name we know."

Since becoming a supervisor of novice IFS professionals, I have realised how important it is to provide an ongoing space for supervisees to grapple with and explore the nature of Self; how it feels to access Self in the moment; how it feels to let Self lead; and how to speak about this in their environments – as well as how not to if that is important. It is possible to come away from a

Level 1 training thinking of Self as a part and describing it as such. (Many trainees come to IFS from reading Janina Fisher (2017), which affects their understanding of Self. In my understanding, Fisher elevates her "going on with normal life" part to be the resource in and for the system, which is not IFS as I know and value it.) IFS therapists and practitioners sometimes confuse "the client's adult" with Self, and, to me, they are not the same. Using the word "adult" with clients can cause confusion as parts can also be, *or appear to be*, adult. In my experience, Self is ageless and can be sensed even in infants. Without evoking shame in either of us, I have learnt to explore with my supervisees: "Is that how you think of Self, as a part?" Or, to say, "No, Self is not a part. Self is altogether different." It is important to be able to have a discussion together about what Self is and how they have already experienced it; and if not, how they can open to experiencing it.

The age update

The IFS intervention of offering an age update to parts may be confusing for some beginners who think that "present-day adult" equates to "Self". Rather, the age update is a way to differentiate past and present. Using in-sight we might say "Ask the part how old it is?" and "How old does the part think you are?" Thus, the part can be made aware that it got stuck back in the difficult past, while time and personhood continued into the present and aged. The age update is also a way to differentiate between resources. The part (often in single digits) becomes aware that the person with whom they are connecting is "a grownup who can help and is available now, even though they weren't there in the past".

How the part responds to this new and updating information will help us determine who is meeting with the part (i.e., whether it is just an older part or Self). Responses like the following suggest the part has recognised the resourcing presence of Self: "I can feel the part's relief", "it's moving closer" and "I feel their head on my shoulder" or "I sense him leaning against my leg" and "he's getting much smaller". If, on the other hand, there is no response to the age update, check again with "How do you feel towards the part now?" and continue with creating a Self-to-part and part-to-Self connection in the here and now, across time.

Spiritual misunderstandings about the nature of Self

Fortunately, I have found it easy to accept cognitively and feel physically the existence of this Self-who-is-not-a-part. This is perhaps partly due to my religious background in which I was aware of and open to something "other" than myself; experiences early on in demos during trainings; noticing shifts after bodywork such as cranial osteopathy, for example. (By saying this, I am not suggesting that all my parts are healed, and all personally know Self. I am very much a work in progress and expect always to be so.)

Not everyone is as fortunate, and you or your clients may be struggling to access Self. As a supervisor, I have come across spiritual ideas about Self that if carried into your work, may get in the way of allowing Self-energy to flow and be present:

1) With a background in mindfulness and/or meditation, you may believe that the one who observes and gives distance to the difficult thoughts or feelings arising inside a person is Self. This is not the case. Hal and Sidra Stone (1989), the founders of Voice Dialogue, make it clear that "the Observer" is often a primary subpersonality or part, which has been my own experience. There is more warmth, connection and a "being" quality to Self than the "doing" quality of coolly observing from a distance (which is usually for safety, preservation or personal improvement).

2) Having previously been on or still on a Buddhist path seeking enlightenment, you may have a self-improvement part who is dismissive of other parts and pressures you to be permanently in Self, as if enlightenment were a journey to be arrived at once and for all. This can cause problems in that this manager may get triggered frequently or trigger a critical part whenever Self-energy is obscured. This part may not understand that Self-to-part relationship (i.e., dual awareness) and Self-leadership of the inner system is what IFS is all about as opposed to the dualistic notion of being *either* parts-led *or* Self-led, with the idea that the latter is a destination to arrive at. True IFS is Self *and* parts.

3) Religious Self-like parts may believe that Self is not enough. Prayerful and religious parts[3] may be used to seeking external help, healing, and redemption. Active members of organised religions may have parts who devoutly believe in the importance of a spiritual hierarchy which may play out on the inside. There may also be confusion for parts unable to work out where Self fits with the Trinity, and so on.

If you recognise yourself in any of the above or have awareness of parts in you who struggle to allow Self to be present and actively leading in your life and work, you may want to seek some support – either through supervision or from peers. Chapter 8, "Working with Self-Like Parts and Clients with 'No Self-Energy'" will also be useful.

Be aware that your own understanding and experience of Self and Self-leadership will grow through reflective practice and ongoing learning. It was a while before I grasped that:

- Self is relational.
- In Self there is safety and belonging

How to talk about Self

My prior experience explaining EMDR and embracing transparency to help co-create a sound working alliance (Clarkson, 2003) with clients helped pre-pare me to think about how explicit to be with each individual client. With some clients it is appropriate to share key IFS concepts, such as Self's healing, transformative presence and nature; and with other clients it is not. I have heard from some practitioners who believe they have been advised not to discuss the nature of Self with *any* clients. I presume this is to allow the client a potentially bias-free experience of Self and to manage any evangelising parts in the therapist. I am all for letting things unfold naturally while I also respect a manager's right to know something of what to expect.

So, getting the balance of not priming too much or too little can be tricky, and needs to be handled on a relationship-by-relationship basis. I am not instructing you to tell all clients about Self; I am asking you to use your own judgment on a case-by-case basis. Also, I will say that I do not stay silent about Self in the presence of a part who is controlling a client's system and thinks it *has to* because there is no help coming and no alternative.

It can also be helpful to remember that although I may think the other person and I understand something in the same way, that may not be the case. Yes, the client (or parts of the client) may be a trained IFS practitioner/therapist, but that does not mean I can take shortcuts in the steps of healing or presume the existence of knowledge across their whole system.

Transition reflection

"It's exciting and satisfying to say to a client (without feeling like I have to persuade them like I used to) 'IFS can help, there is a core Self inside of you.'" (Elise Parsons, trauma informed craniosacral and somatic IFS therapist)

Naturally, your words to describe Self to yourself and your clients will be your own and different to my choice of words. I tend to use the phrase "the You who is not a part" for Self. When doing direct access, I will often use the client's name and perhaps ask the part, "Do you know the Joanna who isn't a part?" or if the part is very young and I know the client well, I might as part of updating say something like: "Oh, it makes sense you have that concern, you think Sean is only four. Well, he grew up and there is a Big Sean who …". Other phrases include: "your core essence", and therapist and speaker Jenna Riemersma (2020), who specialises in bringing the transformation of IFS to people of faith, talks about "the imago dei" or image of God within. In whatever ways we conceive of and describe Self and parts (e.g., the sun behind the clouds; the conductor and the orchestra; the ideal driver for the inner psychic bus full of children; atman; buddha nature; what connects us to nature and the animal kingdom …), is a matter of choice, context, and ecological sensitivity.[4]

A certified IFS practitioner and a leading independent management consultant working across Australia and New Zealand, Helen Telford, presented at the 2021 IFS conference on bringing more Self-energy into the room and to our communities. Helen works with conflicted groups and organisations in the health sector to reach difficult decisions and resolve interpersonal problems, she doesn't use the term Self-energy at all. Instead, she will prime the group by sharing that: "We do our best work when we come from a place of …. curiosity, confidence, calmness, compassion, clarity, courage, connectedness and creativity [the 8 Cs of Self]."

She might then go round the room and ask each person "Which C can you bring to this meeting today?" In her business coaching practice, Helen tells me she offers the full IFS protocol to customers without needing to use the term "Self".

"Discovering" Self and parts

Richard Schwartz's professional transformation

In *Internal Family Systems Therapy* second edition (Schwartz & Sweezy, 2020, pp. 3–24) Schwartz lays out his journey towards the creation of IFS, and his discovery of the ubiquitous, healing Self. This journey began when he was a 20-something aide on a psychiatric ward connecting with young kids/adults. These patients had been let down by the psychiatric services who had made them "the identified patient" without taking into consideration their home environments and past experiences of, say, abuse. This experience influenced him in becoming a family therapist so that he could intervene at a level beyond the individual and alter the family's patterns of behaviour to bring about "cure". As a family therapist, he held a powerful and interventionist role in which he and his colleagues (including those behind the one-way mirror) "played God" in the families' lives. As Schwartz explains, doing family therapy in this way did not work out either for him or his bulimic clients (Schwartz, 2021, pp. 14–17).

Instead, he turned to the clients themselves to teach him what they needed him to know – that an inner system of parts is normal, that parts are not what they seem to be, they are not their burdens and there are no bad parts (Schwartz, 2021, pp. 18-21). In their work together, Schwartz discovered that there was someone else inside, beyond, or other than, the parts. This other that he came to call Self could respond to parts with curiosity, compassion and kindness. Such was Schwartz's excitement at the discovery of this attachment figure inside his clients, that, at first, he over-reacted and downplayed the importance of the therapeutic relationship with his clients. Later, he realised it isn't a question of either/or, but both (Schwartz & Sweezy, 2020, p. 22 and p. 20):

> The primary role of the therapist is to guide, coach, and be a companion to the client's Self as he explores the mindscape. Secondarily, the therapist provides corrective relational experiences. As clients continue to notice and be with their parts, between as well as in sessions, they come to appreciate that they are healing themselves.

> … my relationship with clients is terribly important to our success, in part because it gives them a new relational experience of acceptance and compassion, but also because my ability to be in Self helps their protective parts relax so their Selves can flow in. Then they can give their parts a new experience that is parallel to the one they were having with me.

At the time of writing, I believe this is his current position. As a therapist, Schwartz's behaviours, identity, therapist role and beliefs about how healing occurs have transformed over time. You might consider what aspects of your own professional identity have changed and might need to change. What do you need to jettison? What can you retain as compatible with IFS? How do you now see yourself compared to who you were and who you are moving to become?

There is a reflective exercise at the end of the chapter to help you explore your underlying assumptions taken on during previous therapy or professional trainings. This builds on the exercise mentioned in the Introduction (p. 5).

Richard Schwartz's personal transformation

As well as deconstructing and reconstructing his professional identity and functioning, Schwartz also writes about his personal transformation(s). He shares in trainings, interviews, and his publications how he changed from relating to himself as singular to realising that he, too, like the clients he found challenging, had many parts inside of him. Also, in *No Bad Parts* (2021), he speaks about his spiritual awakening, moving from doing Transcendental Meditation driven by parts helping him to escape his life, to letting go of his anti-religion legacy burden and embracing the concept and experience (for himself) of Self – the same Self revealed by his clients, and recognised by his students.

Parts as consultants to Self

As someone transitioning to using IFS in your practice, you will have experience in asking client's parts to step back, give space, or separate, for Self to be present. You may regularly help your own parts to do the same. Something you may not have come across is that our parts' reactions to things and people can include valuable information; parts can act as "consultants" to our system. For example, at the start of a new therapeutic relationship, I felt parts becoming activated even before the client had finished arriving. Just their arranging of themselves, and their belongings in and around their seat had landed in my system in a noticeable way. I got curious inside myself. Was a part (or were parts) reacting because they were confusing the present person with someone from my past or my outside life? Or was the reaction indicating someone or something in the client's system that was worth noticing? Or was it both? Whichever it is, the activation provides valuable and relevant information:

> *My part:* "They are going to judge us. I don't feel comfortable."
>
> *Self to part:* "OK, I hear you. Judgmental client parts are entitled to be here, and likely to be here, especially while we first meet and get to know each other. Will you let me be curious?"
>
> *My part:* "Hmm, I'll move the other side of you away from them and watch."
>
> *Self to part:* "That's great. I am aware we're often sensitive to judgment so let me be curious about where this is coming from. …. Hmm, thank you, well spotted, I can sense something that might be judgment there underneath the client's amenable surface. … I'm going to welcome such parts of the client in my head and let them know we've sensed them. … I'll also protect you if needs be."

My part: "Sure, and I bet it's relevant."

Self to part: "Thank you for the information and thank you for letting me be present. Remember, you don't have to be here if you don't want to be."

Don't worry if this is a step too far for you on your IFS journey at present. It may come in handy down the road a little. For those of you who are turning towards offering IFS supervision, the idea of parts as consultants may be useful. Here is an example from supervision where a supervisee is talking about her work with a client caught in a cycle of addiction

Supervisee: "We've got a good map of the parts: there are the 'freedom-loving, buzz-addicted parts' who react to the 'responsible, over-stretched parts' and the 'care for others parts'."

Supervisor: "Great. And what parts of you get activated in the work?"

Supervisee: "The part who wants results and to have the addictive behaviour lessen, which I'm aware could collude with the part who brought the client to therapy and wants 'it' stopped."

Supervisor: "OK, and you brought the client to supervision today because?"

Supervisee: "Um ..." (*No response*)

Supervisor: "Well, you've done some parts mapping and I'm wondering if it's time to move on to the next stage?"

Supervisee: "Which would be what?"

(*I'm picking up on "a hole" or "gap" in the process which is showing up in supervision with the supervisee's absence somehow. I'm curious, and, trusting the process, keep going.*)

Supervisor: "What's the missing magic ingredient. I don't usually use that term, which is curious, but anyway ... what's the missing magic ingredient?"

Supervisee: "I ..."

Supervisor: "Self. You've mapped the parts, and have any of them met the Self of the client? I'm wondering if Self is the missing magic ingredient. In Self's presence is where the healing is. And I realise I'm getting and sounding very passionate ..."

Supervisee: "Ah, the client talks about how they'll be bored, have a boring life without doing this."

Supervisor: "Hmm, so a part of the client is concerned about giving up the addictive behaviour for fear of boredom. That makes sense, doesn't it?"

Supervisee: "Yes."

Supervisor: "So, part of the work might be to explore an alternative or replacement buzz for these addictive parts? And, I'm noticing I'm still feeling and expressing in an overly passionate way."

Supervisee: "Yes! The manager that wants it stopped is passionate too, that their way is the right way. They don't want any spiritual healing stuff to go on."

Supervisor: "Ah, and is this part's way working? Is that part getting the results it wants?"

(*Feeling more grounded and that something has opened up now rather than there being something missing.*)

Supervisee: "No, no."

Supervisor: "Maybe see if they would be willing to try it a different way, perhaps?"

Notice how I monitored myself and was curious towards my own system. I didn't on this occasion speak in terms of "a part of me feels/says/thinks". Instead, I noticed and spoke for discrepancies from my usual supervisory speech ("missing magic ingredient") and delivery (super passionate in an unfocused way) – both signs of parts' activity and implicit information. Noticing and highlighting the activation enabled the supervisee to recall and share some missing-to-supervision aspects of the client's process as well as revealing missing aspects of the therapy process (hope-merchanting and getting buy-in for change and trying something different from an important protector).

Accessing the Self of the client[5]

IFS lead trainer Cece Sykes has developed a helpful visual showing a possible representation of the continuum of Self-energy[6] and IFS lead trainer and specialist in working with children and adolescents, Pamela Krause (2013, p. 39), provides a handy table showing the combinations of Self-to-part relating between a therapist and their client. Helen Telford who I mentioned earlier spoke of how sometimes, prior to her IFS transformation, when up on stage working with conflicted groups, a blanking part might blend with her when confronted by audience members. She might look fully present, but on the continuum, she would be down the blended/dissociative end. After training in IFS therapy, and learning how to access her own Self-leadership, she tells us how she has more curiosity and calm available. She is more willing to not know and to make space for Self-leadership in the group members as they take more responsibility for their reactions.

When using in-sight with clients, I prefer *not* to proceed far along the healing steps without the presence of the client's Self. As a result, I have adopted what I think of as a belt and braces approach to the key IFS differentiation question (the 4th F), "How do you feel towards the part?" If I sense the presence of a Self-like part giving a Self-like response, I will employ any and all of the following:

- "How does the part respond when you communicate to it that ... (C quality)?"
- "Who does the part see when it looks at you?"
- "How open is your heart towards the part?"
- "Just check if there are any parts trying to help and have them relax. Let them know you have this."

In this way, I am giving ample opportunity for the client and I to notice that something other than Self or a C quality is present. Also, I will be checking if the work continues down the path of healing. Sometimes, clients spontaneously notice these parts with wonder: "I always thought that was me."

I am comfortable repeating the 4th F many times in a session, not least because in my previous EMDR practice whole sessions featured the same handful of verbal interventions, such as:

- "Let it go, have a breath, what do you notice?"
- "Let it go, have a breath, what are you noticing?"
- "Go with that"
- "Notice that"
- "Notice any and all of that" (if the client revealed conflicting material).

Transition reflection

"There was a huge shift in my practice when I got to know my parts uncomfortable with others repeating themselves and therefore uncomfortable with me repeating myself for fear of the message that might be giving." (Sarah Murphy, Clinical Counsellor)

I urge you to become at ease with repeating yourself – act like a broken record playing the same phrase over and over. If the client finds this annoying or upsetting and says so, great – there's another part you can get to know and negotiate with. I am more than happy to ask even seasoned clients (and clients who are IFS therapists) "how do you feel towards the part?" *every time* a part steps back or gives space. It is important for my system that I take opportunities to check on the client's Self-energy rather than assume that because half a dozen parts have stepped back then Self must surely be present by now. No, a new part may have stepped in, or a part may have come back round. Remember, if Self is present, Self is not going to get annoyed by the question! And I have yet to have a client (or supervisee) complain about how often I ask, "how do you feel towards the part (now)?"

For those of you who would like additional verbal options to check on Self's presence with a part, try these on for size:

- "How close are you to the part?"
- "How is it for the part that you are with it?"
- "Does the part sense/believe/feel/know that you get it?"

Note that these enquiries are about more than just accessing Self. It is important IFS professionals understand *why* we want to access the client's Self, which includes:

- to connect a part (or parts) with Self to form a relationship; and
- to free Self from constraints so that it may be present to lead and heal.

Shortcuts for when many protectors have concerns

If time or patience are in short supply, and the client is likely to have a shame reaction if part after part after part is asked to step back, then there are things you might try. Firstly, you can get the client to ask in advance that parts with concerns about going to the target part step forward and let you know. This is good practice and often what IFS trainers do in demos. Secondly, once you notice many protectors are reacting to the target part, you might want to address all of them together in one go, via in-sight or direct access, which might go something like this (you will want to contextualise it and come up with your own version/s):

> *Therapist:* "OK, Susie, it looks like your parts are a bit stirred up today, shall I speak with them directly to ask them to give us some space? (Susie nods assent) Great. Well, you are all welcome, and I'm thinking that maybe you are stirred up because Susie has had a pretty tough week in the outside world which she's just told me about. It makes sense to me that you might be feeling concerned about us going inside to … (insert the target part). I just want to remind you that Susie has grown up and is 55 years old. Also, Susie-who-is-not-a-part has many, many resources like

calm and connection. She's no longer a little girl at the mercy of out-of-control parents and she *did* survive, thanks to your efforts and perseverance. We would really appreciate it if you could all give some space to let that Susie go to the little one and help her and then many of you might not have to work so hard and could even change job if you wanted to.

"Lastly for now, if you're not sure about giving Susie some space, see if there are any parts in there who've already seen how Susie-who-isn't-a-part can help little ones trapped in time." ... (pause for Susie to listen/sense any responses)

Susie: "OK, some of them have just heard from a part that we've done good work in the past and that they can trust me. It feels calmer in here, like I'm not being bombarded by worried parts."

Another option is to assist the client to work with their breath, body, and imagination to offer Self-energy to the parts. As usual, whether this is of use will depend not least on the client's readiness for, and your comfort in, offering such an intervention – experiment and discover what works for you and your individual clients or customer base. This intervention might be best set up at the beginning of a session.

- (Presuming you have access to your Self-energy) ask the client if they can remember a time when they felt (choose one of the following) any of the C qualities; or felt at one with the world and nature; or felt their energy body strongly; or felt open-hearted and receptive, etc.
- If the client can remember an example, have them describe it briefly, making a point to bring their senses alive in the moment and in the memory. This is so that the client can recall that felt sense of, say, courage, in their body.
- Have the client place awareness on their breath as well as on their felt sense of the quality for a few inhales and exhales (without needing to change the breath in any way). You might want to match your breathing to the client's if this feels natural and comfortable for you.
- Now lead the client in breathing into where in their body they feel that courage and breathing out that quality to where in the body they feel the parts or sense that the body needs more Self-energy (places of tightness or rigidity, for example, or areas they know parts reside) ... not forcing or striving, and with as much of a sense of an invitation as possible. This isn't about making parts feel the courage, it's about inviting them to feel Self's courage if they are ready and wish to.

- Even if just a few parts take up the invitation to notice the C quality on offer with the breath, the client's system may well feel more spacious.

If, and when, the client becomes overrun by protectors as they approach a target part, recalling the above (for example, the C quality and the exercise itself) may help the client send some Self-energy to the parts and help them be willing to "stand down".

Signs of Self's embodiment

As you may be aware, different people experience Self differently. Enquiring of your client how they feel in their body may also provide information about the presence of Self, parts and Self-like parts. If the client can't feel into their body, then access to Self may at first be limited and the work may need to remain for a time with the therapist doing direct access with the client's part(s). In their chapter "A Model of IFS-Informed Supervision and Consultation: Unblending from Struggle into Self-led Clarity", IFS consultants Dan Reed and Ray Wooten (2023) include a checklist of 10 markers to track one's own Self-leadership and that of our clients (see also Chapter 8). Schwartz (2021, p. 99–100) writes:

> I have a set of markers that I check as I go through my day, but I also find them particularly helpful during triggering times. For example, when I am interacting with someone, I can quickly notice how open or closed my heart is and how much compassion I have for them. I'll check to see if I have a big agenda for talking to them or a tone of voice that's constrained or lacking energy. I can also just check for how many of the eight Cs I'm embodying. Different people have different markers and I encourage you to find yours.

Making a repair[7] if needed

If one of my parts is getting (or previously has got) in the way by reacting to a part in the other, then, at some point, if not in the moment, it will be helpful to unblend from my reactive part and make a repair. Making a repair includes speaking for the presence and activation of my part, explaining its presence if appropriate, apologising, and reassuring the client the part has already received or will receive some attention so that it may give space for Self to be present.

Reminder: Self-leadership is the gamechanger in IFS

So, we've reviewed what Self is, what it is not, how to talk about Self and how parts can act as consultants to Self and how clients' parts can be helped to give space. We have touched upon signs of Self's embodiment and the importance as therapist or practitioner (and consultant) of making a repair if one of our parts has caused a rupture in a relationship.

Why have I begun the book with this? Because Self-leadership is the gamechanger in IFS. I'm not saying that IFS is the only therapy that gives access to and increases Self-energy, I don't believe that is the case. I believe that all good therapy increases access to Self in client and therapist. However, IFS is the only psychotherapy I know that makes explicit the active and healing nature of Self's presence and trains therapists to recognise and work from Self.

If you have trained in IFS recently and have the new Level 1 Manual (Pastor & Gauvain, 2020), I encourage you to remind yourself of the section contributed by Barbara Cargill "As a Self-led IFS Therapist, you will…" (p. 141).

The 5 Ps of Self-leadership in action

In addition to the 8 Cs of IFS, the 5 Ps of presence, perspective, patience, persistence, and playfulness are qualities of someone who is Self-led; they signify the opposite of "taking things personally". They are especially significant for an IFS professional in a therapeutic relationship with someone for whom doing IFS comes less easily and comparatively slowly. IFS psychotherapist Gayle Williamson explains the significance of the 5 Ps in her work with Pat. They first met before Gayle trained in IFS when Pat attended a dozen or so sessions either side of a hospitalization for her mental health. Years later, Pat – now in her early 40s – has returned to therapy after further episodes of what the medics call psychosis, she is on medication and has a heavy-hitting diagnosis. However, aided by IFS in which Gayle trained about five years ago, they have been working together for eight months. In that time, Pat's goals for therapy are being maintained: she has not had another psychotic episode, has stayed out of psychiatric hospital and has returned to her voluntary job part-time. Gayle's implicit goals for the work are also being maintained: doing what she believes helps (IFS) and helping Pat to engage in the process of therapy.

Transition reflection

"I've found that the IFS model can be trusted; it provides a container."
(Gayle Williamson, IFS psychotherapist)

From the moment of her return, Gayle recognised the importance for the relationship of embracing IFS concepts and practices, in particular, not pathologising mental distress (Self's perspective); using direct access (presence) to befriend protectors such as the storytelling part, so parts could get to know h/Her, and she them. Together, she and the client have reframed the psychotic episodes as the activity of extreme protectors (perspective). In supervision, Gayle tells me:

> (*Perspective and patience*) "It's easy for clients' parts to avoid by distracting, but I remember it's my job to hold to the model – Pat isn't going to do that by herself. We might not have the ideal momentum of getting permission from protectors using in-sight to go the exiles and then move through the steps of healing. But we are always noticing her parts, their relationships with each other and making contact with them whenever we can. It often happens that I might notice a part and I'll ask would she like to see if we can get to know it. Pat will happily go inside, but quickly return saying 'No Gayle, nobody's saying anything' and then go back to updating me about her week (*a primary protector in action*)."

> (*Persistence*) "So I choose to come in again and say, 'Pat, would it be okay if I tried to speak to that part?' Sometimes she'll still return saying, 'I hear nothing'. And I'll just say, 'that's ok, nobody has to talk if they don't want to.' And we go back to talking generally for a while until I maybe spot another gap where I can come in and say, 'how about if we try talking to *this* part?' So, over the months, we've been talking about and constantly doing bits and pieces of IFS mainly using direct access; she's opened up a lot. She can now talk a little about her childhood, name what she's feeling, even the emotion that's most difficult for her system – anger – which she couldn't do before (*perspective*)."

> *Gayle:* (*Persistence, patience and perspective*) "Pat, do you think there might be a part who doesn't want to go to the sadness this week?" (*She nods.*)

> (*Playfully, with a smile*) "And you can guess what I'm going to say next, can't you?"

> *Pat:* "Yes... you want to speak to it!... Oh, okay then."

And so, Gayle gains permission to speak directly to the part (*presence*) – just for a while – who doesn't want them "doing parts work" this week. In the moment, this doesn't get them further down the steps of healing, but it still has value relationally and in the long-term. From where I sit in supervision hearing about their work, it is as if Pat's system is gradually allowing itself to be more multiple, more multi-faceted – instead of being dominated by one or more protectors. There is more depth to her and to their relationship, as Gayle holds in her mind's eye and open heart the longer-term perspective of inner healing.

Exercises

1) Bringing awareness to your own Self qualities

*   Part of *doing* IFS involves *being* a certain way; it involves being Self-led.
*   Remind yourself of the 8 Cs and the 5 Ps. (Did you forget one or two? If so, is that usual? Anything of interest to consider there?)
*   If you are an IFS therapist or practitioner, bring to awareness your practice, perhaps in terms of a session, a day, a week, or in terms of your relationship with a particular client. If you use IFS as a way of life, you might like to reflect on a specific relationship, issue, or segment of time.
*   Now have some fun and get creative. Divide a pie chart into portions showing any C qualities available. See completed example A in Figure 1.1.
*   Alternatively, you might want to divide a circle or wheel into 8 equal segments, one for each C quality. Now represent each C quality you noticed by placing a mark on each segment from the centre (0 of the quality) to the edge (a lot of or maximum of the quality), to show how much of each C quality you sense you had available for that session/day/week/client. See B in Figure 1.1 for an example.
*   Using a bar chart, draw up to 5 blocks, one for each potential P (or 8 blocks for the 8 Cs), showing the amount you noticed of each P or C by the length along the x axis. See two completed examples C and D in Figure 1.1.
*   Reflect on what you have just created. Are there any patterns you can detect?
*   If the above is hard to do in retrospect, perhaps bear this in mind going forward.

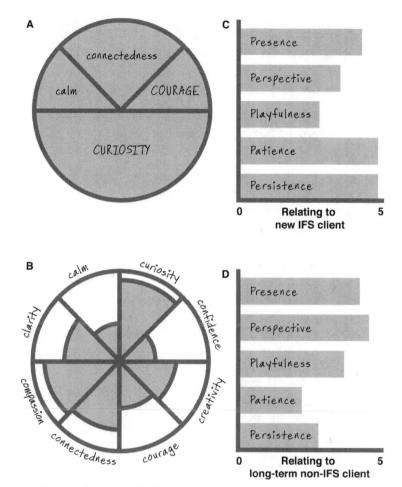

Figure 1.1 Completed examples for Exercise 1

2) Exploring constraints to your own Self qualities

Spend some time with a pad and paper, out in nature or with an IFS peer or colleague, getting into an open-hearted, receptive space, without judgment or urgency, just curiosity, and take each of the Cs and Ps and ask inside questions like:

- Does anyone have strong feelings about presence/persistence …?
- Is anyone blocking my courage/confidence …?
- Who has bad memories about being creative/connected …?

Welcome whoever appears and get to know them and their concerns, build a Self-to-part relationship so that you can recognise when these parts show up in sessions and constrain your confidence or creativity … and so that you can ask them to let you handle things and allow the C quality to flow safely and freely.

If necessary, complete the IFS steps of healing with any little ones who carry burdens and pain around any of these qualities.

3) Considering the nature of your therapeutic relationships[8]

Reflect on one of your therapeutic or supervisory relationships using metaphor and more creative reflections:

- If you and your client/supervisee were washed up on a desert island together what would be happening?
- If you were a fly on the wall in session, what would you be seeing/feeling/sensing?
- Tell the story of the relationship starting, "Once upon a time …"
- If you and the client/supervisee were objects/stones/animals/pictures /a song/a game/a fairytale, what would you be?

Write or share with a partner your responses and see if anything has arisen as to the C qualities (or their absence).

4) Self-assessment of IFS competencies

Either on your own, with a peer or with your supervisor, choose a rating scale (e.g., poor, average, good) and mark yourself on your ability to achieve the foundational IFS competencies shown at A in Appendix I.[9] (Adapt to your context – for example, if "client" is not applicable). This will give you a sense of your current strengths and weaknesses in terms of your proficiency in IFS, which you can review once you have read more of the book or in some other way progressed in your IFS journey.

You might also wish to rate your competencies in B and include items specific to your circumstances and context in C in Appendix I. Are there areas in which you need additional training (whether IFS or non-IFS)? What are your learning edges?

Notes

1 Many years later, I now realise that Self also does not pathologise or demand change, and it sees beyond the burdens and extremes to a part's true nature.

2 Schwartz writes about the dual nature of Self as an active and boundaried inner leader and "an expansive, boundaryless state of mind … a kind of 'no self' state" (Schwartz & Sweezy, 2020, p. 45).

3 See Steege (2023), who writes about common categories of religious/spiritual protectors.

4 By "ecological sensitivity", I mean being sensitive to the patterns and balances of relationships between all the elements of an environment or system – in this case a person's inner world. (See Schwartz & Sweezy, 2020, pp. 5, 18–19, 21, 23, 24, 29, 41–42, 204.)

5 Although a sign of Self's presence is lack of attachment to an agenda, in IFS therapy and IFS supervision, my therapist parts have the agenda or intention of accessing Self-energy in the client and my Self aligns with what Schwartz and Sweezy write (2020, p. 54): "The Self … does have the intention and the ability to bring healing, harmony, balance, and connectedness to any system it encounters. The larger goal of IFS is simply to give us all more access to our Selves and to bring more Self-energy to our planet." If we are doing therapy or working on ourselves with a stronger agenda, then it is likely a part is driving the work.

6 See the Self Spectrum: Degrees of Consciousness (Sykes, 2017, p. 37).

7 IFS lead trainer Fran Booth has written about acknowledging our parts with others in her chapter, "IFS Consultation: Fostering the Self-Led Therapist" (Booth, 2023).

8 With thanks to the Centre for Supervision and Team Development and their training module "Therapeutic Supervision", details of which can be found in Shohet and Shohet (2020).

9 These are only based on and do not equate to the current list of competencies assessed in the IFSI certification process.

2
Giving yourself and IFS some time

Introduction

This chapter begins with a model of learning that may be useful in navigating your transition to IFS. The chapter also touches on what IFS is, brought to life by way of a real-life case study in which supervisee Lucas struggles to move forward in his practise of IFS and in his offering of IFS to his client. I encourage IFS beginners to befriend their professional parts and become adept at helping clients buy in to IFS. Included are extracts from supervision sessions with Daniel, who uses in-sight to unburden a part bringing fear to his client work. I also refer to Schwartz's consultation with Anna, encouraging her to develop her own "patter" to help her client buy into IFS. Lastly, you will be stimulated to reflect on what IFS is not and what "doing IFS" means for you. Exercises at the end of the chapter help you attend to your personal and professional deconstruction and reconstruction as your IFS skills and understanding grow.

Transitioning: Conscious competence learning model

Learning is not easy; it can trigger our anxiety and fear, frustrate, and even destabilise us as we feel we have lost one professional identity and have yet to form a new one. I have discovered that I and other therapists with whom I have worked find we feel "professionally homeless" for a while during this deconstruction and reconstruction phase of the learning transition. We neither fit in where we used to feel at home, nor do we know what our new home will look like, or even whether we will make it that far. Such feelings and disorientation are normal and can be welcomed! I have taken comfort over the years in having a "map" of the stages of learning – the conscious competence model (Broadwell, 1969), which is often depicted as a ladder to ascend.[1]

DOI: 10.4324/9781003243571-4

In this model, the four stages of competence are:

1. **Unconscious incompetence** – we don't really know what we don't know, we may already have reached level 4 in another modality or profession and be feeling secure in that identity and practice.
2. **Conscious incompetence** – we are aware of how little we know of the new modality, and it may feel like we have a long way to go to reach level 4.
3. **Conscious competence** – we have acquired the skills and knowledge we need in the new modality though they have not become "natural" and some concentration is needed.
4. **Unconscious competence or mastery** – we can use our new skills effortlessly, they are "in our bones" and "second nature" and we may even have begun to teach or support others on their learning journey.

What different learning journeys may look like

We all learn at different speeds and in different orders. My system likes *slow*, and mastered IFS in roughly this order (with continuing reflection along the way):

*   Read "the red book". (Schwartz, 1995)
*   Watched someone else doing it who knew what they were doing (Levels 1 and 2).
*   Signed-up and studied via the Online Circle.
*   Experienced IFS as a client.
*   Tried the new modality with low-risk clients.
*   Tried out a couple of supervisors I didn't stay with and a couple I did.
*   Accessed more confidence working with clients.
*   Carried on experiencing it as client (including in supervision).
*   Signed up and studied via the IFS Continuity Program (which I still do each month).
*   PA-ed for Level 1 and Level 2.
*   Level 3 training.
*   Went for Certification (therapist parts beginning to relax and trust my Self and the client's Self).
*   Reading widely.
*   Becoming an Approved IFS Clinical Consultant.
*   Writing about IFS supervision to help marshal my thoughts and review what it is I do.
*   Continuing to work with clients and supervisees.

You may of course progress differently, which is just as valid, and will also have its own challenges. Certainly, I am currently working with supervisees who have done things in this order:

- Read the red book (or Earley, 2012).
- Applied IFS in real-life with clients.
- Received supervision.
- Experienced IFS themselves in supervision.
- Level 1 training.
- Certification.

In the last Level 1 training for which I PA-ed, the trainer advised the trainees to allow themselves three years to focus solely on learning IFS before they tried to vary it or integrate it with another modality. In his view, it takes that long to learn any modality. Interestingly, this amount of time seems standard and comes up elsewhere. My professional body, BACP (British Association for Counselling and Psychotherapy), will not accept anyone for counsellor accreditation without a minimum of three years of experience as a counsellor (plus meeting all their other requirements). When I accredited in EMDR, that professional body also expected three years' hands-on experience before becoming eligible to apply for accreditation. Learning IFS takes a minimum of three years' application, reflection on practice and supervision. I think of it in this way:

- Basic training is just that: basic – it is *not* sufficient to make a sound practitioner out of anyone.
- Learning on the job is where the real learning takes place.
- Learning to do something new means unlearning what gets in the way of that new learning.
- Proficiency comes through practice and reflection on that practice on your own and with more experienced and knowledgeable others.
- It can take a while before the supervisory relationship becomes helpful.
- Becoming an IFS therapist is more than just learning some techniques (see Chapter 1).

Becoming at home with a new modality also involves learning to assess your own abilities and competence. Although I now feel at home and at ease with IFS, I continue to assess my abilities as an IFS therapist in terms of:

- My own Self-energy being available.
- Multiplicity thinking in terms of the three categories of parts + Self.

- An awareness of where I am in the flow of the model and why.
- A sense of trust that the client's Self and I will have clarity about when and where to go to next.

Feeling the discomfort but doing it anyway because ...

I recommend you consider what keeps you hanging on in there in your transition to IFS. What and who are your anchor points helping you face and embrace the confusion, fear, setbacks and successes as you move towards feeling at home in and with IFS? If you don't know what your reasons are for holding to IFS despite the ups and downs of the journey, it might be difficult to help your existing clients to transition to using IFS. It might also be hard stepping out with courage to take on new clients asking for IFS.

On my own IFS journey, I was fortunate to "win" two demos to be client with Schwartz himself. I experienced Self's healing, wholeness, and presence early in my learning journey which cemented my commitment to the IFS model and paradigm. Yes, the deconstruction and reconstruction of my professional identity was at times deeply frustrating, anxiety provoking and baffling. And I came out the other side intact. I was willing to feel the discomfort and keep going because I knew IFS heals and transforms. I'd felt and experienced that; and if that was possible for me, then I could help it happen for others.

A case example

A supervisee, who I will call Lucas, is qualified in Humanistic Integrative therapy. We have been working together for many years, as I was his external placement supervisor during his counselling training. Since qualifying, Lucas has become interested in IFS, attending two days of IFS training, reading Janina Fisher's book *Healing the Fragmented Selves of Trauma Survivors* (which though not an IFS book, can often steer people towards IFS, as it focuses on different parts) as well as Jay Earley's *Self Therapy*, which he likes. Our supervisory contract has been extended to include working with IFS concepts and practices as he seeks ways to incorporate IFS into his practice.

Transition reflection

"I had the impression it was only through working with exiles that change, or relief can happen. I'm learning that working with protectors can also be really powerful." (Volunteer counsellor)

Lucas is back working in person with Jake after a long break in sessions due to the start of the pandemic in 2020. In their first batch of in-person sessions, Lucas was excited to take in his collection of stuffed animals from which Jake could take his pick to represent his parts. The anxious part was "the problem" that had brought Jake to therapy, and they had agreed a number of sessions to work on this together. Both therapist and client were pleased with the parts work they had done. Along the way, Jake had learnt that other people also had parts; and when someone was horrible to him, he knew it was a part of them speaking and acting, not the whole of them. This was useful to him. Lucas occasionally "coached" Jake to be compassionate to his own parts but creating Self-to-part relationships on the inside had not been attempted.

As they return to working together in person, they re-contract. Jake wants to be more assertive and make a fledgling intimate relationship work. By the time Lucas meets with me online for supervision, they have four more sessions left of their agreed allocation. Lucas updates me on their sessions since our last supervision and recounts all the psycho-educating he has done, how he has recommended Jake watch various IFS videos which the client has not done. "He made excuses, blaming his dissociating part," the supervisee tells me. Nonetheless, they have a trusting relationship and Jake found the "counteractive" (Ecker et al., 2012) work Lucas offered in the last session helpful. By counteractive, I mean that when Jake spoke of feeling abandoned and worried the relationship has failed if the new man doesn't text back swiftly, Lucas offered/taught him a new way of thinking and feeling about this issue. He asked how Jake's significant other relates to him when they are in person (attentive and connected), and advised Jake to focus on that reality rather than believing the "negative" reality when there is a long gap in texting.

Lucas tells me that usually at this stage of a counselling relationship he focuses on exploring with the client how they can be their own counsellor and take responsibility for their own life after counselling has finished. Silently, I wonder if Lucas wants my help in trying to teach his client IFS in four sessions. I ask Lucas what he requires from supervision: "How can I help Jake take more responsibility for himself in relationships?" My initial response, which I chose not to share was: *It might help if you stopped taking responsibility for him and let him take responsibility for himself.* I remind my system that previous challenging in supervision of Lucas's preference for more counteractive therapies (such as CBT or mindfulness) rather than transformative therapies (such as IFS) have not encouraged him to use IFS more broadly. And while the supervisee lacks a fuller understanding of and ability to use IFS, he is naturally going to offer what he already knows to do. At present, Lucas has not consistently attempted to facilitate the client's Self-to-part relationships. Based on my existing knowledge of him, I believe that this is because Lucas himself lacks confidence in and relationship to Self. Some of the supervisee's therapist parts have yet to be befriended and yet to free Self to lead. I decide to offer IFS-style supervision of facilitating a U-turn.

> *Emma (Supervisor):* "Before you expect him to change, how about we see what parts of you are getting caught up with his and the ending of the relationship?"
>
> *Lucas (Supervisee):* "OK."
>
> *Supervisor:* "Shall we do a map or list of the parts that feature strongly in this relationship?
>
> *Supervisee:* "Yes. (*Closing his eyes and taking his time*) There's a teaching part. I like to teach, and I've realised I talk a lot in sessions. A helping part, and the part who feels inadequate around relationships and says it's not sure we have anything to teach this client about relationships." (*Opening his eyes and looking to me to guide the process*)
>
> *Supervisor:* "What's their fear of letting You lead?"
>
> *Supervisee:* (*Eyes closed, going inside*) "At the end of our allotted sessions, he won't be fixed."
>
> *Supervisor:* "OK, is that a fixer part speaking or one of the parts you've already mentioned?
>
> *Supervisee:* "It's the teaching part."
>
> *Supervisor:* "Shall we see if you can get to know this one a little? (*Lucas nods and closes his eyes*) As it says that about the client not being fixed in the sessions you have left, how do you feel towards the part?"
>
> *Supervisee:* "I have some sympathy with it … I'm quite blended."
>
> *Supervisor:* "Sure, ask the part if it will give you some space so you can get to know each other."
>
> *Supervisee:* "That's the prime difficulty – separating from the part. This is difficult for me and yet I'm trying to teach it to my client."
>
> *Supervisor:* "Absolutely … Continuing with befriending your teaching part, do you have a sense of the part in or around your body? (*Supervisee nods*) How do you feel towards the part as you notice it there?"
>
> *Supervisee:* "Connected and understanding."
>
> *Supervisor:* "See if the part can sense that and sense you there."

Supervisee: "Yes, it says it can sense that it will be OK if it steps back when I'm with the client." (*Opens his eyes after a while*)

Supervisor: "That's great, and as you imagine being with the client next time, what do you notice?"

Supervisee: (*Turning inwards again*) "I'm talking less, and I notice it's easier to be in Self when the client is talking and I'm witnessing his story with compassion rather than when I'm teaching something." (*Supervisee opens his eyes*)

Supervisor: (*Pausing, noticing how the supervisee returns to the room*) "And how are you now? Are you back?"

Supervisee: "I'm feeling a bit dissociated."[2]

Supervisor: "Ah (*in a welcoming way*), does that make some sense to you? (*Supervisee nods and we pause*) I wonder if this parallels[3] what happens for your client?"

Supervisee: (*Nodding, seems present and calm*) "I wonder. I've just done something that feels new and that is hard, and the client tells me they dissociate when they come to watch a video that might help them change or have a different perspective on themselves ..."

We left it there. However, let's review my supervision and see what other interventions I might have offered. What came to your mind as you read what happened? (You can be as critical as you like, and as your system will allow. Having opinions about what is "good practice", and "bad practice" is using your professional judgment, which can help you grow as a practitioner.) The following might have been useful and relevant for someone with Lucas's level of and proficiency in IFS:

• Raising the polarity I was sensing between Jake and Lucas (and between Lucas and I): I don't know how vs I'll teach you.
• Voicing the polarity I was sensing inside both Jake and Lucas: I want to change/learn new skills vs I don't want to change/learn new skills.
• Helping Lucas practise the 6 Fs in a role-play.
• Teaching IFS theory about Self's lack of agenda vs parts controlling the agenda.
• Speaking for my parts, including the one who had the strong instant reaction.
• At the point where I continued with befriending the target part, I could have explicitly given Lucas the choice to continue or stop what we were doing.

Do you have a sense of what you would need in supervision or which intervention you would prefer or find helpful?

Discerning what IFS is

If Jake was your client, what key IFS concepts would you be acting on? Or if you were the supervisor, or a peer in a supervision group, what key IFS concepts might you highlight as you review the case together? How might these key concepts direct Lucas's next steps? What might you have done differently? Here are some initial thoughts:

IFS is a constraint-releasing approach

The next step in their working together might be to use IFS to explore the parts getting in the way of Jake being assertive. (These parts may or may not have shown up in the parts mapping using the soft toys.) After all, in theory Jake has access to Self-energy and the natural leadership and assertion that brings. Working with this in an IFS way would not be the same as teaching assertion techniques, which I know the supervisee has done in the past with clients.

IFS is a systemic approach

As we know, the client's system is made up of protectors (managers and firefighters) and exiles as well as Self. (There may also be legacy burdens, cultural burdens and unattached burdens to consider.) Jake's system may well include active polarisations between parts which Lucas has yet to become aware of: be assertive vs let the other lead; get close vs stay distant; take responsibility vs abdicate responsibility/seek rescue. Would you know how to work with a polarisation between parts using IFS?

Parts attract parts and Self resonates with Self

It can be hard for a client to access Self-energy if their therapist is leading with a part.[4] Lucas the supervisee and his client Jake may well have polarised parts in the lead in this relationship: I don't know how vs I'll teach you. How might you notice this if you were the therapist?

IFS is a transformative, not counteractive, therapy

Exiles and protectors can transform (Schwartz & Sweezy 2020, pp. 163–164) or "be loved into transformation" (ibid p. 250) by Self. Thoughts, feelings, beliefs, memories can transform through the steps of healing of IFS. You will probably need to do more of your own reading around the intricacies of transformation, but the exploration of the differences between counteractive and transformative therapy continues below.

Seeking buy-in to IFS

In the IFS Continuity Program (Schwartz & Rich, 2020) month two live call, Schwartz gives consultation to someone working with a client who has previously had Dialectical Behaviour Therapy (DBT). He is hope-merchanting to the consultee, Anna, encouraging her to develop her own "patter" in getting buy-in to IFS from a part who, for its own protective, well-intended reasons, is resisting Self and the transformation that IFS can bring.

Schwartz explains that he would tell such a part he can help it and the ones it protects get out from where they are stuck. His patter also includes a message of collaboration, saying that the work will go at the part's pace rather than the therapist's, his own, or another part's. Interestingly, sometimes Schwartz might seek collaboration through letting the part know it's in charge or "the boss" (see Schwartz & Sweezy's list of reassuring things to say to protectors, 2020, p. 138).

The consultee finds this a helpful idea as she is aware there are protectors in the client who have learned DBT skills and can function, so the client appears "fine". Schwartz responds by re-emphasising that IFS is not a counteractive therapy (as DBT might be called) and although the part with the DBT skills (a manager) helps the client function better, the underlying wounding (the exiles) driving the extreme system still needs healing. Once that happens, the part using DBT could take a break or change its role.

Transformation: A major selling point

Protectors work perpetually to prevent what they fear happening. In IFS, we do not teach protectors new ways of working, thinking or managing, although we might negotiate for different behaviour towards other parts in the system and for buy-in to the transformational sequence of the IFS healing steps. In this way, IFS is a transformational not counteractive therapy as outlined by Ecker et al. in *Unlocking the Emotional Brain* (2012) and as described by Peter Afford in *Therapy in the Age of Neuroscience* where he writes about psychotherapy in general (2020, pp. 36, 56, 58–60, 99, 112, for example).

Ecker et al. detail what they call the Therapeutic Reconsolidation Process (TRP), which unlocks, erases, dissolves implicit memory and lifelong emotional learnings or schema that drive problematic behaviours, symptoms, and reactions. It's not the language of IFS, but TRP can also be considered transformative rather than counteractive and IFS is one of the therapies that can achieve this meta process.

Who would not want to help clients to transform their inner worlds rather than have them suppress, overcome, push away or otherwise counteract their symptoms, thoughts, feelings, etc? But like Lucas from earlier, and his therapist parts who enjoy teaching, you may have parts who get something from a counteractive approach – perhaps it offers a sense of being an expert or having something concrete to offer in the moment rather than risk failing to help the client "go inside". Perhaps this is the first time you have heard the term or heard about TRP. Buying into IFS involves letting go of the counteracting tendencies that come from parts. It involves negotiating with and helping your protectors (who are anti-vulnerability) to risk the vulnerability of letting Self lead in your system and in the client's system.

As Schwartz and Sweezy remind us (2020, pp. 102–103):

- most protectors will not change their behaviour until the part they protect is healed;
- neither managers nor firefighters can heal themselves or other parts;
- parts cannot change other parts; and
- only Self can truly transform the inner world.

These are all factors that could, if more widely accepted, impact the popularity of counteractive forms of psychotherapy.

Befriending therapist parts to access more Self-energy

I'd encourage you to take your time learning IFS, building up your skills, and freeing your confidence. This may mean working with parts to ask for space while you learn, practise, and develop, as well as tending to any exiles who may become ready for healing. Parts you may wish to negotiate with for space, or tend to with compassion, include:

- Critics/Shamers
- Judges
- Perfectionists

- Need to know/understand/work it out parts
- Freewheelers (*I can't do it wrong if I do my own thing*)
- Independent learners (*I hate being told what to do and follow a script*)
- Comparers (*Why can't I do it like the trainer did it in demos?*)
- Drama Triangle parts (rescuers, persecutors, victims)
- Exiles whose feelings of shame and unworthiness are triggered

Here is an example of supervisee Daniel and I working together to unburden a part colouring his experience of a client. The supervisee and I have been working together for many years and his orientation is Humanistic Integrative. He has become interested in IFS, has completed some introductory training, and read several IFS texts. He has not attended a Level 1 training. One of the reasons I mention this is to point out that we have a robust and open relationship in which we trust and respect each other; another reason is because it provides an example of using IFS in supervision with a supervisee who is not fully trained in IFS.

The supervisee has been working with an elderly male client in person for some time. The client's wife is terminally ill and lives in a home; while the client, who has his own noticeable health problems, lives alone with some outside help, including my supervisee. Daniel is himself of mature years and they have contracted to help the client "cope", which is shorthand for "not get emotional and cease functioning".

Meanwhile, the global pandemic has arrived, and the client is no longer able to visit his wife in person nor have in-person counselling sessions. The supervisee has agreed with the client a weekly phone-call together, which is sort of counselling and sort of not. Daniel has received a worrying email from his client, which he brings to supervision, and I read it when he shares his screen. He asks me what I've picked up from his case presentation and from reading the email. I reconstruct the dialogue from there:

> *Supervisor:* "Firstly, I get a sense of how well the client is managing in real terms and how you are both concerned that he might have a 'breakdown' and I am aware that I don't know what that means for each of you. I sense that for the client this might mean 'becoming emotional', while for another client it might mean 'becoming psychotic' or 'having hallucinations' or 'reaching for the bottle'. Without knowing what the client means, I'm thinking it might be difficult to respond. If it's the fear of becoming emotional, then normalising feeling out of control and unable to cope might be helpful as well as normalising not wanting to feel like that. What do you think 'breakdown' means? Is it likely he needs to contact his GP?"

Supervisee: "I think the client is concerned about becoming emotional. He usually responds well to a mindfulness exercise when I lead one. I could see if he wants to do that, though on the phone it might not be as straightforward."

Supervisor: "How would it be if you validated his emotions *and* his fear of his emotions and wanting to remain strong?"

Supervisee: "So, I should agree with the client that his life is crap, and he doesn't know how he's going to be able to keep going?"

Supervisor: "That's a very strong response to what I just suggested."

Supervisee: "Yes, I did that on purpose. If I was him, I wouldn't want to live."

Supervisor: "This is really, really important, Daniel. How do you think what you've just shared might be affecting you and your work/relationship with him?"

Supervisee: "How do you think?"

Supervisor: "I'm not going to answer that. ... What parts in you come up around working with this client?"

Supervisee: (*Slowing down and becoming more focused on himself*) "It brings up a part who is working really hard to make the client's life less crap, giving him tools, coming up with ideas."

Supervisor: "A part who wants to rescue the client?"

Supervisee: "Yes, and there's also a part who is afraid that one day when he has a 'breakdown' or it's all too much, he'll harm himself.

Supervisor: "Ah, I'll say that back to you but a bit stronger: you think the client's life is crap and if you had his life you wouldn't want to go on. Is that near enough? (*Daniel nods*) Would you like to work with the part of you inside who holds those beliefs?"

Supervisee: "It's not a part."

Supervisor: "Hmmm, well, it's not Self. ... Find this part of you and see if it will give you some distance so you can have a conversation together."

Supervisee: "I see a young me whose gran used to take him with her to visit an old people's home to see her crippled friends."

Supervisor: "How old is this part?"

Supervisee: "Under seven."

Supervisor: "How do you feel towards the part?"

Supervisee: "Protective and that this probably wasn't a good thing for this boy."

Supervisor: "Let this young you know you feel protective and caring towards him and see how he reacts. (*Silence*) Does he know you're there?"

Supervisee: "Maybe."

Supervisor: "How do you feel towards the part?"

Supervisee: "Accepting."

Supervisor: "Let him know and see if he responds."

Supervisee: "He's smiling."

Supervisor: "Great, and how old does this part think you are?"

Supervisee: "Oh, he knows I'm 67."

Supervisor: "Does he know you're a counsellor and you work with people with difficult lives?"

Supervisee: "Yes, he knows that."

Supervisor: "And how is that for him?"

Supervisee: "Mostly good but some things worry him. He doesn't want to be hurt; he doesn't want to be like those old people."

Supervisor: "Does that make sense to you? (*He nods*) Let him know you get that and ask him what else he wants you to know about how that was for him."

Supervisee: "The smell, the smell of a hospital and old people isn't pleasant, and it's a very bad situation, they're not able to do anything, it's frightening for him."

Supervisor: "Let him know you get all that and see what else."

Supervisee: "He wants nothing to do with old people."

Supervisor: "Yes, and my guess is it's difficult for him – you working with this elderly client."

Supervisee: "He doesn't want to grow old."

Supervisor: "Daniel, do you have a response to that?"

Supervisee: "I don't want to either."

Supervisor: (*Checking the supervisee's Self-energy*) "How do you feel towards the part?"

Supervisee: "Compassionate."

Supervisor: "Send that to him and let him know from me that he doesn't have to grow up and grow old. Yes, *you* have grown up, but he can stay his age if he wants to."

Supervisee: "OK. ... He's OK with that."

Supervisor: "What else does he want to share with you?"

Supervisee: "He's afraid of deformity."

Supervisor: "Does that make sense to you?"

Supervisee: "Yes."

Supervisor: "Let him know you get that."

Supervisee: "He's feeling better now."

Supervisor: "Great, is there more he wants you to know?"

Supervisee: "No."

Supervisor: "Ask if he's stuck back there in that situation and would like to move to somewhere more comfortable for him."

Supervisee: "No, he's not stuck there, he can still play with his friends, he's OK."

Supervisor: "Great, so would he like to let go of all that he's shared with you about that situation?"

Supervisee: "Yes, he would."

Supervisor: "Great, so let go to …?"

Supervisee: "He wants to put it into a hot air balloon and let it float away."

Supervisor: "Great, help him have that happen."

Supervisee: "It's going and we're waving to it … it's all gone."

Supervisor: "And is there anything he'd like to invite in to replace what he's let go of?"

Supervisee: "No, he's happy playing with his friends."

Supervisor: "How about when you're working with this client, let him know he can play with his friends then."

Supervisee: "Yes, he'll leave the old people to the grown-ups."

Supervisor: "OK, great, is it OK to stop there and come back to the room?" …

Supervisee: "So, what's my aim next time I work with this client?"

Supervisor: "Yes, great question. Let's try an experiment. Imagine your next contact with the client … and what do you notice?"

Supervisee: "I feel some compassion towards him and that it's better not to let my parts' fears get mixed up with his fear. I'm clearer on what's mine now so we can deal with whatever his might be."

The client and supervisee went on to work together with more ease.

Discerning what "doing IFS" means for you and how to "package" that for buy-in

Earlier, Lucas was grappling with how to bring IFS into a particular thera-peutic relationship and piece of client work. Depending on your context, you will also need to consider what doing IFS means to you, how to "package" it, and how to respond to enquiries from those wanting it, and so on.

I work and write in the Southwest of England, aware that in the UK, coun-selling is, for the most part, an unregulated profession.[5] Except in the case of applying for certification when a person's bona fide skills in IFS and Self-leadership need to be demonstrated and externally verified, anyone can incorporate IFS into their work and call themselves whatever they like. Bodyworkers who are trained in teaching yoga or Tai Chi or who are reflexologists, acupuncturists and craniosacral therapists may have greater access to Self-energy in their work and carry on as they have been doing. Other bodyworkers may transition to becoming IFS practitioners and offer therapy as a standalone addition to their bodywork. Some people retrain and study counselling or psychotherapy at master's level with the future goal of becoming a certified IFS therapist rather than a certified IFS practitioner. Other therapists have had a module of IFS as part of their basic therapy training. Others are certified therapists working in schools, for example, who may never call how they are or what they do (e.g., speaking for parts) IFS.

At present in the UK, choice rather than the demands of professional bodies dominates as to how one describes one's credentials. There is also now more choice in IFS training routes. As the popularity of IFS continues to grow and applications for places on official IFS Institute trainings outweigh availability, you may opt or have opted to attend an alternative training. However, the IFS Institute's three-level training offers a gold standard, and both the UK and the US official IFS therapist directories now request that those listed indicate their highest level of IFSI training. Also, clients may want to know: "Have you done official IFS training?" If you haven't, then I hope you would be able to answer honestly and explain why you believe you are sufficiently trained and able to offer IFS in your chosen way. Here are various responses a client could be offered on enquiring about IFS therapy with an IFS therapist or practitioner:

- "I learnt IFS as part of my undergraduate training, it's not the same as the official Level 1 training but how about we try working together for a few sessions and see how things go then review? Also, I have IFS supervision and feel confident in my full use of the model."

- "I'm an EMDR practitioner and I've done extra training with PESI in IFS parts work which I use alongside EMDR as needed. I'm not qualified to offer you pure IFS and wouldn't want to. How does that sound to you?"
- "My core professional training and practice is as a yoga teacher, and I've recently retrained. I've completed the first level of IFS training with the IFS Institute and had lots of practice in using the model. I'm happy to work therapeutically using the whole IFS protocol if your parts allow that and can come to trust my Self-energy and yours."
- "I hear how keen you are to have IFS therapy to work on your addictions and complex trauma. As you see from my website, I have completed the institute's Level 1 IFS training. However, I only feel confident working with certain clients at present. Please see my website's Links page for details of other practitioners and directories."

A beginning IFS therapist might say to a placement provider or employer:

- "I'm learning to incorporate IFS into my practice, and at this stage, I only feel right working with protectors, not with exiles. Please bear that in mind when you assign clients to me."
- "I know I'm the resident trauma expert and I don't expect that to change. However, it's going to take me some time to feel competent using the whole IFS protocol and, until I'm ready, I may work with some clients using more than one approach. Meanwhile, I'm practising with a small group of peers from my training to increase my skills."

As professionals, we each need to take responsibility for our practices, be transparent about our credentials, abilities and check out our client's expectations and assumptions. This is especially important as most clients shy away from asking therapists about their qualifications and competencies.

Personally, when I say I "do IFS" it means I feel confident enough in the model and in my access to Self-energy that I can offer the whole protocol to some, or most, clients should they want that. All clients may not want or need me to take them through all the steps of healing and nor, for example, have I always been successful in having client's gatekeeper protectors give space for the client's Self to emerge. Nonetheless, I consider that I am still "doing IFS".

An IFS session probably looks different with each client with whom I work. In a way, it should – as although IFS can be described as a protocol, I am still creating a unique relationship with every client and every part. Together we will be relating to discrete parts in the client, each of which has unique needs, fears, history, perspective, and beliefs, etc. and will need a personalised response from my system.

> ## Transition reflection
>
> "I tell clients, I know only pure IFS therapy, so in one way I have less to get in the way." (BS, certified IFS practitioner and experienced PA)

In writing this, I'm hoping to encourage you to be accountable and aware of your current level of training and proficiency. But I also want to offer some soothing for any of your protectors, who may be doing some comparative, rule-book, or catastrophic thinking inside your head. "Doing IFS" may mean different things to your parts and it might be helpful to find out what some of their expectations are, as they might be getting in the way. Here are some examples of parts' extreme reactions:

- *I'm doing it wrong, my IFS trainer got to an exile every demo, I can't get clients into Self-to-part relationship with protectors, let alone exiles.*
- *I have to use all 6 Fs every session with a client.*
- *If I don't get through all the healing steps, I'm not doing IFS.*
- *I feel stupid doing direct access; I think I'll just give up on IFS.*
- *I preferred my old therapy model; I didn't know I wasn't doing it right then as there was no protocol to follow.*
- *I can't mess this up, my work manager is suspicious of IFS anyway.*

All such parts are welcome and can be helped to relax. The attrition rate can be high for people doing post-qualifying training, especially for those not used to a therapy with a protocol. One of the reasons for my writing this book is to try and help you stick in there and work at "doing IFS" with self-awareness, evolving competence and Self-energy, all of which may increase as you take note of what IFS is not.

Discerning what IFS is not

Your transition to IFS competence will be increased by you attending to what IFS is not, and how it differs from some therapies and is like others in some respects. For example, one of the things I like about having a protocol to follow in both EMDR and IFS, is that there is a "bottom line" aspect to the work. An IFS therapist articulated something along these lines recently:

> I like working with IFS compared to doing "talking therapy". You know, I'd listen and be with clients and hope that in a few years that would help them feel better about things. But we/I wouldn't know if it was because the external circumstances had changed over time or because our work had had an effect. Now I can tell them, well, we've talked to that part and done that work… It's easier to know when therapy is working or not working. I can feel when it's off and I know when a part has yet to unburden, etc.

Something about the tangibility of IFS is appealing to him.

It's not that other therapists, professionals and "ordinary people" don't have access to Self-energy, they can and do. Non-IFS therapists may also help their clients access more Self-energy. Take mindfulness, for example. Mindfully observing the internal world (thoughts, feelings, urges, sensations, etc.) from a distance is not IFS. The goal of such mindfulness could be said to be becoming aware of emotions, thoughts etc., and allowing them to be in awareness without needing to change or interact with them. Taking up a witnessing or observer position and stepping back from a need to change the internal world can be helpful. This process may even be seen as an aspect of IFS. However, IFS offers much more: the creation of Self-to-part relationships which means creating a relationship to the emotions and thoughts in the body and the parts who hold them. IFS is about bringing parts and Self together, not having Self watch parts from a distance. This is an easy mistake to make as parts getting in the way of Self-to-target part relationship are so often asked to distance or "step back".

Doing mindfulness and IFS may have some of the same outcomes such as improving self-regulation and decreasing stress, but the goals of each thera-peutic process distinguish them from each other (for the goals of IFS, see p. 100, Chapter 4). In my view, a working belief in and experience of Self together with the skills to help Self relate to parts in a healing way is what makes IFS what it is.

Transition reflection

"When I drop IFS, the therapy can be easier. The analytical parts in the client and I are really happy to analyse together, the parts of the client that want to 'wallow in it' are happy and the parts who don't want to change are happy and if they are happy my parts are happy. But nothing happens, we're just talking." (NM Integrative psychotherapist working with IFS)

IFS is not Hakomi, Focusing, meditation, prayer, Clean Questions, Schema therapy, Transactional Analysis nor Narrative Therapy, although there may be similarities and common ground between them. Differentiating IFS from other forms of therapy is part of becoming proficient at IFS.

Being willing to share, from Self, what is and is not IFS

Sometimes, clients come for IFS who are experienced in a different form of therapy. This might be because they have had years of a particular form of therapy or because they are therapists themselves who work using a different modality. The client may have parts wanting to do IFS their way or understand and think about IFS processes in a particular way. Generally, if it's not getting in the way of doing "true" "clean" or what I think of as "plain vanilla IFS" as taught in the IFSI trainings, then I might let things be. However, if it gets in the way of the fundamental Self-to-part relationship, then I am likely, in time, to raise the issue – speaking *for* not *from* parts. For example, if a client is either wholly blended with parts or "blissed out" on Self I might enquire if I can share with them what I have noticed of their process and say, "an aim of IFS is to have Self be with the part which involves you being aware of both aspects of yourself at the same time. Am I right in thinking that part or parts of you are working for that not to happen?"

Another example I can think of in which I might explain how IFS differs from a client's expectations of therapy might be around integration. Sometimes clients are up for identifying parts and say, "they just need to be integrated". If I sense these words are coming from a part who wants other parts gone from the system because they want "integration" to mean "becoming mono minded with me in charge", I may mention that in IFS integration means something other than they might think. We cannot get rid of parts; we can help them heal or transform. The concept and language of "integration" is not particularly dominant in the IFS lexicon; rather we talk of harmonising, which happens as a result of the IFS process. As Schwartz and Sweezy (2020, p. 97) describe it: "When we help extreme, isolated, polarised parts to disarm and trust the Self, they integrate and harmonise, causing the feeling of fragmentation to decrease rather than increase."

There is more to becoming an IFS therapist or practitioner than being "in Self"

Most therapy trainings (and IFS is no exception) do not have the time to help attendees reflect on what they may need to keep and what to let go of from their old professional selves and previous trainings in order to embrace IFS fully and efficiently and *become* an IFS therapist/practitioner rather than merely *do IFS*.[6] Similarly, there is little time to explore what of attendees' previous trainings and personal and professional selves align with IFS concepts and practices. These enquiries are invariably left to supervisors like me who are willing to join with supervisees in attending to such significant and life altering personal and professional identity shifts, with the aid of all that IFS has to offer.

In this second part of the chapter, I hope to inspire you to begin reflecting on what you might need to let go of in terms of your existing therapeutic/healing/professional behaviours, beliefs, identity, and role. Also, don't forget, doing IFS isn't about getting rid of your parts, silencing them nor even convincing parts to change. All parts are to be welcomed and appreciated as unique individuals operating from a place of positive intention towards their system. Our pre-IFS therapist/practitioner/professional parts may have skills that are still valuable. Equally, whatever their level of experience, training, and dedication, through no fault of their own, parts cannot do, be, or transform as Self does. It is in the best interests of our parts to allow Self to lead in our own systems as this enables Self to lead and be active in our client's systems.

Psychotherapy training brings about personal and professional change

Training in any form of psychotherapy involves personality change. Indeed, so commonly known is this that my initial training came with a "health warning" that marriages might become destabilised as one partner changed and the other remained the same. My "health warning" to you as you read this book and train in IFS, is that the profound self-change necessary in becoming an IFS therapist/practitioner/professional may not only destabilise your external relationships and systems, but it will also necessitate some level of personal and professional deconstruction and reconstruction. It is my hope that reading this book can be a companion to you and help you undergo those shifts consciously. In addition, for those of you who have come to IFS training after already qualifying and practising as therapists, I hope the book will give you the desire and confidence to befriend your system and especially those protectors who learned to do therapy differently. They may be invested in not letting go of the old ways and old ideas for long enough for you to learn by practising plain-vanilla IFS, or IFS on its own terms (not merged into something else or watered down in some way).

Deconstructing and reconstructing

My journey to becoming an IFS therapist and consultant has been a long one and Table 2.1 outlines some of the therapy-based experiences/learning and influences that have tilled the soil in which the seeds of IFS have grown

Table 2.1 Pro-IFS influences

Breakthrough/breakdown experience and first experience of therapy	*Humanistic Integrative Training[7] and Voice Dialogue Therapy[8]*	*The Work of Byron Katie[9]*
• Emotions can hijack personality and grab the driving seat. • Extreme emotions pass and fighting against them doesn't help that process. • I don't know from the outside who I am on the inside (so how can anyone else know just from looking at the outside?). • Calm, clarity, curiosity, connection, courage, confidence received from and modelled by the two therapists leading in-patient group psychotherapy.	• Experiencing a few main subpersonalities, including my inner critic and the Observer. • Rational Mind separates and I realise it is not "me". • Learning that inside there is something other than just subpersonalities. • Learning about Drama Triangle parts, Victim, Rescuer, Persecutor, resonates with my system.	• Beginning to glimpse that reality is self-created and neither singular nor monolithic. • Truth is subjective and beliefs can be validated as true while simultaneously not being true. • It is possible to recognise and reclaim projections. • Loving what and who is in front of me is a process not a fixed end point.

Table 2.1 Cont.

• Encouragement to be curious towards what is on the inside and creative in expressing that. • My past affects me in the present whether I am consciously aware of it or not.	• Healthy Triangle ways of being appeal: vulnerable, responsive and responsible to myself, owning my potency. • I am not who others have said/say I am.	• Others are in process and not fixed. • Tough love feels real and better than conditional love.
Developmental Transformations (DvT) form of Dramatherapy[10]	*EMDR*[11] *therapy and training*	*Process-oriented supervision training*[12] *and practice (the seven-eyed model)*
• All parts are welcome and equal • Being is inherently unstable • Embodying, enacting, expressing a part/role can be fun and playful • Physically feeling the difference resulting from the practice (more presence, agency, choice, connection) • The therapist is not the mechanism of healing, the processes are • Encountering another helps me encounter myself	• Trauma exists in the present tense • Dual attention – one foot in the past and one foot in the present aids healing • Emotional or psychological healing is innate, just like physical healing • The therapist is not the mechanism of healing • Trusting the client's self-healing helps me remain non-attached and more available • A protocol helps me stay present, connected, and compassionate towards the client	• Parallel process is inevitable and spotting and working with it can be helpful • Everything is data (curious non-attachment is key) • People find people frightening and I want ways to relate that ameliorate that for me and others • My relationship with fear is in process • My professional authority gets constrained on the inside • Valuing transparency, equality, autonomy, and reflection

and flourished. It isn't necessary to know the ins and outs of the therapies or trainings I mention, but if you are interested to know more, website details and references appear in the endnotes. Reflect on your own therapeutic, healing, professional and spiritual journey, and experiences up to now using the exercises at the end of this chapter, together with Appendix II.

Obviously, this is a look in the rear-view mirror at life, but perhaps you can see how some of the above made me "ripe" for IFS. In my first experience of therapy, for example, I experienced my own multiplicity at first hand: stable and functioning at times, emotionally hijacked at others. I also had my first experience of Self-led therapists.

Conclusion

As someone whose foundational training is Humanistic Integrative, I feel lucky that I escaped the extreme positions of other therapeutic modalities. For example, in the psychodynamic tradition, the therapist is taught to be the reparative parent and significant attachment figure for a client/ dependant who is often viewed as possessing major developmental deficits. At the opposite end of the scale, there are those therapists who are taught to be more like a blank canvas with strict boundaries around not self-disclosing, wearing the same clothes each weekday so that clients with appointments on Tuesday always get the same presentation of the therapist. Somehow, and more by luck than judgment (thank you, universe) I chose to attend a training course in which I embraced the concept of self-healing about which Maslow writes in his seminal work *Toward a Psychology of Being* (1998, p. 55):

> Every human being has *both* sets of forces within him. One set clings to safety and defensiveness out of fear, tending to regress backward, hanging on to the past, ... *afraid* to take chances, afraid to jeopardise what he already has, *afraid* of independence, freedom and separateness. The other set of forces impels him forward toward wholeness of Self and uniqueness of Self, toward full functioning of all his capacities, toward confidence in the face of the external world at the same time that he can accept his deepest, real, unconscious Self.

My Humanistic Integrative training introduced me to the idea of choosing the nature of my therapeutic relationships[13] and I escaped a lot of needless pressure by having permission to believe in the client's potential for self-growth and self-healing, no matter how wounded the person. My parts have not had the worry of how to single-handedly reparent my clients nor how to somehow make up for all the deficits they experienced as neglected, abused children (many of which I too experienced). I believe this enabled me to access more Self-energy which in turn enabled my clients to access more Self-energy and self-healing of their own.

Exercises

1) Reflecting on previous training and existing practice

- You might like to do this with a peer or peers, in supervision, with a colleague or on your own.
- Have to hand writing or art materials and large sheets of paper, or sand tray/small world items.
- Explore, express, plot answers to the following questions.
  a) In your core training or previous experience, what were you taught, or what did you learn and embrace about the nature of the therapist/ healer/professional role and the therapeutic/healing/supervisory relationship?
  b) In your core training or previous profession, what were you taught, or what did you learn and embrace about the nature of healing and change?
  c) In your core training and/or postgraduate supervision training, what were you taught, or what did you learn, embrace, or keep to yourself about the nature of psychological damage and psychological pain?
  d) In your previous training and studying, what were you taught, or what did you learn about working with trauma?
  e) In your core training, or previous experience what were you taught, or what did you learn about multiplicity? How do you understand multiplicity now?

(To prime your thinking, see Appendix II which features common responses to the above explorations, together with endnotes providing and signposting you to key IFS information.)

2) Beginning to explore how Internal Family Systems therapy *aligns with* or *diverges from* your existing foundation

- You might like to do this with a peer or peers, in supervision, with a colleague or on your own.

- Have to hand writing or art materials and large sheets of paper, or sand tray/small world items.
- Take your responses to questions 1a to 1e, and discuss them with someone familiar with IFS.
- Consider how your responses *align with* or *diverge from* IFS theory, concepts, and practice. See Appendix II for endnote references which provide and signpost you to key IFS teaching related to the words, phrases and concepts I include there to prime your thinking.

You might also find the following helpful as sources of information:

- Supervisor/consultant
- IFSI training
- PAs assisting on trainings
- The IFS Institute website (videos, articles, podcasts etc.)
- Published IFS texts (see IFS Institute bookstore)
- Endnotes throughout the book

3) Considering what to let go of and what to embrace further

- You might like to do this with a peer or peers, in supervision, with a colleague or on your own.
- Have to hand writing or art materials and large sheets of paper, or sand tray/small world items.
- Comparing and contrasting your findings from questions 1 and 2, is there anything (a concept, theory, or practice) from your past ways of working that you might need or want to let go of as part of your personal and professional life transforming with IFS?
- Comparing and contrasting your findings from questions 1 and 2, is there anything (a concept, theory, or practice) you want to embrace more fully as part of your transitioning to IFS?

Notes

1 See for example: ukcpd.net/collegemembers/conscious-competence-ladder-developing-new-skills/

2 In his trainings, Schwartz makes it clear that dissociation is not pathological but the activity of parts and can be worked with as you would expect. The supervisee uses non-IFS language but could easily have used the language of parts: "I feel

some blending with a dissociating part," for example, and I could have asked to speak with it as a part.

3 Parallel process is an important concept in therapy, which can be noticed and interrupted in supervision (see Chapter 9; Hawkins and Shohet, 2012; Redfern, 2023).

4 If the IFS professional has plenty of Self-energy, that acts like a tuning fork so that the client can begin to vibrate with or access their own Self-energy (Schwartz and Sweezy, 2020, p. 278).

5 At the time of writing, regulations exist around adoption-related counselling, and legislation is being sought to end the practice of conversion therapy in the UK, while non-counselling titles and roles such as "Clinical Psychologist" and "Dramatherapist" are legally regulated and protected.

6 One of my psychotherapy influences, a trauma specialist and dramatherapist, David Read Johnson, writes (1999, p. 59): "It is conceivable that a two year Masters program and a six month internship might prepare a student for *doing* creative arts therapy, but it is clearly not enough to prepare a student for *being* a creative arts therapist … What will help our graduates achieve this goal is to experience closely-held relationships with senior therapists for several years."

7 My accrediting professional body lists brief explanations of different therapies here: www.bacp.co.uk/about-therapy/types-of-therapy/

8 See www.voicedialogueinternational.com

9 See www.thework.com

10 See www.developmentaltransformations.com

11 See www.emdrassociation.org.uk; www.emdr-europe.org; and www.emdria.org. Also see Bruce Hersey's websites (www.brucehersey.com and https://www.emdr ifs.com) for IFS-informed EMDR consultation trainings and more.

12 See www.cstdbath.co.uk and www.cstdlondon.co.uk

13 For example, see Clarkson, P. (2003) *The Therapeutic Relationship*.

Part II
Barrier to transitioning
Not grasping key IFS
concepts and practices

3
Understanding the why, the what and the when of the IFS model

Introduction

This is the first of three chapters forming Part II of the book which focuses on reducing the potential barrier to successfully transforming your practice, work, vocation etc., of not grasping key IFS concepts and practices – after all, if we have failed to fully understand a concept or practice, then we will probably not be getting the results we hope for and this could be discouraging.

Unlike much of the book, which pays attention to the "who" of the IFS model (Who am I talking to? Who is driving my/the client's inner psychic bus? Who else helps maintain the symptoms/problem?), this chapter details *why* we do certain things in IFS and *when*.

The exercises in this chapter spotlight parts activated by learning, learning preferences and reflecting on how far you have come.

Knowing why we do things can help

I imagine I'm not the only person who finds it easier to learn a new skill if I know *why* things are done in X way or Y order. Also, if more than one thing gets the same results, then it is useful to know the answers to questions like, "Why use A not B?" and "When do I use B rather than A?" How easy it is to misunderstand and get things confused can be demonstrated with reference to a group supervision session of a cohort of trainees learning eye movement desensitisation and reprocessing (EMDR). Confusion occurs around two different elements of EMDR, which both seem to have the same effect.

> *Trainee A:* "This EMDR is great. I had a new client this week and it went really well. They only had the one session and reached SUDS

DOI: 10.4324/9781003243571-6

(Subjective Units of Distress) of 0 out of 10 at the end of that first session. They never came back. They didn't need to, I guess."

Supervisor: "Tell us more about that."

Trainee A: "Yes, I always Install a calm place[1] in the first session. Then they'd been telling me about their problems and their history, and they were getting distressed. As it was near the end of the session, I coached them into their calm place and it all went: no more distress; like magic!"

Supervisor: "Anyone want to respond or comment on that?"

Trainee B: "I also had great results with a client I've previously been doing talking therapy with. We had successfully Installed their safe place and the other phases that come before starting the bilateral stimulation (BLS). After the first set of BLS I asked them what they noticed, and they said they were chilled and calm and had no distress at all. It was amazing!"

Supervisor: "OK, let's stop there and revise what we think we know ..."

So, Trainee A had learnt **what** a calming resource is – a resource to bring calm and containment to a person's system. The trainee had also grasped the **when** by using it to help safely bring a session to a close in helping stabilise a distressed or triggered client. However, they had not understood the difference between the calm brought about through using a calming resource, the "calm" or "numbing" that arises through internal blocking of access to distress, and with successful completion of the Desensitisation phase[2] when the client has successfully activated neural networks holding the pain, distress and dysfunctional elements of memory and reprocessed them to resolution (in an IFS sense to a full unburdening, including retrieval and redo if needed). They hadn't grasped **why** they needed to lead the client through the whole eight phases of the EMDR protocol, not just apply a calming resource, which is only part of that lengthier therapeutic process.

Trainee B had grasped the **what** and the **when** of moving to Desensitisation after the earlier phases of EMDR. They had yet to fully grasp the **why** of the Desensitisation phase, which is not to bring or expect instant "calm" or "numbing" but to facilitate the client in maintaining their window of tolerance so that they can revisit/relive and "go to" or "be with" trapped or frozen trauma, pain, and grief, etc., to metabolise and digest it (or in IFS language, to witness and unburden).

Learning *what* to do can be a useful starting point; understanding *when* and *why* we do what we do, i.e., the function of what we do, is important in consolidating learning and getting the successful outcomes that IFS can bring.

Table 3.1 The 6 Fs

1st F	Find the part in or around your body
2nd F	Focus on the part
3rd F	Flesh out the part
4th F	How do you Feel towards the part?
5th F	BeFriend the part
6th F	Address the Fears of the part

The 6 Fs

Below we explore the purpose or function of these important elements of getting to know a part (see Table 3.1).

I remember during one of the weeks of my Level 1 in 2014, practice groups were tasked with focusing on just the first three of the 6 Fs: find, focus, and flesh out. I didn't understand why this was required and I didn't enjoy the experience. One of the practising pairs spent what seemed like ages on the 3rd F. As they did that, inside my parts were vocal:

- *But that's witnessing before the 4th F, isn't it?*
- *They're doing it wrong.*
- *I'm not practising doing it like that when I'm in the therapist role.*
- *We haven't established it is Self speaking, so who is telling us about this part if it's not Self?*
- *I must be missing something!*

Looking back now, I see my problem as arising from not understanding the purpose of the first 3 Fs, especially flesh out. But it was early days for me, after all, and everything was not necessarily going to make sense straight away. Let's look at this further.

Fs 1 to 3 – Differentiating[3] using find, focus on, and flesh out

On the other side of that period of confusion with the 6 Fs, my understanding now is that find, focus on, and flesh out are intended to help *differentiate the target part*, which means to help the client and therapist become aware of it as separate from the client. These first three Fs help the individual understand that the part's feelings and beliefs are not their own. And, if something initially shows up for the client as an emotion or a body sensation, finding it, focusing on it, and fleshing it out is intended to help *differentiate* it *as a part*. For example, some clients (I am often one of them), on going inside, always begin by noticing body sensation. "Applying" the first 3 Fs to the sensation(s), i.e., just openly noticing, and placing attention there, invariably leads to a part, a recognisable subpersonality. Susan McConnell (2020, p. 26) explains this well:

> "Fleshing out" means to get to know more than one aspect of a part. However a part first appears, it is only once we know the part as more than a sensation or more than a feeling that this subpersonality takes on the impression of being a part we can relate to as a person with a history, behaviors, hopes.

Fs 1 to 3 – Embodying using find, focus on, and flesh out

It is worth noting the "embodiment aspect" of the 3 Fs, by which I mean the facet of the model that is intended not only to help locate parts in and around the body, but to ascertain how the target part uses, affects, and controls the client's body. Arriving at such information via direct access or through your own observation, helps to "give body" to the part, which in turn helps it to be differentiated and recognised as a distinct part. This can be useful for parts-detecting in future therapy sessions and in life, helping the client to notice who is driving their inner psychic bus. Here is an example featuring Jason, a supervisee, and Percy, his client:

Supervisor: "How would it be if you, Jason, play Percy's part and I play you, the therapist, doing implicit direct access?" (*Jason nods*)

Therapist (Played by me the supervisor): "Percy, is it okay if I point out some of what I notice about you, how you hold your body for example?"

Client (Played by Jason): "Sure, sounds a bit odd but you are the expert, so I'll go with it."

Therapist: "Great, thank you. Well, I'm noticing that, right now, your voice is even, and you speak in a 'clipped' kind of way, your eye contact is direct and professional, you hold yourself still and upright and I get a strong, 'no-nonsense' vibe from you. Does any of that seem accurate?"

Supervisee/client: "Yes, he's just like that! Oh, sorry, I'll get back into role as Percy's part: Yes, I'm a professional, I get things done, I've a business to run. Your point is ...?"

Therapist: "Well, I wonder if you remember last week when you got upset about your dog having to stay over at the vets – you'd just come from there? (*Jason nods*) Momentarily, your voice was different, soft and uncertain, you were curled over with your gaze fixed firmly on the carpet, you seemed very sad ... (*Jason is looking confused, and I ask him to bear with me*). Well, that was what therapists like me would call a part of you."

Supervisee: (*Coming out of role*) "I have done that, we use parts language, it's just this 'controlling' part doesn't know it's a part."

Supervisor/therapist: "Sure, I get that. Shall I continue talking to you as Percy? (*Jason nods*) And you, this part of Percy who is the professional businessman who wants a job done right is recognisably different to the part of Percy who was hurting about your dog. You came in very quickly last week to make sure the sad one didn't linger for long. Even though I mentioned you were in the right place here in therapy to get emotional about something you had every reason to get emotional about."

Supervisee/client: "You said 'part', are you telling him, oops, me, that I'm a part?"

Therapist: "Yes, I am. I understand and experience you as a successful businessman, and an important part of Percy's life who may even have brought him to therapy. (*Jason nods*) Also, and you may not know this, there is a You, a Percy who is not a part who can take care of that sad part, so you don't have to feel embarrassed by or concerned about it. I would like to introduce you to that Percy one day."

Supervisee (Out of role): "Hmm, that all seems too easy to me."

Supervisor: "Sure, and that's partly why we do things like this in supervision when we're not with the clients we find triggering, it's easier in some way."

The 4th F – How do you feel towards the part? during in-sight work

On the face of it, this seems to be a straightforward question. However, without a meaningful understanding of *what the question is for*, IFS professionals may find themselves "personalising the question" or failing to notice that they are asking a variation on the question based on their therapist parts' previous learning, which might need to be let go of or eased back on. Let's look at the **why** of this question. The reason for persisting with the question in its original wording is because "How do you feel towards the part?" serves an important function of differentiation; of unblending the part from Self. The answer gives vital information about the presence of Self (revealed by an indication of one or more of the C and P qualities) or about the presence of another part reacting in some way to the previous part. It's sometimes a good idea to add the words "right now", as in "How do you feel towards the part right now?" to make clear that we are not looking for how the client generally feels towards a target part, we want to know how much Self is present *at this moment*.

Without differentiating part from Self, there can be no mutual two-person relationship. This explains why those who are skilful in or used to mindfulness and meditation may initially struggle with IFS because they can be used to being either in a part (the monkey mind as some people call this, for example) from which they are trying to move away, or in an observing or blissful witness state that a part of them may be seeking. Whereas in IFS, part and Self are differentiated one from another in the hope that they can then turn and be with each other, connect and communicate in a two-way relationship.

Differentiation is thus an important aspect of the integration that IFS brings[4]. For example, without first differentiating (find, focus, flesh out, feel towards) an exile, it cannot consciously progress through the healing steps of IFS. The very role of protectors is to keep exiles hidden or exiled, i.e., undifferentiated or "lost in the system".

The following are unworthy replacements to this crucial unblending question and need to be given a backseat:

- How do you feel about the part?
- How is the part feeling?
- How does the part feel about you?

Using the first replacement question above, "How do you feel about the part?" is to invite a thinking part's response "It's okay" or perhaps "Well, I don't like it." Similarly, at this point in the process (4th F), to ask "How does the part feel?" is to invite witnessing to occur before knowing that a Self-to-part relationship has been established – this may not go well. Also, asking the part how it feels about you (i.e. the client) instead of the 4th F question may or may not indicate if Self-energy is present. Parts often react with anger towards Self or distrust so such a response would not necessarily indicate a part's presence.

Something else to be aware of is that, once you are using the correctly worded 4th F question, things may still not run smoothly. If you don't know what the question is for, and why IFS places such emphasis on it, you may be prone to accepting answers from the client that grind the work to a halt rather than facilitate the flow of the model. Clients will often answer "How do you feel towards the part?" with "I think …" answers, or "It's doing X, Y …" or "I remember when A, B, C …" or "It's telling me about …" I encourage all those learning IFS to practise *not accepting those answers without further enquiry*. When you meet any of the above responses, it is important to persist with your curiosity. One of the ways I have learnt to do this is by incorporating the client's answer into my rephrasing of the initial question:

- As you think … how do you feel towards this part?
- As the part does X, Y … how do you feel towards it?
- How are you feeling towards the part as it does X, Y?
- As you recall A, B, C … how do you feel towards this part?
- As the part tells you … how do you feel towards it?

If the client reports feeling something other than the C qualities towards the part, you have an opportunity to develop your skills in asking the reactive part to give space (go into a waiting room etc.) or making it the new target part for a while. If no parts react, then we move to the 5th F.

The 5th F – befriending the part[5]

We are taught during IFS training that the primary attachment relationship is the Self-to-part relationship in which the Self of the client is the primary healing agent of parts of the client. However, it may take some time before the novice IFS professional "knows this in their bones". This F is when we help the client more firmly establish and deepen that Self-and-part relationship. It's where, essentially, the client and the part get to know each other better. There are certain questions we ask a protector – either through direct access or in-sight:

- "What is your role/job in the system?" or "how are you trying to help Mary?" (it's necessary to use your therapist-Self qualities of patience and persistence here and keep enquiring until you really understand the part's role and positive intention for the system.)

- "How long have you been doing this job?" (It's often good here to encourage the client to notice any images or memories they may be shown by way of answer. This question and the next also helps differentiate past from present.)
- "How old are you?"
- "Do you like doing your job?" (This begins to open up the idea for the protector that it may have options now. It can also be powerful for protectors to realise how exhausted they feel.)
- "If you could do something else in and for the system, what would you prefer?"'

Also, because befriending is about creating a two-way relationship, we can be curious about the part's relationship with and responses to the client's Self. Using in-sight, we guide the client to ask questions such as:

- How old does the part think you are? (Parts are often surprised and relieved to see that the client has grown up.)
- Does it feel you get what it is sharing? (Parts are like small children who feel so much better if we can attend and attune to them.)
- How does the part respond when you send it appreciation for how hard it has been working for the system? (It's likely that the part has been starved of appreciation.)
- What needs to happen now? (Especially helpful if a part reacts adversely to Self's presence, say with anger or rejection. The client's Self can respond appropriately whether that is with an apology or assurance that the relationship can build slowly, or that Self doesn't need the part to change but it can once the part it protects is safe and healed).

Checking on the hook-up (which in IFS refers to the two-way Self-and-part relationship) is an important element of befriending because it enables a protector to recognise that Self is different to whoever hurt the client in the past and unlike parts who might be critical or controlling towards the part inside. Self is different, it validates the part's thoughts and feelings and sends appreciation for its dedication, hard work and positive intention for the system. This curious and appreciative befriending process helps the part notice that Self values and cares for it, is worth trusting, can be available to it, and in time can heal the part(s) it is burdened with protecting – the exile(s).

The 6th F – addressing a protector's fears[6]

With the client accessing Self-energy, the therapist guides the client, or uses direct access, to be curious about the protector's fears, i.e. 'What are you afraid will happen if you stop performing your role?' Exploring protector fears is important for various reasons:

- The part's responses may give valuable information about the exile(s) it protects (see the example of Sol below)
- The replies can provide important clues about another part(s) the protector is in conflict with or is afraid of (i.e., it will reveal a polarisation; see the example of Jayla below)
- It enables client and therapist to begin addressing those fears and hope-merchant which builds the trusting Self-and-part relationship
- It can help therapist parts not get hooked into believing rather than validating
- It's an important part of gaining permission to go deeper into the system to the exiles

Schwartz and Sweezy (2020, pp. 137–138) provide an example of a client, Sol, using in-sight to get to know a critical part inside of him. Here the part reveals its fear that if Sol keeps making so many mistakes he won't be liked. The therapist is curious about who wouldn't like Sol which reveals the exile this part protects who is burdened by feeling less than Sol's ideal older brother.

Another example might be of working with a client's dissociating firefighter (or another soother or distractor) who steps in at home when the client's husband is critical.

> *Therapist:*   "Jayla, ask the part what it's afraid would happen if it didn't numb you out when Colin criticises you."
>
> *Client:*   "It says if it didn't do what it does, I'd get angry (*as the IFS professional, you would notice/parts-detect that the firefighter is talking about another part who would get angry*) at my husband, which he wouldn't tolerate. The part says the conflict would get out of hand and then the relationship would be over, and we'd be done for."

Although the 6 Fs are "basic building blocks" of IFS, there is a lot to understand regarding why you follow them. Perhaps allow yourself some breathing time to fully take in the above. Maybe have a walk around the block (this might help your nervous system digest and integrate any new learning and make neuronal connections or associations). Then take some time to reflect on your practice with the 6 Fs and consider if you need to do further reading, practising, raise something in supervision and so on.

Getting buy-in to doing IFS

There are other occasions (in addition to during working with the 6 Fs) when addressing protector fears are especially important (and exile fears too, depending on who has shown up). One is when working with Self-like parts (see Chapter 8) or dominant parts who may fear unblending to allow Self to come forward to meet and be with them. Using direct access, I might ask such a part, "What are you afraid would happen if you gave some space for the Jocelyn who isn't a part to come and say hi?"

Transition reflection

"The clients I had before I trained in IFS I think of as 'legacy clients'. I'm having some tough love conversations about how and if we continue working together." (GH, accredited psychotherapist and IFS therapist)

Another occasion when it is important to address the fears of dominant parts is during contracting (see Chapter 4).

Some therapist parts with prior training may need negotiating with as you seek permission to try using aspects of the IFS model or share the laws of inner physics, etc. (See the example of Fiona in Chapter 6). Registered Social Worker and Clinical Counsellor, Sarah Murphy calls these parts "fallback parts".

Asking parts to step back and allow Self to be present

There can be confusion and much frustration about this intervention for IFS professionals and for the parts they are asking to step back. I'm grateful to my first-ever IFS trainer, Mike Elkin, who, when he was teaching about befriending a protector, had a particular emphasis and used the unblending wording: "Ask the part if it is willing to go to a conversational distance."

This wording emphasises both differentiation and relationship. After all, conversations are best from a conversational distance. If someone is physically too close and in our personal space, parts can feel threatened and will blend. Also, with my eyesight, I cannot clearly see someone who is too close to me, which also inhibits a productive/positive conversation. If a person is too far away, then talking is challenging also.

Elkin's teaching helped me realise that it is okay to relate to parts – all, and any parts – even if they aren't the target part and they make themselves known in response to the 4th F question. In fact, it can be helpful to use such wording as it suggests a part is welcome and will be talked to, if it wants. There are other ways in which to ask this important differentiating question and make it relational, for example: "Okay, so it seems a frustrated part is here, see if it will step back/give you some space to be with the other one. If not, let me know."[7]

Parts taking it personally if a part will not step back

It's possible you may have parts that get triggered when a client's parts don't step back. You may have seen Schwartz wade through parts like a pro and feel you are doing something wrong if things don't go as smoothly. Here are some thoughts on this:

- Know that you are not alone in not having the same success as Schwartz (he's been doing what he does for decades, you haven't).
- Believe me when I say it's likely not to be personal on the part's behalf.
- Things might proceed more easily if your part that is invested in parts stepping back gives You more space to make the request without attachment to that particular outcome.
- Somehow communicate that the part has a choice about whether it steps back or not, that you are negotiating not demanding.
- Make it clear you welcome the opportunity to get to know the part if it won't step back.

Hopefully your IFS training will have highlighted how to get to know a protector and I won't repeat all of that here.[8] Rather, I will share some general principles of relationship-building inspired by the non-IFS but parts-friendly book on negotiating, communication and styles of human interaction, *Rapport* (Alison & Alison, 2020):

- Parts, like humans in general, desire autonomy[9] – which includes having choice.
- It makes sense that some parts will want to be met, listened to, understood, and appreciated before doing what we ask.
- Your Self is better at building rapport (and thus gaining co-operation) than your parts.

Parts trying to "do it right" or who are otherwise attached to an outcome (i.e., having a part step back) may create what these authors know as psychological "reactance" (p. 98), which is a threat response due to a part feeling its behavioural freedom is being controlled or constrained, or it is being "made" or "expected" to change.

Creating safety is crucial and includes giving safety updates

This is not necessarily taught during IFS Level 1, but it is something I frequently bring to client work, especially with those who have a history of any sort of complex, developmental, relational or one-off trauma. Basically, I draw attention to whatever aspects of safety I can for the part with whom I or the client (or supervisee) is speaking. The reason I do this is to help the part feel safer. From supervision, here are three different examples of working towards creating *inner* safety:

Attending to the sequence of working with parts

Below is a direct access role play with a supervisee showing that working with another part first might help the target part feel safer:

> Supervisor, Emma, playing the therapist: "Welcome, you are Jesse's anxious part, is that right?"
>
> Supervisee playing the client's part: "Y – e – s,"
>
> *Therapist:* "Welcome, I guess it's a bit anxious-making speaking to me? (*Supervisee nods*) Well, I'm not here to make you feel bad, I just want to be curious and get to know you a bit, would that be okay? And, in case you are worried, there are no wrong answers."
>
> *Client:* "Okay."
>
> *Therapist:* "Thanks. I'm wondering how old you are, if you know – and if you don't that's okay, too."
>
> *Client:* "Nine, I'm nine."

Therapist: "Ah, and you work really hard for Jesse, I hear, (*Supervisee nods*) which sounds kind of tiring.

Client: Mm hm.

Therapist: Do you know how old Jesse is? (*Supervisee pauses then shakes their head*) I wondered about that. Jesse is 32 years old now. Can I tell you about him? (*Supervisee nods*) He shares a flat and has a job, and he's coming to therapy to see me because he wants to help you (and other parts inside) so you don't have to work so hard and feel so anxious all the time – if that's what you'd like. I like him and I think you might too. Would you like to meet him?"

Client: "He won't be angry with me, will he?

Therapist: "No, I'm pretty sure the Jesse who is not a part is going to like you. It's another part inside who maybe wants you gone and would feel angry with you. Would you like Jesse to have a chat with that one so you feel safer in there?"

(*Supervisee nods enthusiastically as a penny has dropped*)

Supervisee no longer playing their client: "Okay, I'm getting a sense of the lack of safety on the inside now, as well as in Jesse's outside world that this part is experiencing."

We move back into dialoguing.

Sometimes, therapist parts can be so keen to impress client's parts with how safe they are, they may forget that much of a client's feelings of danger may derive from the inside and from past experiences. This is especially likely if the client has a history of a suicidal part actively trying to kill the client, or parts have acted in ways that have brought the system into great peril (by being forcibly sectioned or jailed perhaps). External constraints and dangers in the lives of clients also need attending to, of course (see Schwartz & Sweezy, 2020, p. 26, and the concept of constraining environments).

Attending to therapist overwhelm in supervision

It's our last session before a seasonal break and Jordan is only just on time, which is not like him. He is distressed about something that has happened at home and focusing on client work is impossible. He realises the thing that has gone wrong in the present has "joined up with" past devastations. We verbally contract in the moment to work with a three-year-old part and see how far we get in the hour. In addition, I have an unspoken goal or meta-contract for this piece of work, which is to help any parts that show up to feel some safety somehow.

Transition reflection

"For me to offer IFS therapy ethically as an IFS practitioner without previous therapy training has meant doing Level 2 and 3 training, subscribing to the Continuity Program, attending targeted IFS workshops, being a PA, going through the certification process, and having ongoing supervision and therapy." (BS, certified IFS practitioner and experienced PA)

Jordan finds, focuses on and fleshes out the target part: "He's three years old and all alone with feelings that are too big for him." (*He tells me what these are.*)

Supervisor: "Will he give you some space so you can be with him?"

Supervisee (*Taking time inside to check this out*):   "No, I'm feeling really blended with him."

Supervisor: "Okay if I talk with him directly?"

Supervisee: "Yes, we can try that."

Supervisor: "Hello little one, I'm sorry you're so distressed. You're only three and you have these big feelings to manage. (*Supervisee is nodding*) That sounds scary.

(*More nodding. I let the part know that I'm aware of some of what is going on for him and check I've got it right. He nods.*)

I'm wondering, how is it to be speaking with me?"

Supervisee: "Alright but now I'm feeling tension both ends of my body, at the sacrum and at the back of my head across my shoulders."

(*Jordan now has space from the three-year-old and describes his present-moment experience.*)

Supervisor: "Okay, see if these sensations will relax so we can return to the boy, and if not, let me know."

Supervisee: "No, these need attention."

(*I'm guessing these might be parts who are polarised with each other in their protection of the three-year-old, but I keep that to myself.*)

Supervisor: "Sure, who shall we start with?"

Supervisee: "The tension at the sacrum."

Supervisor: "Notice that tension, see if you can flesh it out some more."

Supervisee: "It's telling me it feels unacceptable and ugly and scared."

Supervisor: "And how do you feel towards It?"

Supervisee: "Open and available."

Supervisor: "Great, let it know that and see if it can really feel you. ... See if this part can really feel your safety."

Supervisee: "I'm telling it that I accept it and want to hear from it. It's really focused on the other tension, in my head and shoulders."

Supervisor: "See what it wants to tell you about that."

Supervisee: "That's what's trying to get rid of this one and making it feel unacceptable."

Supervisor: "Does that make sense to you?"

Supervisee: "Yes."

Supervisor: "Let it know and see if you want to say anything to this part about that."

Supervisee: "Yes, I've let it know it makes sense and I've told it that I'll speak with the other part, and I'll keep them safe from each other. They don't have to be scared of each other."

Supervisor: "Great. What needs to happen next?"

Supervisee: "This part is okay for now and wants me to speak to the other part."

Supervisor: "Great, can you find that one in your head and shoulder area?"

Supervisee: "Yes, it feels familiar, I often get this bodily tension when I'm with clients."

Supervisor: "How do you feel towards it?"

Supervisee: "Yes, open to hearing from it."

Supervisor: "Great, let the part feel that openness and ask it to tell you about itself."

Supervisee: "This isn't going to work. I can't do it." (*It seems a hopeless part has jumped in.*)

Supervisor switching in the moment to implicit direct access: "You're right, you can't do what needs to be done. Parts can't get rid of other parts, and you can't help the little three-year-old in the same way that the Jordan who isn't a part can. I know you want to help and wish you could."

Supervisee speaking about the hopeless part: "It's relaxed a little."

Supervisor: "Thank it. See if this one and the other one would both be willing to relax and give you some space to get back to the boy for a few moments before the end of the session."

Supervisee: "Yes, they are relieved they don't have to do anything."

Supervisor: "Great and do you see the little one again?"

Supervisee: "Yes, I feel warm towards him. ... He can feel it this time. He likes that, he doesn't feel so all alone. ... He's sitting next to me now."

Supervisor: "Lovely, really help him feel your warmth and your safety and your welcome. Just be with him. Nothing to be done right now but enjoy being with each other."

Supervisee: "He feels calmer." (*Pausing*)

Supervisor: "Lovely, when you are both ready, come on back to the room."

Supervisee "I feel noticeably different than when I arrived. That was so good to experience the difference it can make for a part to feel Self-energy and presence. For the parts to know that they aren't the ones expected to do IFS with other parts either on the inside or the outside."

Supervisor: "Awesome, that was a great piece of work."

Psychoeducation

I might explain to a supervisee: "Young, wounded parts often don't feel safe. They feel alone or caught in a scary polarisation, or scary situation from which they cannot escape. However, the client also exists in a present-day reality. Sometimes it can be helpful to explain to a part at a level they can understand that there are these two realities existing at the same time. For example, in my therapy, I'm working with a polarised pair of protectors who are six years old and stuck in a scary past situation in which they feel trapped. For them, time stood still, and they don't know they've been doing what they do for over 50 years. When the me who isn't a part was able to be with them, it was really moving and relieving for them to know that I/they did survive, that I/Self is available to them, and they don't have to be alone any longer."

Inner polarisations in beginners

Reflecting on my own journey as well as being witness to the journeys of many non-IFS and IFS novice therapists over the years, I have discovered

Table 3.2 Learner polarisations

Let's wing it/I like to go with the flow	Do IFS by numbers/by the book; I like to follow the rules
Follow the client	Tell the client the answers/what to do or know better than the client
(In supervision) I don't really want help but tell me anyway	(In supervision) I need the answer and I need it now

common, often unspoken, polarisations of parts around learning (see Table 3.2).

One part of the polarity is averse to really following a protocol or what it perceives as "the rules". This part prefers to "wing it" and be free to make it up as they go along. This might show up as the therapist passively "following" the client (rather than following the flow of the IFS model) because that's what the therapist parts believe therapy involves and is a way to get the least blame when it doesn't work. The supervisee might come to supervision saying a version of, "the client won't close their eyes so there's no point doing IFS". There is often another part polarised who embraces the idea of a protocol or map to follow. It wants a script for every circumstance and uses language and concepts taught by other people because it wants to learn to do IFS therapy "properly" and wants "to get it right". For this part, "doing IFS by numbers" is the way to get the least blame if therapy does not go well. The supervisee might come to supervision saying a version of, "Well I asked all the protector questions on the sheet but ..." Unfortunately, while these parts are dominating the novice IFS therapist or practitioner, things are unlikely to go smoothly. It is likely these polarised parts intend to protect against shame but if they block Self-energy, shame is likely to result (and shame has already happened and is lodged in the system).

As with any polarisation, a way to take the heat out of the extremes, is to get permission to go to the exile(s) they protect and bring transformation and healing to them, so the protectors can relax. Alternatively, it may be possible to negotiate with the polarised parts so they give the therapist space when with clients so Self can lead. A third option is to negotiate with the extreme parts so that their skills can become assets rather than liabilities. For example, successful IFS involves embracing spontaneity (Let's wing it could really help here) *and* following the model (doing IFS by numbers is a great way to learn, especially initially). In my experience, both supervisee and supervisor need to have patience and persistence and get permission to do inner work with supervisee parts in supervision.

The what

In concluding, I want to highlight a particular aspect of **the what** of IFS that often seems missing early on in a person's practice. Really flowing with the model can be helped by recognising that *negotiating* is a major aspect of "the what" of IFS. Successful therapy, coaching, teaching, business – if not all relationships – includes an aspect of negotiation: negotiating one's way through stuckness; with protectors for permission to go to exiles; with exiles to not overwhelm; with parts to give space for Self's presence to be more fully felt, and so on. Don't worry if this doesn't make sense at first, or feels out of your reach; there are many different aspects of "the what" of IFS that you can take time to become familiar with and comfortable using.

Exercises

1) Reflecting on learner polarisations

Either on your own, with a colleague(s) or in supervision, consider the learner polarisations in Table 3.2. Do you recognise parts inside you like these? Consider how your system likes to learn new thing. Is it through reading, writing, listening, watching? Do parts like to learn by thinking and in abstract ways to start with before moving on to learning by doing? Do parts like to dive straight in and learn by practising and discovering something for themselves? Are there parts polarised with your preferred ways of learning?

2) Reflecting on learning preferences

Consider the three examples highlighted in the earlier section "Creating safety is crucial and includes giving safety updates". Which example did you relate to most (the direct access piece, the inner therapeutic work, the psychoeducation)? Does your choice of example reflect a preferred learning style? How might you use the concept of the safety update in sessions with clients if you don't already? Would you prefer to come up with what to say in advance or do you trust parts to allow Self's clarity to come forward in the moment?

3) Reflecting on how far you've come

a) Either on your own with a journal, art materials, sand tray or small objects, etc., or with a peer, spend some time looking back on your journey ... seeing how far you've come.

You might want to create/draw/write a timeline beginning with when you first came across IFS and plot points that come up/stand out for you between then and now. Or maybe you want to begin the journey even earlier, when you first knew you wanted to be a therapist ... Be spontaneous, don't think too much about each point, just enough to represent them.

After you have created your timeline, sand tray, picture, etc., reflect on it, being curious towards and about it and what parts have to say to you.

b) If you are working with another person, perhaps ask that person to interview you, being curious about your journey and helping you reflect. You might want to contemplate, and explore Why, What, When and How questions of your own transforming:
- How have I changed between then and now?
- What have I enjoyed along the way?
- What has been challenging?
- Where am I headed?
- Who inside me needs attention?
- What in the job on the outside requires attention?
- How has my understanding of Self developed over time?
- What are my learning edges regarding the model?
- What can I contribute to the IFS community?
- What needs to happen next?
- How will I know I am ready to begin working with exiles, not just protectors?
- When shall I sign up for Level 2/begin supervision/seek certification ...?

Notes

1 If you aren't trained in EMDR, you do not need to know what this means, although the question of "to resource or not to resource" often comes up in IFS trainings. Self-energy is not part of EMDR's conceptual frame and, understandably, therapists may have parts fearful of being with a client who is revisiting their

grief, pain and trauma. During Phase 2 Preparation, resources of various kinds are therefore activated, heightened, and made accessible at will to the client. In EMDR this is called "Installation" and it gives an emotional resource or life raft to which a client turns if and when they feel uncomfortably overwhelmed. In IFS, Self is an innate resource that does not need to be installed but accessed and connected with. IFS also preferences the no-overwhelm contract over resourcing.

2 As an IFS professional, you don't need to know this. However, if you are interested, the eight phases of EMDR are: 1 Client History; 2 Preparation (including resource development and installation); 3 Assessment; 4 Desensitisation; 5 Installation of a Positive Cognition (PC); 6 Body Scan; 7 Closure; 8 Re-evaluation.

3 The concept of "differentiation" is important especially in working with trauma. "To differentiate" has two meanings both of which apply to IFS: 1. To recognise or ascertain what makes (someone or something) different – "ask the part to notice how you (the You who isn't a part) are different to the abuser you grew up with"; 2. To make or become different in the process of growth or development – "the body sensation differentiated into a young pre-verbal part". Verbs similar to differentiate are: transform, metamorphose, evolve, change.

4 HCPC-registered dramatherapist and certified IFS therapist Martin Redfern brought this to my attention.

5 See Ch. 10, "Feeling Toward, Befriending, and Exploring Protector Fears" (Schwartz & Sweezy, 2020).

6 See Box 10.5 (Schwartz & Sweezy, p. 146) which details 11 common manager fears.

7 See Endnote 2, Chapter 5, which highlights Tamala Floyd's adaptation for the BIPOC community of the standard "step back" approach.

8 See Boxes 7.5 and 8.4 (Schwartz & Sweezy, 2020) and Module 2 of the IFSI Level 1 training manual about working with the protective system (Pastor & Gauvain, 2020).)

9 Autonomy relates to being self-governing and having self-directed freedom and moral independence. See also Endnote 6, Chapter 5. It is an important (though white, Western and individualistic) ethical principle and forms part of the code of ethics to which I adhere. If you are coming to therapy from a non-therapist background, what ethical code of conduct will you adhere to and align with? If you have not thought about this, perhaps you could explore this with colleagues. See also Ch. 3, Alison and Alison, 2020 (especially pp. 90–108), in which the authors lay out their four core foundations of rapport one of which is autonomy.

4
Learning how to contract with multiplicity in mind

Introduction

This chapter begins with some of the processes I have learned pre- and post-IFS that help me contract successfully as a self-employed therapist in private practice. It moves into a more IFS focus on therapist parts which, if unacknowledged, may get in the way of successful contracting. An example of reflecting on a non-IFS contract from an IFS lens is included together with a sample intake form, as well as learning by reviewing a consultation session offered by Schwartz as part of the IFS Continuity Program. There is a brief exploration of meta-contracting and implicit contracting, which will be of relevance to non-therapists, as will the exercise at the end of the chapter "Contracting and your inner team".

The term "contracting"

At its most basic, the term "contract" refers to a mutually agreed focus for the work, arrived at through negotiation between the relevant parties who will be engaging in the work together. I prefer to think in terms of "contract*ing*" as it is an active, non-mono umbrella term covering all the elements in this chapter (and more). If your system struggles with the legalistic terminology, there is other wording you can adopt. IFS senior lead trainer, Chris Burris (Burris & Schwartz, 2022), for example, teaches how to arrive at a "workable agreement". Also, it is important to distinguish the words and concepts we use when discussing cases in supervision that only belong in supervision as they are *not* all transferable for use in the therapy relationship. I don't believe I generally use the terms "contract" or "contracting" with a client, while I do with supervisees.

DOI: 10.4324/9781003243571-7

Processes involved in successful contracting (any modality)

Arriving at an appropriate therapeutic contract may not be easily nor quickly achieved. In addition, most trainings either do not specifically teach contracting, or they may model working therapeutically with a bare minimum of contracting along the lines of "go with what is present and see where we get to". The latter is great for the purposes of a demonstration or in a practice group, but may not work so well in a real-life clinical setting. This approach also works well for those who have been practising for many years and know that whatever comes up they can respond appropriately and effectively.

I was fortunate that my early experience as a therapist was as a volunteer in a placement where the work was short-term, either four or ten sessions. This really honed my contracting skills so that the client and I could mutually agree our parameters for a piece of work that would fit the timescale allowed. Mostly, clients left at the end of their allocated sessions having achieved what they had set out to, which felt good to both of us. The client had a good experience of therapy on which to look back, should they decide to undertake further therapeutic work in the future. My contracting skills were honed further after I earned accreditation with the British Association for Counselling and Psychotherapy and began to get EAP (Employee Assistance Programme) work, which was six sessions in duration. Below are some of the things I learned that still apply even now when my primary modality is IFS. They can be adapted for your circumstances and style.

Differentiating between wishful thinking and reality when contracting

One supervisor was fond of saying things like "you're in the real world now, not a classroom" and "you haven't got a magic wand". Somewhere along the way, I made this useful and learned to ask of clients, "so, if I had a magic wand you could use (which I don't unfortunately), what would you want to be different or to have happen by the end of our time together"? In this way, I would ask for the "wishful thinking" upfront, which we could then "deconstruct" to drill down to something more "real".

For example, a client might share: "I want to process my mother's death." We have begun the contracting process. Next, I would want to be curious and uncover some of what the client means by that. After all, the reality is that I do not and cannot know what they mean by their words, nor can I know what is happening for them that makes them think they have not already processed the loss. I also do not know the origin(s) of the words, which may reflect the agenda of someone else in the client's life (family member, boss, the media, a cultural or societal expectation). I want to bring into conscious reality in the space between us what lies behind or under those words, "process my mother's death" which could be "code" for:

- "I need help, I'm drowning my sorrows in two bottles of wine a night."
- "I'm numb, I can't feel anything since she's died, I want to start feeling again."
- "I hated her and I can't take that anywhere, I've never told anyone about the abuse ... I wonder if you might be able to handle that?"

Presuming that I have the same understanding as the client of those words "process my mother's death" is not a sound therapeutic option for me, and I hope not for you either. Once I have a sense of what the words mean to the client, I may still not be ready to agree a contract. I also need to know more about who my potential client is (which will be becoming clearer as we explore the contract together). Only then might I begin the process of agreeing what we might work on together, and how.

Being curious about a potential client

Another contracting principle is to hold back on agreeing the contract until I have a sense of who I am moving into relationship with. This comes naturally to me (thank you, parts) as I have a deep aversion to promising more than is possible, I like to underplay things, and prefer to be pleasantly surprised. I also want certain information to help me determine what to offer and agree to work on and what to refuse to work on or suggest the client takes elsewhere. Some of the things I am curious about include:

- Is this the person's first experience of counselling? If yes, what signals am I picking up about where they think change comes from – do they have an internal or external locus of control[1]?
- If this is not their first experience of counselling, were their previous experiences positive and successful or dissatisfying?
- How has the client come to be here – have they been sent by their doctor? Has a spouse or family member, such as a parent, an investment in their outcome? Are they here reluctantly, desperately, hopefully, realistically? In IFS terms, which part(s) brings them to therapy, and who and what does that part see as being the problem?

- Are they here because they want someone or something else to change and think therapy can make that happen?
- Is the client "psychologically minded", by which I mean do they have some sense of self-awareness, a desire to get to know their inner world? Or are they used to change happening only in the outside world in a concrete and measurable way?
- Do they claim an unremarkable childhood – "fine", trauma free, with "great parents"?

As well as gaining some idea of the client I might be working with, and their approach to therapy, I also bear in mind the practical arrangements and "reality-test" those somewhat.

Considering the practicalities of working together

- What might get in the way of the client engaging with the process? Can they really make this time each week and pay the fee? How smooth or bumpy was the initial enquiry and booking process between us? Can I really commit to seeing them at this time at this fee each week; and if so, for how long?
- If I can only offer short-term work, is the problem/goal too large or too complex for short-term counselling? If yes, is there perhaps a portion of it that we can work on in the short-term? Would exploring the blocks in the way of their goal be worthwhile in the time available? Would offering a positive counselling experience and signposting to a more targeted service be welcome and appropriate?
- Is the issue likely to be trauma-related and, if so, is doing a piece of "pre-trauma treatment" or "pre-therapy" relevant and likely to be valuable and therapeutic before signposting elsewhere?

Having gained a sense of the client, the practicalities, what they expect or hope from therapy, I evaluate that information with as much Self-leadership as possible to avoid the pitfalls of having parts make choices, which I move onto next.

Neither discounting nor elevating oneself

In my experience, beginning IFS professionals may need to unlearn unilateral or compliant contracting, in which a part (or parts) of them treats the client as if they have placed an order off a menu, which the therapist then fulfils. To agree to whatever the client wants in the therapeutic contract is to elevate oneself as having powers of delivery that may not be realistic. It may also elevate or put too much emphasis on the needs and desires of particular parts in the therapist, such as rescuers, pleasers or desperate-not-to-lose the-client parts. Paradoxically, compliant contracting that "follows" the client in this way also discounts so much the therapist has to offer. To avoid dia-loguing about the therapeutic contract with a client or clients is to discount one's own expertise, training, instincts, and the input of Self and parts of your system and the client's.[2]

A metaphor from the food service industry might help illustrate this further. Pre-pandemic, I used to enjoy going to a local festival in the summer to hear the music, see the stalls selling interesting goods and eat speciality food to which I would not usually have access. I would go up to the mobile food supplier, look at their menu, place my order, make payment and have, my order fulfilled – and I'd tuck in! Therapy is not like food service: saying yes to whatever the part of the client in front of you at the start of the therapeutic encounter requests is to act a little like that food vendor, who just fulfils my order without question. As a therapist, I am not like that food vendor in that therapy clearly isn't as simple as ordering a takeaway meal; and a food vendor has the power to fulfil a food order that a therapist does not have in the therapeutic relationship.

Assessing therapist–client fit

In that real world my supervisor referred to, from my supervision experiences, it seems that beginning IFS professionals often don't spend enough, or any, time determining which clients they might or might not work well with. This is understandable as they want the experience, and they often want it between the modules of training. Similarly, those who are new to IFS but experienced as therapists in other modalities, are often so keen to transfer their current caseload to working the IFS way that they struggle to differentiate between clients with whom they can make good headway and those with whom they may struggle, at least initially. In my view, therapist parts often put the system under a lot of pressure by not making better choices regarding who to take on as an IFS client or who to transfer to working using IFS. Some therapist parts may believe they don't have choices in this. Below is an example.

A beginning IFS practitioner takes on a client who has previously been in therapy with many different therapists to "combat their addiction". Yes, this might look like a chance for a great experience for both with IFS. However, if the therapist had reviewed the case, in terms of the bullet points below, would they have proceeded and taken on the client?

- A background of multiple prior therapeutic experiences – none of which has succeeded – might suggest what?
- Do the client and therapist both have parts who see IFS as a "wonder therapy" likely to succeed where other therapies have failed, and is this realistic?
- Do the client and therapist agree on what "successful therapy" looks like?
- Has the novice IFS professional discussed a timeframe during which to review how the work is going and determine if the therapeutic dyad is a good fit?
- How likely is it that there is trauma underlying the presenting problem and, if so, does the novice IFS practitioner feel equipped to work with traumatised exiles and a hard-hitting protective system?
- Does the supervisee feel they have adequate (i.e., IFS-informed) supervision?

Transition reflection

"I'm employed and don't get to choose my caseload. When the work is very demanding, I remind myself about the value of clients as tormentors. Finding my balance between being realistic and a hope merchant is a challenge." (Sarah Murphy, Clinical Counsellor)

Would I have taken on such a client at the beginning of transitioning to becoming an IFS therapist? No indeed. As I often say to my supervisees, with sincerity, playfulness, and compassion: "Ouch, these are really heavy-duty clients you are learning to do IFS with. If I had a magic wand, I would find you some straightforward work with which to start. That way you could build up your trust in, and have a positive experience, with IFS."

This is partly why the IFSI training is so experiential, and why trainees are encouraged to form practice groups with each other. It's also why IFS supervision can be helpful as a place to practise and learn IFS, including contracting.

Contracting with multiplicity in mind

Contracting is multi-relational

Ideally, contracting is as multi-relational as possible, both *inter*personally (between therapist and client) and *intra*personally (within each person). Frank Anderson and Cece Sykes (Schwartz et al., 2021), teaching about how to work with clients using addictive behaviours or substances, illustrate this clearly. A part (or group of parts) in the client may be pushing in therapy for the system to stop using, and parts in the therapist may want to comply saying: "You've come to the right place; we can fight this addiction together." However, as IFS professionals, it is not our job to side with the managers against the firefighters to make them stop (i.e., a counteractive approach). Sykes and Anderson speak to this in the live call, month one of the IFS Continuity Program Trauma and the Addictive Process, saying that in IFS not only do we get permission to heal the wounds in a client's system, but we focus on creating compassionate Self-to-part relationships on the inside for *all* the parts involved in addiction (see also Sykes, 2017 and Wonder, 2013).

Additionally, it is important to attend to parts in the therapist or practitioner who are activated at the idea of taking on the client and the issue(s) they bring. It's particularly beneficial at the contracting stage of the relationship to bring as much Self-leadership as possible.

We can look at therapeutic contracting in a way that considers both or all parties in the relationship (each of whom are multiple). Many of the authors in *Internal Family Systems Therapy: Supervision and Consultation* (Redfern, 2023) write about Self partnering with parts who bring into, or highlight, information that is helpful to the therapeutic relationship.

Bearing in mind the locus of and responsibility for transformation

During my Humanistic Integrative counselling/psychotherapy training, I learned that ideally, the locus or place of evaluation,[3] change and control is within the client. The therapist is not the source of change, though they may act as a catalyst for client change. Unfortunately, some therapist and practitioner parts don't know or believe this, or they seem to forget it when learning IFS. Perhaps due to the stress of the new way of working, parts who may not have been active for a while become triggered. I have witnessed many IFS therapist or practitioner parts who like to be in control, make the client better and so on. These parts want to be "the agent of change". This is understandable and can be validated and met with compassion. And, these therapist parts don't have to change, but they do need to not run the therapy.

Transition reflection

"I find myself, or more accurately, my therapist parts sometimes collude with manager parts who fear the client getting to know their substance using part in session." (Sarah Murphy, Clinical Counsellor)

The other day, a supervisee spoke for a fixer part who feels strongly that they want to fix the client. This part has been trying to rescue broken people all of its life (I'm guessing that's 40 or so years now). I welcomed that part and said it was doing nothing wrong; there is no shame in being a fixer part. However, if this and other therapist parts persist with their positive intentions, hopes and functions and take over in therapy sessions, they will get the opposite of what they are striving for. A fixer therapist part doing therapy will successfully constrain Self's transformative healing in the client, *not least because they are already constraining Self's presence in the therapist.*

In IFS training, students are taught that Self is the transformative agent and particularly the Self of the client. Often, this makes sense in the training room and is less easy to put into practice in real life as therapist parts take over and do what they usually do. Over the years of working in the UK (with mostly white European clients and supervisees), I have found there is a cluster of parts that can dominate in the therapy room. This group of parts is represented by Karpman's Triangle, also known as the Drama Triangle (Karpman, 1968; Redfern, 2021, 2023). At each point of the triangle is a part (or in Transactional Analysis terms, a "role") – victim, persecutor and rescuer. When a person "lives on the Drama Triangle", their relationships with others (and inside themselves) are dominated by the drives of these parts. In my experience, three of the dominating drives of these Drama Triangle parts are likely to get in the way of personal transformation: the drive for others to change; the imperative to avoid any and all vulnerability (in oneself and in the other); unfamiliarity, even discomfort, with curiosity. Learning about and studying these parts as they have shown up in my system(s) and in those of my clients formed a bridge as I transitioned from working integratively to learning "plain-vanilla IFS".[4]

The reason I am raising this here is because although I adhere to the IFS ideal that our clients are our *tor-mentors* (see more in Chapter 10), I also welcome advance planning and conscious choice. At contracting stage during your initial consultation(s) or assessment session(s), it might prevent a lot of stress, hard work and hours in supervision[5] if therapists could detect when therapist parts on the Drama Triangle (rescuer-, persecutor-, victim-type parts) are making choices and taking on clients without Self's input and without consensus from the rest of their inner system. The presence of Drama Triangle parts at contracting stage can be detected by any of the following, (and more):

- A sense of desperation, "I really need the money/hours/experience".
- Rushing to agree or decide a contract before getting to know the client (or not contracting at all).
- Making promises like: "I know you've been let down before, I will be here for as long as you need me."
- Offering reassurances such as: "I hear you've had a lot of therapy, well IFS is more effective and faster, it will be great."
- Stretching boundaries: "Well, my practice is full, but I'm sure I can fit you in somewhere."
- Silencing parts who might polarise with any of the above statements, who might say if invited: "It's not realistic to promise always to be there for any client,"; "And just where in the diary is another client going to fit?" and "I know my supervisor wouldn't approve of me taking on this client, but I can handle it, she needn't know."

When I started seeing clients in 2003, I had no choice about who I worked with (someone else assessed clients initially before they came to me and matched them to my stage of development). I was strongly aware of my own Drama Triangle parts, looked out for them in others and got good at detecting them. I often taught clients about the Drama Triangle and the Healthy Triangle (Redfern, 2021, 2023) and, in doing so, I got permission for both of us to look out for these parts inside of ourselves, in our relationship, and in relationships outside the therapy room. This was/is in the service of unblending.

As therapists, bearing in mind our own multiplicity and having space from our therapist parts as we contract are important, as is knowing that the locus of change resides in the client's system through and in the presence of Self (theirs and ours).

Contracting with IFS in mind

It is likely that at the beginning of your journey as an IFS therapist you will not yet be used to the important concept that protectors provide coping and survival strategies, whereas Self heals. This concept may be completely alien to your clients and to parts of you. Until that concept is "in your bones", I suggest that curiosity is the main go-to at the contracting stage. I offer the following questions in the hope you bear these in mind at this stage:

- Which part(s) brought the client to therapy?
- What does the part that brought the client to therapy say they want?
- What does that mean and what do they really want?
- What parts are *not* being spoken for?
- What parts are in opposition to the part who brought the client to therapy?
- If I agree to the client's request for therapy, am I contracting with only one part?
- Is there a risk to agreeing such a contract?
- Is there a part in me who wants to agree to whatever the client says around contracting?
- What is my part afraid would happen if they didn't agree in this way?
- Who in me is *not* being noticed or consulted?
- Is it possible to offer IFS therapy *and* agree to restrictions placed on it by the client's fearful managers (see below)?
- Would some hope-merchanting and/or psycho-education about IFS and its primary goals be appropriate before agreeing a contract?
- Which specific Cs and Ps would I hope to bring to working with the client?
- Which of the 8 Cs and 5 Ps might the client bring to this work?
- What might my IFS supervisor/colleagues say about this contract?

Schwartz and Sweezy's chapter entitled, "Setting the Table for Treatment" (2020, pp. 95–110 is useful reading on contracting. Here's an excerpt (p. 108):

> When a client describes her problem we ask questions about her inner experience around the problem and feed back what we hear, adding the phrase "So one part of you . . . and another part . . .
>
> Throughout the process we look for the client's inner polarities, which can involve a manager and a firefighter or a manager and a manager, . . .[6]

Below is an example of a non-IFS trained therapist working with an unsophisticated client (i.e., has never had counselling before) who lacks some emotional literacy.

A manager-dominated contract and relationship

Therapist part(s) sometimes accept contracts that see them "shooting themselves in the foot!" They often agree to anti-therapeutic terms and conditions from their clients' protectors: "I don't want to dredge up my childhood"; "If there is silence, I expect you to keep the conversation going"; and "Don't expect me to shut my eyes or meditate, I've done that before, and it doesn't work." To accept such terms at face value without exploring the protector fears behind such statements and looking at what might or might not be workable will work against the relationship and the IFS therapeutic process. Rowan and Jacobs (2002, pp. 130–131) phrase it like this:

> There is a fear here, a fear of social disorganisation. If the boundaries of control were broken, all kinds of bad things might happen. The fear in the therapist is of disorganisation of the self, or of the client, or of the relationship between them; and catastrophic expectations on the part of the therapist that make them restrict their work to what is safe and unexceptionable. One of the favourite slogans at the instrumental stage is: 'We don't pretend to know better than the client. We let the client set the agenda and the aims.' This assumes, of course, that there is just one type of client, the rational one who makes a clear contract.

> "But perhaps it is sometimes the irrational one, the neurotic one, who makes the contract with us, with the rational one nowhere to be seen?

Help me cope

Let's explore the example of supervisee Daniel, who frequently brought a particular relationship to supervision because of their ongoing struggles. "Help me cope" was Daniel's agreed contract with his client. Daniel is Integratively trained, with some understanding of IFS. He wants to move towards working in a more IFS way but currently favours a cognitive-behavioural style of working with this client, which involves:

- Countering or reality-testing negative thoughts;
- Encouraging endorphin-producing behaviours;
- Encouraging social contact and creating/using support networks;

- Teaching distraction techniques or practising of ones the client already uses; and
- Teaching self-soothing and resourcing skills.

Let's consider from an IFS perspective the therapeutic contract "help me cope" and the therapeutic relationship. Here are possible questions I would ask myself together with likely answers:

Q: Who brought the client to therapy?

A: A manager wanting help keeping exiles and exiled pain locked away and who wants to keep coping. This part may not like some of the coping mechanisms of polarised parts, such as not getting out of bed in the morning and doing nothing.

Q: Who in the therapist accepted that contract?

A: A therapist part also frightened of the client's emotions and/or a therapist part who has yet to buy into the idea of inner transformation, the importance of curiosity, and who prefers counteracting (see Chapter 2). There may also be some exile activation around fear of being in the client's situation (alone, infirm, bereaved, in the latter years of living).

Q: Which parts are not being attended to in this contract?

A: The exiles (in either client or therapist); the part on the opposite side of a likely polarity who can't cope or doesn't want to cope.

Q: Is this therapeutic contract "help me cope" likely to be successful?

A: In the short-term perhaps. In the longer-term and in the sense of any sort of change or transformation in the client's system it is unlikely unless the exiles unburden spontaneously. Alternatively, things may get so overwhelming that more of the client's system becomes available for therapy and to meet with Self.

Q: Is there a risk for the client in agreeing such a contract?

A: If/when the keep me coping protector fails, and the client becomes more emotional than the system can tolerate, the level of internal shame is likely to increase, burdening exiles further. If there is a polarised can't cope part, it's possible they may take irreversible action such as suicide to end exile pain if it does flood and overwhelm the coping part.

Q: Is there a risk for the therapist in agreeing such a contract?

A: Parts in the therapist who want change, not maintenance, may get impatient and frustrated. If the therapist is assuming the help me cope manager is the only part to attend to, then suicidal ideation or action may come "out of the blue" and be distressing for the therapist. The therapy relationship may become never-ending and therefore a burden to the therapist.

Q: Which of the 8 Cs are available in working with the client on this? Are they truly Self qualities or do they indicate the activity of therapist parts?

A: *Connectedness?* – being with the client (but it may be part-to-part not therapist Self to client part and certainly not Self to part inside the client). *Creativity?* – is it Self's creativity or therapist parts coming up with creative ideas to help the client's coping protector stay in overall control?

Q: Which of the 5 Ps are available in working with the client on this? Are they truly signs of Self's presence, or do they indicate the activity of therapist parts?

A: *Persistence?* – or is it therapist parts helping the client "keep his finger in the dyke" and prevent the water/emotion breaking through? *Patience?* "the client keeps on coming back, they must be getting something out of it" may indicate therapy as insurance policy in case the client takes a turn for the worse and Can't Cope takes over, rather than a more actively transformative experience.

Q: Are there C qualities missing in the work with this client?

A: *Curiosity* – asking the part "What are you afraid would happen if you didn't cope?" *Courage* – to move towards the exiles or discuss this as a possibility. *Confidence* – believing in the existence of the client's Self and the possibility of healing and hope-merchanting for such.

Q: Are there P qualities missing in the work with this client?

A: *Perspective* – an overview of protectors, Self and exiles in the system and therapeutic dyad. *Playfulness* – it's all very serious (interestingly in our most recent supervision, the supervisee realised the client shows Self's presence when he laughs and they are playful together). *Presence* – the therapist is very "active" while the client does a lot of "reporting about" rather than both being in each other's presence in calm connectedness.

Of course, the therapist – incorporating a CBT approach – has done nothing wrong in agreeing to this contract. But I hope it is thought-provoking as an example of how not to contract as an IFS therapist.

IFS consultation with Schwartz

During month four's live call of the Continuity Program module on Self-led Sexuality (Schwartz & Rich, 2020), an IFS therapist consults with Schwartz seeking clarity on how to proceed. Her client has a complex history and current circumstances of eating issues, trauma, and dissociative behaviour. Takeaways from their conversation, which provides a mini-masterclass of case conceptualisation and parts-detecting from Schwartz, is bullet-pointed below:

- With IFS you don't need to work it all out and know it all beforehand, instead you bring appropriate curiosity.
- Guessing out loud about what's going on in the client can be problematic if you are off track, as parts who are listening may lose trust or feel misunderstood.
- Preference direct access with parts who are afraid of you talking to and getting to know other parts.
- Remember to keep the exiles in mind/view/at heart as extreme protector activity in the present relates back to and was formed from what was going on in the family of origin.

Bearing multiplicity in mind during all aspects of the work

Having come to IFS late in my psychotherapy career, I was fortunate to have had a lot of experience in general contracting as well as contracting EMDR-style for a targeted piece of trauma work (the Assessment phase, in EMDR parlance). I only intend to share some general ideas here, which those who have trained in IFS without a psychotherapy background may find helpful. Please note, this is not intended to teach you how to do an in-depth trauma assessment with your clients. If you are new to IFS, I recommend you practise IFS with less traumatised clients first, if possible, to prevent putting too much pressure on your therapist parts while learning a new modality. Also, please note that the suggestions or practices that I have used successfully may not work for you, your circumstances, and your clients.

In my view, the less experienced you are, the more you need to ask and be curious about, and with, a client. This is *not* so you can accumulate an impressive mountain of history with which to wow your supervisor or supervision group. This is to help you begin to parts-detect, get an overview of the client's system across their history and in interactions with the other systems in their life, and perhaps begin to hear from any of your parts with concerns or reactions to what is being learned.

Initial consultations

Remember, as with any aspect of IFS, it is helpful when Self is in the lead. It is less likely for an initial consultation session to go well if your system is led by parts wanting to find the problem to fix, needing to work it out, fill out the form properly or get a move on; Self's curiosity and open-hearted non-attachment are key. Leading from Self while in communication with your parts, it is probable that you will be able to attune to your client, noticing how easy or difficult it is for them to respond to your enquiring. Adapt the process to meet your client's needs, your own and, if possible, those of any additional stakeholders such as the organisation you may be employed by.

Table 4.1 shows a form that can be used as part of an initial consultation session or couple of sessions with potential clients. (Remember, you are looking for signposts or trailheads to which you may return for further enquiry.)

You will see that three areas are emphasised in bold type. These headings are where keeping an eye and ear out for parts is especially important. However, enquiring using any of the items on the form can yield significant information about parts (and Self's presence or absence). For example:

Medical history

Includes the client's birth story if they know it. Who told them about this? How did the parent(s) cope if there were challenges? If the client is female, has she had traumatic experiences either giving birth or during her own birth; is she menopausal? This section can often provide clues about the existence of very young and traumatised exiles.

Counselling/psychotherapy history

Includes asking about the client's relationship to their emotions and how feelings were expressed, hidden, or managed, etc. in their family of origin. This can yield information pointing to firefighters, exiles and managers and their relationships to each other, as well as highlighting possible legacy burdens. It can give you a heads-up about how willing to be vulnerable the client is likely to be or whether plenty of hope-merchanting might be needed down the line.

Table 4.1 Initial intake form

Date 1st Session:	Age:
Preferred Name:	Gender pronouns (and outline of significant history related to gender/ sexuality/ identity):
Does the client live alone? If not, with whom do they usually reside?	Does the client have disability or special educational needs?
Have confidentiality limits been explained to the client?	Emergency contact details:
Presenting problem	**Symptoms** (does the symptomatic part(s) seem to be a protector or an exile?)[7]
Psychiatric history in outline only (including impact of same):	Medical history in outline (including own birth details if known, as well as details around giving birth if relevant, relationship to their body, and ability to sleep):
Trauma history outline (including that related to race/ability/difference):	Counselling/psychotherapy history outline (including relationship to emotions):
Risk history and risk issues (assess for external safety, inner safety and readiness/timing to begin and do some therapeutic work):	Current risk level (low/ medium/high):
Self-medicating – do any of the following contribute to the client's problems: drugs/alcohol/gambling/debt/ poverty/diet/weight/exercise?	Any periods off sick or incapacitated in the past?
Support networks and resources (including access to Self[8]):	Number of sessions initially contracted with client: Number of sessions before first review:
The agreed focus:	

Table 4.2 IFS brief initial intake log

Which part(s) brought the client to therapy?	Which part(s) are they polarised with inside the client?	Who in you is reacting to parts in the client?
What parts in the client's system don't want or fear change?	Does the client have access to Self?	Do you have access to Self?

Periods off sick or incapacitated

Asking about this and getting the response, "Hell no, and I'm not about to now, that's why I'm here so it doesn't get to that. And how many more questions are you going to ask?" gives information about a part or parts of the client and potentially about parts in you who respond ("Yikes, no pressure then!"). Asking the same question to a different client and finding them turning gently inwards with curiosity, taking their time, and then responding, "Well, actually, I hadn't thought about it until you asked, but every year at this time I get sick in one way or another and have to take time off work. I wonder what that's about?" also provides information about how they relate to their inner world and might relate to you. Similarly, your system will probably respond differently to this client, and you may get a sense of how much Self-energy is currently available to you both.

Contracting and history taking give us information about parts in the client and ourselves. Remember, being curious about parts who may be in the client and in ourselves is not the same as letting our "work it out parts" have a field day. To satisfy the part in me who likes to make things extra clear and concise, see Table 4.2 which gives a shorter and more IFS-only list of things to look out for and log when exploring from a Self-led place an IFS therapeutic contract with your client.

To conclude this chapter, I touch on two areas that inform who I am and how I operate as an IFS therapist, but which may never be explicitly discussed with my clients.

Meta-contracting

In case I have not already said this enough, IFS is not about transcending or getting rid of parts. We cannot operate in the world without both our physical bodies and our parts (though we can operate and even succeed without access to Self). Using IFS with clients or oneself is not about working towards being in Self 100% of the time nor is it about achieving enlightenment. For me, the clue is in the title: Internal *Family* Systems. According to Google's online dictionary, a *family* is a unit that lives together formed of one or more parents and their children. IFS is about helping Self, and parts be a more harmonious, smooth-running, co-habiting unit (which may also help our bodies be more at ease).

As we are contracting with our IFS clients and agreeing a focus for the work, which might be quite tight or narrow and may span just a few sessions or be open-ended, I also hold in mind the goals of IFS therapy (Schwartz, 2021), which are to:

1) free parts from their extreme roles, so they may return to their natural states;
2) restore trust in the Self;
3) achieve balance, harmony, and wholeness; and
4) become more Self-led inside and in the external world.

These will not necessarily be explicit in our contracting with clients, and our clients do not have to agree to them. However, they form part of what I think of as therapeutic "meta-contracting". Non-therapy professionals who use IFS may also hold these goals in mind when working within their contexts and they too may not share these goals explicitly.

The implicit contract

How much contractual detail remains implicit and how much is explicit will probably be determined by whereabouts in the world you are reading this. If you're in the US, then my guess is that you will have a rigorous client contract setting out many of the contractual obligations you will fulfil in the relationship. If you are in the UK, then you may not have a written contract with your clients (though this is getting less usual these days) and may not cover some items in a verbal contract. My system implicitly "contracts" with clients, supervisees, and supervisors the following, none of which appear in my documentation (this list is not exhaustive):

•   Punctuality, including starting sessions on time and ending sessions within agreed parameters.

- Reasonable flexibility in scheduling if possible and with enough notice from the client/supervisee, and similarly keeping rescheduling of appointments by me to a minimum.
- Completing any requested paperwork within a reasonable timeframe.
- Taking responsibility to check payment, chasing late payments as necessary, and timely sending of receipts.
- Working in a private space, not eating during sessions, not answering the door or phone during sessions.
- Not making the client my friend either during or after the therapeutic relationship.

The items in the bullet pointed list are things agreed/contracted to internally and viewed by my system as part of "doing my job". As I write this, I am sending appreciation to my team of parts who work to adhere to such contracting. You might try the following exercise on internal contracting to meet your own team.

Exercise

Contracting and your inner team

I have been fortunate to have experienced various professional transitions and to have accompanied many supervisees who have made the journey from student to qualified and/or from working in one modality to another. There are certain aspects of the work that often trigger parts and this exercise is designed to help you get out ahead of some of that inner conflict before you start contracting with your clients in your new way of working. You may wish to do this alone or with a colleague, peer, supervisor, or group.

Think of your inner system as a team and call a meeting of parts as you might schedule a team meeting at work, a family meeting at home, or a gathering at a place of worship or community. If you prefer, you might think of this as an inner "away day" or "team building day" in which case you could be out in nature with your team. Alternatively, you might get cosy by the fire or do this first thing in the morning with a coffee and pastry in your office.

Note that your system may want to address all agenda items in one meeting and split the time accordingly or it may want to be more organic and see how things go, in which case more meetings may need to be scheduled. See if a part wants to volunteer to take the minutes, which includes noting who attends and making notes of what is agreed.

Ask your parts to give space so Self can preside, and/or do whatever helps you access Self inside. Depending on your inner world, you may wish to build Self-to-part relationships with active inner critics or shamers in advance of the team meeting as they may feel solely responsible for motivation and feel threatened at the idea of a team meeting presided over by Self and in which responsibility is shared among the team. Make sure if there are parts polarised on any agenda item that you hear from both sides, ideally in the same meeting if you can.

Adapting to suit your individual circumstances, let parts know the intention of the meeting is to provide a time and space to:

- Receive some appreciation, acknowledgment and to be held by Self;
- Enable parts to get to know of each other's existence and roles;
- Listen to what parts have to say about the agenda items;
- Address any concerns parts may have about their responsibilities, roles, items on the agenda (for example, the part in charge of designing and building the website may be feeling out of its depth or under-appreciated);
- Have Self mediate between parts who are polarised on any of the issues under discussion (for example, a part may have the understanding that saying yes and taking on every client that enquires is important, while another part may be taking you out with a migraine regularly as it silently yells *Just say No already!*);
- Appreciate all parts' contributions and see if they can appreciate each other's responses;
- Recruit volunteers to take responsibility for acting on agenda items (for example, an admin part may like the job of sending out invoices and keeping track of the bank balance now you will be charging for sessions, rather than working as a volunteer); and/or
- Allocate resources, including time, for the parts to act on the agenda items.

You might explore together the following agenda items (and any your system adds) one at a time:

> **TIME:** boundaries of the meeting; the length of the working week and working day; expectations regarding weekends and holidays; work/life balance issues and wants, etc.
>
> **MONEY:** rates; raises; billing; tax returns; cancellation policy; maximum number of clients; number of concessionary places available; running a waiting list or not.

SCHEDULING: online or paper; level of flexibility; short-term or long-term contracts or both; mix of clients to supervisees; time off and notice for holiday periods.

MARKETING: website; speed of returning calls; networking; directories to join; creating a niche or not.

ADMIN: client documentation (contract, privacy notice); invoicing; receipts; memberships; living/professional will arrangements; filing; data protection; insurance.

CPD/CE (Continuous Professional Development/Continuing Education): budget; attending events; running events; keeping logs for certification/audit purposes.

SUPPORT: childcare/elder care arrangements; self-care; professional support such as therapy and supervision; peer support; referral systems in and out.

Notes

1   *Locus* is Latin for "place" or "location" and the terms "internal locus of control" and "external locus of control" are taught in psychotherapy and psychology trainings. Someone with the former believes that they have personal control of their own life, and the latter will believe that their life is controlled more by factors outside of themselves. Originally conceived by the American psychologist, Julian B. Rotter (1966). I have adapted this to thinking about "locus of change/transformation".

2   Ann Drouilhet (2023) writes about this in her chapter on consultation to IFS therapists working with couples.

3   This refers to the place from which a person makes a value judgment, i.e., do they trust their own judgments and evaluations about themselves, others and the world or do they take in judgments from external authorities.

4   "Plain-vanilla" IFS is the term I use for what I think of as "pure" IFS and others might call "clean IFS". By that I mean doing IFS that would be recognised as such by others who *only know* IFS. I'm not suggesting you never integrate IFS into other ways of working, nor integrate other things into IFS. I am suggesting that you be clear about what you call what you do (see Chapter 2). Also bear in mind that IFS is a complete psychotherapy model and you may not feel the need to integrate it with anything else, nor integrate anything with it.

5   My parts struggle sometimes with what they perceive as having to work extra hard with supervisees in supervision to make up for their earlier poor choices at contracting, when, for example, rescuer parts have taken on clients that activate other parts who feel like a victim to a persecuting client (part).

6 See also Pastor and Gauvain (2020) in which they suggest that a person may be drawn to therapy by what I think of as a self-improvement manager wanting help to create lasting change. Meanwhile, other parts may be wishing they were anywhere other than in a therapist or coach's office or Zoom room!

7 Schwartz and Sweezy (2020, pp. 101–104) explain that whether the symptomatic part is a protector (has a job) or an exile (not doing a job) is one of two important things to assess.

8 The second important aspect of an IFS assessment according to Schwartz and Sweezy (2020, pp. 101–104) is how much access the client has to Self.

5

Differentiating between key IFS concepts and practices

Introduction

IFS has differentiation[1] at its core and running through every level. It's there on a conceptual level as we take on board that human nature is multiple not mono, and on a practical level the work involves differentiating one part (or group of parts) from another part (or group of parts), Self from part and part who wants to be Self from Self. In this chapter, I suggest that for a successful transition to IFS, therapists, practitioners, and all professionals do well to differentiate between:

- Empathising with and having compassion towards;
- believing a part and validating the part's reality;
- what needs to be known (that Self is present, for example) versus what does not need to be known (for example, all the minute details of content or story[2]);
- what a novice IFS therapist and practitioner does and doesn't need to know in advance.

Exercises at the end enable you to consider change in IFS, your relationship to content and provide ideas for self-supervision.

Differentiating between compassion and empathy

As part of successfully transitioning to IFS, I believe it is important to reconsider relying on empathy as a *primary* way of "being with" and of conceptualising therapeutic healing. You may have been taught that only accurate empathy from therapist to client will engender therapeutic personality change in the client (Rogers, 1957[3]). Those of you with a psychodynamic training may

DOI: 10.4324/9781003243571-8

hold to a deficit model of psychotherapy in which therapists need to provide what the client never had thus potentially over-inflating the significance of therapist empathy in client healing. Also, many of us turned to becoming therapists to offer others what we never had ourselves in our formative years, including empathy. I suggest that it is Self's presence, which includes compassion and the other C and P qualities that we never received ourselves, which we do well to offer to others now (whether, clients, family members, colleagues, business clients, etc.)

Compassion is probably best understood through sensing and getting to recognise it for yourself. I experience compassion as openness to and acceptance of the other without leaning into and towards them. I feel a sense of depth and breadth as well as a containing encompassing, and largeness. There is resourcing and grounding and I do not need anything from the other. On the other hand, when I am empathising, it feels more of a social event in which I need something from the other, for some sort of exchange or transaction to take place. Susan McConnell (2020) describes compassion as an open-hearted presence.

Schwartz and Sweezy (2020, p. 262) write: "There are neurological and psychological distinctions between empathy (*feeling with*) and compassion (*feeling for*)." They draw our attention to research involving brain scans using fMRI, which show that compassion activates reward circuitry in the brain whereas empathy activates pain circuitry. This may help explain why IFS therapists sometimes report feeling enlivened after sessions rather than depleted.[4]

Self-to-Self and Self-to-part connection feature compassion for/towards the other, but an over-emphasis on empathising or identifying with the other is generally due to parts' activity, as is sympathising. Both empathy and sympathy are often more about soothing the "giver's" pain than transforming the receiver's pain and have a subtle distancing feel to them (see Pastor & Gauvain, p. 132). Understanding and sensing the differences between therapist compassion and empathy is important in doing IFS as individual parts may respond differently to therapist empathy.[5] As therapists, we also remember that we are Self detectors as much as we are parts detectors. See Chapter 8 for an example when Susan McConnell (2020), in addition to the 4th F, asks the client where in her body she feels the compassion. This highlighted that a part was active, rather than Self.

IFS is not a deficit model of therapy. We believe that a person has within them what they need to heal. Self naturally already possesses the ability to create relationships with parts and to meet their relational needs, which include eight highlighted in *Beyond Empathy* (1999) by Erskine et al. writing about integrative psychotherapy:

- Security
- Valuing
- Acceptance
- Mutuality
- Self-definition
- The need to make an impact
- The need to have the other initiate
- The need to express love

As the authors explain: "When the eight needs ... are attended to, consistently and with sensitivity to which need is in the foreground at any given moment, the overall experience is one of being loved." (ibid., p. 151).

Empathising is often what our parts do because they think it will help the other, bring about change, and because they can then feel good about themselves for doing what "a good therapist does". On the other hand, Self is not affected by the need to be a good therapist! Self validates parts as autonomous[6] individuals, each with a right to their own thoughts, feelings, beliefs, agendas. This is a loving and transforming act and way of being in which change is not expected or demanded, and yet becomes possible.

Lastly, offering empathy can contribute to keeping a part/client stuck because it can seem like we are buying wholesale into the reality of the part, (Erskine et al., 1999, p. 57, my emphasis added):

> In an empathetic response, the therapist feels what the client is feeling. He or she metaphorically crawls inside the client's skin and shares the client's affective experience.

> "Oh, that's too bad" or "You must have been furious!" are common responses to our friends' stories about themselves. Such responses represent empathy; most therapists are trained[7] to do this sort of thing as a part of "active listening." It is a part of our training that we would do well to deemphasise *as we learn to inquire in a way that goes beyond empathy.* (p. 31)

Differentiating between validating and believing

Validating a part (particularly during befriending and relationship building in the IFS steps of healing), is a natural outcome of the nature of Self which recognises the self-contained and sense-making nature of the part and its existence. Interestingly, validating a part has implicit within it the subtle suggestion that change is possible. I am grateful to a client for articulating this,

> Client: "The part didn't like it when you said that makes sense because it hears that something else might also make sense."

> Therapist: "Yes, indeed, and that is partly why I used those words. My belief is that perhaps the part's current truth may not always feel/be true for this part. That doesn't take away from how much sense it makes now in the system as it is. And the system may change."

Validating a part's experience is not the same as "buying into" its story as "the only" story

Validating is an important aspect of listening to and honouring a protector for the job it has been doing valiantly for the system for so long (Schwartz & Sweezy, p. 135). Validating can be accomplished therapist's Self to client's part via direct access as well as via in-sight from client's Self to client's part. What do we mean by validating? The dictionary definition refers to demonstrating or supporting the truth or value of something – important in IFS and also needing to be unpacked a little.

IFS therapists and their clients validate the *subjective truths* of each individual protector and each individual exile such that each part's truth(s) can co-exist with/alongside another part's truth.[8] All parts have value and significance in the system. No one part is inherently dominant – the protector who says, "I have to shame her to keep her small, so she's not noticed and abused again" is as worthy of validation and recognition as the protector with whom it may be polarised, who says: "I'm in therapy to reclaim my power, taken from me by my childhood abuser, and this ongoing negative inner voice." You will have noticed from your training, reading and watching videos that there are certain phrases that validate the truth of parts and acknowledge the value of what each part brings to the system. When said by Self, they will have a softening effect on the extremity of the protector. In Table 5.1 are some validating phrases and questions addressed to the first protector mentioned in this paragraph.

Table 5.1 Examples of a validating approach

Direct access	*In-sight*
"It makes some sense to me that you feel safer when she's small and shamed."	"Does that make sense to you [client]? … Let the part know you get it."
"I'm hearing how hard you've worked all these decades and how important you have been to her survival."	"How do you feel towards this part as you hear how hard it has worked? … Send that appreciation and Self-energy to the part."
"If you didn't have to do what you do, how else would you like to serve the system?"	"Ask the part, if it could change its job, what might it prefer to do?"
"I'm pretty sure the client would like to acknowledge you for all that you've been doing. How would it be if you gave some space so she could come and say hi and thank you?"	• "Does the part get that you really get it?" • "How does the part respond to your appreciation and presence?" • "How is it for this part that you are with it like this?"

To validate in IFS is to accept as:

- true (small 't') not True (big 'T');
- true for the moment not True forever; and
- true for the part not True for all.

One of the reasons my system so values IFS is because of the active embracing of multiplicity and multiple truths. There is the more objective truth of what can be recorded in a photo or on camera perhaps, although even that is interpreted by an individual's brain and senses. My yellow rose may look very different to your yellow rose for example. But I think you get it when I say there are objective, factual truths we can all, usually, agree to: "It is raining", "We had porridge for breakfast." Then there is the subjective truth of an individual involved in an experience which could be filmed or photographed. In fact, there is the subjective truth of each individual part of each individual person …

As I have made the transitions from ignorant of therapy to integrative psychotherapist to EMDR practitioner to IFS therapist and supervisor, my relationship with truth has developed and changed. I realise that before therapy, I only had the tiniest awareness of my own personal truths. I had taken in the message that to look beneath the surface was forbidden and dangerous. Also, as a sufferer of developmental trauma and single-incident traumas, some parts in my system were frozen in time with "truths" that never actually happened. Many of my parts "knew" or "believed" I was about to die and updating[9] them with the co-existing reality or "truth" that I am (as of the time of writing) also still living, has been hugely transformative. Somehow it reminds me of a text from the Old Testament, that I paraphrase: "God said, 'Let there be light' and there was light." Parts inside of me "declared" at times "We're going to die" and it "became true" and has run as truth in the background throughout my life.

> **Transition reflection**
>
> "I sometimes forget that not everyone thinks in parts. I might speak for a part and colleagues can believe that's the whole of what I think." (Sarah Murphy, Clinical Counsellor)

As a beginning counsellor, I recall being taught in college and on placement to treat what the clients said as true, to believe them. At the same time, we were reminded that we were only getting one side of the story, especially if the client had come with relationship problems. So, we also had to take what clients said with a pinch of salt. Looking back, I believe they were trying to teach this idea of validating the client's experience while holding the content lightly. An example: a client, trying to hold back the tears, says of his late wife "I'm glad she's gone – good riddance – the kids and I are better off without her" is speaking a partial truth. He speaks for part of his system and may even be speaking for part of a part in that system and sharing one small aspect of its current/uppermost feelings/thoughts about the loss. For me, as therapist, to grab hold of that one sentence and wholeheartedly accept it, and agree with it as the only truth, would be to do a disservice to the client and their multiplicity. Also, doing this would be coming from a part trying to help in some way, not from Self.

Relating to an angry teen part

Validating rather than believing can be a hard concept and skill to get. Below is a reconstructed example of a beginning IFS therapist relating to a client's "angry teen" part:

Angry teen: (*Shouting*) "I hate her (*the client*) she's endangering us all the time. She won't do what I tell her."

Novice therapist: (*In a calm, adult voice*) "You need to stop shouting, we can't help you if you shout. It's abusive to the client and to me."

Angry teen: "You're just like all the others, telling me what to do, none of you ever help her change anything, you're useless. If it wasn't for me, she'd have keeled over years ago."

As you can see, the therapist's intervention, although taught by some schools of therapy and designed to prevent re-traumatising clients and keep them in their window of tolerance, actually escalated the part's behaviour. By saying what he did, the therapist "buys into" the presentation of the part as bullying and dangerous. My guess is that a part in the therapist was frightened and reacted to try and control the part for "protective" reasons. As is the way with protector behaviour, it often gets the opposite of what's intended and hoped for, and this angry teen part ends up feeling as unsafe as ever in therapy.

Here is a replay with the therapist persistently bringing Self's curiosity towards the part and recognising that parts are not what they seem.

Angry teen: (*Shouting*) "I hate her (*the client*) she's endangering us all the time. She won't do what I tell her."

Seasoned therapist: (*In a confident, courageous way*) "That sounds scary! Tell me how she puts you in danger? What do you mean?"

(*The therapist's Self isn't afraid either of the presentation of the part or the content "something dangerous is happening". Self goes towards the fear with curiosity and that helps the part feel safe enough to continue sharing.*)

Angry teen: "She's still in touch with the narcissistic stepfather."

Seasoned therapist: "And that is dangerous how?"

(*Notice, the therapist doesn't assume he knows what "narcissistic stepfather" means.*)

Angry teen: "The stepfather puts us down verbally all the time and demeans us."

Novice therapist: "Well, we can certainly work together on ways to be assertive with the stepfather and maybe even help the client stop seeing him so much."

(*The beginning therapist may have a part active who wants to resource or teach the client to be more assertive and create boundaries not realising that this would counteract*[10] *the behaviour of other parts in the client's system. The therapist's part continues to react to the client's part's intensity, and to the content it shares, this time buying into the idea that the stepfather is the problem.*)

Seasoned therapist: "And that behaviour from the stepfather hurts, is that right? It's the hurt you want to stop?"

(The more experienced, or seasoned, IFS therapist uses the content to leverage the IFS process of getting buy-in to the internal transformation that is IFS therapy.)

Angry teen: "Yeah, the pain gets bigger and harder to manage and … I have to kill her (*the client*), to stop the pain, it's the only solution … but people keep interfering and taking her to hospital … then she comes out and has to go see the narcissistic stepfather cause he's the grandfather and supports the kids financially. And there's this other part in here who *still* wants to win the stepfather's approval – I hate her too!"

Seasoned therapist: "Phew! I hear what you're saying. It's getting really desperate. What if I told you that we could go to the young parts inside that you protect, and the part so attached to the stepfather, and help them let go of the pain they're carrying and have been carrying for all these years? Then it wouldn't hurt so much being around the stepfather, and you might have more choice inside about things. Does that sound like something you could go for?"

Angry teen: "Maybe."

Seasoned therapist: "OK and before we go to the little ones you protect or speak to that other part you hate, I'd want your permission …"

(Note the experienced therapist picks up on the inner polarisation that is driving some of the extremity. The permission-seeking is also important. This part is a potential ally on the inside and its agreement to proceed, and to speak to the other part with whom it polarises re the stepfather is sought – itself a form of validation and respect.)

Parts and words are not always what they seem

In interviews and trainings, Schwartz often reminds us that parts are not what they seem, they are just little kids even though they might seem big, scary and entrenched in extreme, even life-threatening, behaviours. This concept that parts are not what they seem is an important one in IFS (Schwartz & Sweezy 2020, p. 266) as is what I have been explaining about truth not being what it seems. I also believe that words are frequently not what they seem. In IFS, we choose words carefully, instrumentally and with Self's clarity. Words that are less validating which I would encourage you not to use include the phrases, "That's fine" and "It's okay you feel/believe/think X, Y, Z." To me, these words feel passively accepting of the part's status quo, which is not a message an IFS therapist wants to convey. Also, how often is what the parts tell us truly okay? Hardly ever! Much of what our parts have experienced is and was not "fine" or "okay". If you are using these words, I understand you have a positive intention, but those words do not have the same function or depth as telling a part: "It makes sense to me that you feel/believe/think X, Y, Z." Our words ideally will convey the messages: "*I, Self,* see/sense/experience you, part; and you and your presence are acceptable to me, and your experience and relationships make sense to me. I am here for you …"

As I have elsewhere in the book, I urge novice IFS professionals to understand the "family" nature of Internal Family Systems therapy. For many years, I didn't grasp this aspect of IFS, it wasn't until I started supervising in earnest that something clicked for me. I made the link between Self as the primary attachment figure[11] (Schwartz & Sweezy, 2020, p. 84) and good-enough external parents. If the external good-enough parent witnesses two children fighting each other, I would hope they would listen to each child's side of the story and seek to validate each child's individual experience. This good-enough parent would not just let one child dominate the other and dominate their own attention. To do so, would not be leading the external family from Self.

In summary

Each of the above processes – empathising, having compassion towards, believing and validating – can be employed therapeutically when used for a reason and with conscious awareness.

Letting go of content and the need to know what's true

Although not all processes are created equal, favouring *a process* in psychotherapy is often preferable to favouring *content*. There may be times when hearing details and stories is highly significant in relationship building; in the witnessing healing step of IFS; when engaging storyteller parts of members of the BIPOC community (Floyd, 2023 and Endnote 2); perhaps in grief counselling when memories of the lost loved one are shared; or in counselling in which the client has never had a voice before perhaps due to narcissistic wounding. However, in many therapeutic modalities, including IFS, verbal content can get in the way, especially if it is "talking about", "talking to avoid" or "talking to maintain the status quo". For more on this, I recommend Ch. 3 of *Therapy in the Age of Neuroscience* (Afford, 2020).

Part of maturing as a psychotherapist is learning that content may not be "where it's at". Yes, it is important; but in terms of the IFS model, knowing the function of a part and having the answers to specific strategic questions is more important than encouraging a general content splurge. For those of you for whom IFS is your first major post-graduate training, the draw towards history and details might be hard for you to drop. I was lucky in coming to IFS late in my career after embracing various psychotherapy modalities in which I learned to let go of a need for client content. Similarly, my experience as client prior to IFS gave me an understanding that truth is relative, mutable, and different on the inside than on the outside. Below are some examples from my journey.

Transition reflection

"I have therapist parts who are horrified at the idea of hopemerchanting. They say to me *What! You are going to say you can help? You have to stay in the place of not knowing and follow what emerges.* ... I'm glad you (the supervisor) spoke for how you would hope merchant with clients. That gives my parts permission to try this." (GH, accredited psychotherapist and IFS therapist)

Developmental Transformations (DvT)

In this form of improvisational Dramatherapy, the therapist is the "play object" of the client or group of clients and joins with them in a mutually created "playspace" in which client material is embodied, enacted, played with, ignored, exaggerated, redone, played out by someone else, messed with, and so on. In a DvT group, the therapist may have read or listened to something of each individual's clinical history, but other group members will not have this prior loading, nor will context or history generally be shared in the playspace (after all, that's not exactly playful, it would also be taken as an attempt to move from DvT to a form of talking therapy).

Experiencing DvT as a client and group member really informed me of the reduced importance of content in healing in this context. Here I share three highlights from my time as a group DvT player. The first was when I ended up judging someone else in the group. I did this loudly and with great gusto. In IFS terms, I was blending with a judging part of me (or a part wanting to act at playing "the Judge") and using my body to gesticulate and convey what my words were saying. The small group responded by lining up to be judged – yippee! Then, I imagine partly because I had experienced such glee in the role, others in the group took it in turns to "play" judge and I joined the queue of those to be judged. My second example also took place in a small group, some physical calamity was being enacted into which I inserted myself as a pretend emergency response vehicle. I demonstrated what I was by my actions and by my (very sad) "Nee naw, nee naw" sounds. Others in the group enjoyed my emergence and joined in by loading the patient into my ambulance and off we went "nee-nawing" in conga formation (which felt wonderful!). The third example does not strictly show an example of DvT but relates to a game commonly played amongst DvT-ers, "The Fucked Up Game" where each group member lays out the "reasons" why he/she is the most fucked up of all the group members present. The group participants then line up (sitting or standing) from most fucked up to least. Well, one time I won! Again, it felt great. Yes, there was some truth in my rendition, *and* I was hamming it up, exaggerating and so on. I was learning that the truth and content are things with which to play.

Don't get me wrong, in the above examples of DvT sessions, content was present and it was important (both for me and for my "playmates"): parts of me have felt crippled by the judgment I perceived as a child and by the judgment my inner Frankenstein's monster critic used to enforce; I have called the emergency services to a house fire only to be told three times by the responder that the building was not on fire despite the building being ablaze as we spoke (yes, really!). I have had recurring nightmares for most of my life of needing to and trying to ring the emergency services but being utterly unable to do so. However, in DvT, it was the messing or playing with the content and relating to it from a different, playful, distancing angle while enjoying others' reactions to it that made the play feel healing.

Making the implicit explicit in IFS

When considering content, bear in mind that therapy is also about making the implicit explicit and transforming the felt sense of what is true and real. Those of us who have a history of healing from trauma and working with clients with trauma know that there are different sorts of truth that seem to come from different places, what I think of as top-down or bottom-up. For example, I hold physical tension along the tops of my shoulders and back of my neck. I know in a cognitive practical way that it's time for a myofascial release session. Once on the couch, Helen Watts, a sports massage and JFB myofascial release therapist, works with my body, and a new "knowing" seems to arise and form in my head. It says: "That's from when I was a forceps delivery." Both the release of the tension and my system's making sense of it brought relief and felt significant.

I share this because memory,[12] truth, and reality are complicated concepts, and what our parts believe and understand about them can affect how we interact with our parts and others'. From an IFS perspective, here are some practical pointers:

- Parts each have their own truth as they know and experience it, which may differ from that of another part.
- In the inner world, led by Self, we can validate a part's experience (If we hear a voice saying, "That's not right, that didn't happen", then we can meet it with curiosity when the time is right).
- Transformation of memory is possible even if there is no evidential proof in the external world of what a part believes it experienced.
- It is possible to heal traumatic experiences that we, or a part(s), are "too young to remember" ("I'm feeling the foetus's terror and it's not too much; she knows I'm there").
- Self does not relate to a part's truth like everyday outer-world attachment figures and adults, who might disbelieve or discount what a child has to say because there is no proof or because it's inconvenient, etc.
- Discovering and believing something on the inside (e.g., "I was abused") does not have to be acted upon in the outside world (though it might be) nor does it become untrue if it is shared and the other doesn't believe it (e.g., "It can't have happened as he was dead by the time you were seven").[13]

Getting to know what you need to know

At the start of your IFS professional practice, it can be tricky to get a feel for what it is okay *not* to know and what it's *not okay* to not know. In the IFS Continuity Program's live call with Schwartz (month three of Schwartz & Rich, 2020) someone asks him to comment on a demo in which he had not asked the part to clarify the burdens as they were released. Schwartz replies that he doesn't feel the need to know these details. Rather, it is important in his eyes that the burdens (whatever they are) are let go of. Similarly, if the part knows and shares, that's okay too. So, the "content" comes second to the "process" of unburdening; almost an optional extra as it were.

But are there things in IFS that it is important to consider or "know" as much as it is possible to know? Yes, I believe there are.[14]

Transition reflection

"Being relational and open-hearted, boundaried, helping clients take responsibility, following the model, and looking after my parts – it's a lot." (BS, certified IFS practitioner and experienced PA)

Who is talking?

When I'm working with an IFS therapy client, I aspire to know who I'm speaking to; and as a supervisor, one of the questions I frequently find myself asking is: "Who was talking?" or "Who said that?" Sometimes, the supervisee can answer, sometimes not. Presuming you are talking to the "sad part" because that was what you agreed with the client at the outset of the session is no guarantee that this is who you will get to speak to. Unless you check somehow (whether internally by asking yourself if this seems like a sad part or by asking the part directly, "Are you the sad part?" or "Jake, can you ask the part if it is the sad one; I'm sensing another part may have come in here") then you may well end up telling me about it in supervision and I'll say something like, "That doesn't sound like a sad part to me, does it to you?" or "Who was talking? It sounds to me more like a part that doesn't like the sad part and wants it gone." Another reason a supervisee sometimes can't answer is because, at the time when they were with the client, they had presumed the client's Self was talking because the part had been so convincing. However, now, hearing themselves talk in supervision, it begins to dawn on them that they may have missed a part who wants to be known/seen as Self.

I hope it goes without saying (I have parts who like to state the obvious!) that I like to know who is speaking out of my mouth, too. Hopefully as therapist I will be experiencing a critical mass of Self. In supervision, I often feel more freedom for parts to blend and speak. I'll say something with passion and, as I listen, I realise, "Hmm, that sounded forceful, someone in me feels strongly about this, I'll just thank them and ask for a bit more space." Or I might tell a supervisee: "I'm feeling angry, and that feels important and relevant, does that make any sense to you, in relation to this client?"

Are the client and I doing it right?

In my experience, it is remarkably common when learning a new protocol-based approach for parts to presume an understanding of the protocol only to find in practice that it isn't going quite right (which is where having supervision comes in handy). Alternatively, parts can easily assume that because what we and our clients do in session is not the same as we witnessed in the demos during training that we, the client, or both are "doing it wrong".

Doing explicit direct access, for example, for the first few times can be challenging for our parts and for our clients' parts, especially if we have been working together for a while doing a different sort of therapy. In this reconstructed, composite, example, a supervisee raises her direct access concerns:

Supervisee: "So, the direct access started off alright and the client is speaking saying 'I this, I that' and then they shift into 'She this, she that', and I don't know if that's okay or not."

Supervisor: "What do you think was going on?"

Supervisee: "Well, I don't know if it was a sign of unblending, moving into in-sight and Self is now speaking for the part."

Supervisor: "What else are you concerned it might be?"

Supervisee: "Maybe a self-conscious part has stepped in and it's another part telling me about the part."

Supervisor: "And I guess this is where I can't know which it was because I wasn't there. Could we talk about how you might get curious in the future or how you might respond next time it happens, instead of just being put off or dropping the direct access because 'it's not going right'?"

Supervisee: "Sure."

Supervisor: "Great, so in these situations, you could try a version of what Schwartz says, 'Just let the part speak' or 'Just let the part use your mouth'."

Supervisee: "Hmm, or?"

Supervisor: "Or you could speak inside with your parts who are getting self-conscious and concerned that it's not going right, or the client is doing something wrong. If they stepped back, you might get more clarity and confidence."

Supervisee: (*On a relieved outbreath*) "That makes sense, and I can always ask the client 'Who is speaking now?' if it feels like it's a different part."

Supervisor: "Yes, absolutely. One of the ways I can tell when another part comes in and starts telling me about a part is when the content or the tone shifts. If the tone has suddenly become negative, then a part in opposition to the part I was speaking with may have taken over."

Supervisee: "In which case, I can ask it to wait and return to the previous part or make it the new target part if necessary."

Supervisor: "Yes, exactly. And then if your parts are giving you more space, and you think Self may be speaking for the part, you can use the key differentiating question, 'How do you feel towards the part as it tells you this?'"

Supervisee: "Can we role-play?" ...

Telling the difference between Self and parts

If I had to choose what was the most important thing to "know" in IFS, I would say that coming to know/feel/experience/trust the difference(s) between Self and parts is the most crucial. Once I and my clients are experiencing a critical mass of Self, then clarity, confidence and courage abound. One of the great things about IFS for me is that my need-to-know parts, don't need to work so hard. Once the client's Self is in relationship with the client's part, I merely "guide" the conversation and help them stay in relationship.[15] I like to use the question, "How do you (the client) respond to the part?" (I am always willing to give a response if the client prefers this and I often offer that as well.) It is very special to hear the client's Self relate to the client's parts. Schwartz often talks about sessions with clients who have a lot of Self and how he mainly just gets out of the way.

What assumptions or partial truths do parts hold about IFS?

Parts of me used to hold and I believe others' parts may hold certain, often unconscious, assumptions about IFS, such as:

- IFS is always safe.
- It's a very forgiving model, it's not possible to get it wrong.
- Anyone can do the Level 1 without a therapy training so anybody can do IFS easily.
- It's faster than other therapies.
- It's gentler than other forms of therapy.
- Even though I've never worked with traumatised clients before, now I've got IFS I can.

- It's the only therapy I'm ever going to need/use.
- IFS therapists don't need to make formal assessments of clients nor know any client history because we work from Self, and we know our clients have Self.
- IFS is a self-correcting model; I can take more risks than I'm used to.
- IFS therapists/practitioners don't have to honour the same boundaries as other therapists.

It is understandable that our systems might hold such beliefs. Our therapist parts want to believe they've found the latest "wonder therapy", or our improver parts want to tick the box alongside "Complete the most sought-after therapy training" so we can list it on our website, etc. Also, it makes sense that parts hold these beliefs. For example, in the demos on trainings, the trainer undertakes no formal assessment nor takes any client history. As mimicking is a major way in which we learn, I can understand therapist parts who might extrapolate from that they don't need to do those things for themselves with clients. However, as I hope I've been making clear throughout this book, thinking about why we do what we do or don't do certain things and why others do and don't do things is vitally important. Taking on someone for a potential ongoing therapist—client relationship is different to doing a one-off demo in a group training setting. Here is some of the context enabling a trainer to take the risk and not enquire about the trainee's history and bypass an assessment[16]:

- The trainer is immensely experienced in the model (if you are a novice, you are not)
- There is a group present, which hugely increases the Self-energy available.
- Volunteering for a training demonstration is a form of self-selection that is likely to make the trainee/client favourably disposed to giving IFS a chance.
- If the experience proves difficult, the trainee/client can be helped by PAs, peers, their own therapist and/or supervisor if they have them; they are unlikely to be isolated.
- If the experience is less than positive, the trainee/client is unlikely to make a formal complaint as parts might fear jeopardising successful completion of the training course.
- If something is challenging in the work at the time, the trainer is likely to be able to maintain Self-energy.

- If something goes awry or is challenging, it can be used as a learning/teaching point and still give benefit to the participant in the demo and to the rest of the group.

Rather than unthinkingly following the practice of your IFS trainer, you may want to tailor how you do parts work to your circumstances, experience, tolerance for risk, confidence, professional support, and ability to maintain Self-energy with certain client groups compared to others, and so on. Schwartz himself speaks to this in a talk between himself, Michelle Glass and Stephanie Mitchell (2021) on IFS and the window of tolerance.[17] He shares that in highly traumatised systems the threat of exile overwhelm can trigger firefighters who do dangerous things (suicidal parts, self-harming parts, and addictive parts). So, it is important to know in advance of going to any exiles if there are any such firefighters in the system. Ideally such a part would meet with the therapist and the client's Self in advance so its fears can be addressed, and any individualised safety plan negotiated. Michelle Glass gives an example of working with a client's exile, which was deep underground. Permission was granted for Self to go down to the exile and unload the perceived threat before the exile was welcomed up to the surface.[18]

Similarly, in highly traumatised systems the threat of abandonment by the therapist can trigger firefighters who do dangerous things. Unfortunately, these dangerous activities can be frightening to the therapist who may feel victimised and respond from parts who jointly persecute the dysregulated client and rescue themselves (now a dysregulated therapist) by making the boundaries around the work even tighter, and even threatening to or actually ending therapy. Rather than let our own push-pull/get close-withdraw parts get involved in case management or risk control, Schwartz tells Glass and Mitchell how important it is that parts of the client who may be backlashing are met with Self-energy. These parts need to know we care about, even love them, and that they matter[19] to us.

Also, although Self doesn't need to develop, knows what parts need and how to look after them on the inside, Schwartz also speaks to the wisdom of therapists assessing the level of safety and danger in the client's external reality.[20] As he and Sweezy write (2020, p. 42):

> Because system levels echo each other, a therapist should not work with a client's internal system without thoroughly considering and addressing the person's external context.

Exercises

1) Considering the concept in IFS of parts not needing to change

In response to the 4th F how do you feel towards the part? I tell client parts that respond to the target part "I hear you; and I'm not asking you to change, you can still hate/dislike/pity, etc., the other part. And I'd like you to give us space to get to know it more if you are willing."

In supervision I can sometimes find myself reminding supervisees: "Remember, parts don't all have to like each other or agree with each other. That angry part doesn't have to stop being angry with the other one to give space for Self to be present and heal what needs healing."

As a therapist/practitioner/IFS professional, what do you make of the idea that: "Parts don't have to change" and "I'm not asking you to change"? How do you think these fit with or contradict the transformative nature of IFS?[21]

2) Considering your relationship to content in the psychotherapy room

Think about how your core modality, previous profession, or current work relates to client content (psychodynamic, person-centred, integrative, NLP, CBT, coaching, mentoring, mediation, business models, etc.):

- What content were you taught to collect?
- When is that content collected?
- What happens to that content when you are with your client?
- What happens with that content in supervision?

Now consider the IFS work you have done with clients:

- Do you require content from the client before you agree to work together? If so, what content do you need?
- Do you require content from the client in session before you agree to "go inside" or do direct access?
- Does the client like to share some content at the start of each session? If so, what purpose(s) might this serve?
- Do you gravitate towards "gathering" content at any of the 6 Fs or steps of healing?

Next, if the following seems relevant or useful, consult with your parts, either on your own or with a peer, in supervision, etc.:

- Schedule some time to go inside to be with your system. In your own way, let your system know: "Now we are using IFS, we will not be focusing on content in the same way we are used to" and notice any reactions. These reactions might be in the form of thoughts, exclamations, questions, body sensations or changes, emotional twinges, memories, and urges. These are trailheads for your attention.
- Welcome these reactions and note them down in some way so that you can spend time with each trailhead.
- Choose a particular trailhead and use the 6 Fs to find, focus on and flesh out any parts and ask yourself how you feel towards each one that shows up. From a place of Self-energy, dialogue with what is there to learn more about their reaction to a change in content-seeking in the therapy room.

3) Self-supervision

If you are working towards IFS certification, it is likely that you have arrangements in place (or will have) to record therapy sessions. Even if you are not working towards certification, reviewing recordings of sessions is a great source of learning and means to reflect on your practice, and improve. It may also be helpful to share the recordings with your supervisor. (If it's not possible or appropriate to record clients, perhaps you could record yourself facilitating a peer or colleague.)

If you film both you and the client, make sure to review yourself, not just focus on the client. Alternatively, you could just film or record yourself. Here are a few suggestions about how to review the material:

a) Visual review with the sound off and only watching yourself

- Watch the different expressions that cross your face.
- View the position of your head and any movements it makes.
- Notice any tension you can see, any holding.
- If you can see the whole of your body, note how centred and upright you are, if and how you shift from this, moving forwards or backwards.
- Take note of your breathing pattern if you can, be curious as to how it matches, or doesn't match the client's breathing.

- Recall and look out for any shifts to your expression, body position or posture and determine as best you can whether the shift is conscious or unconscious. If conscious, what were you trying to achieve, and did it happen?

b) Visual review with the sound off and watching client(s) and therapist

- Look for any mirroring that takes place on your faces, your body postures, and positions.
- Watch for matching movements, see where they initiate, i.e., who follows who.
- Review for repetition of movement, expression, posture, breathing patterns in any of the participants.

Reflect on what you have noticed: does this indicate parts in the driving seat; how could someone tell from the outside that Self is in the driving seat; did you have a part activated by a similar part in the client(s); who do you recognise; who is new to you?

Reflect on any action you wish to take after this review, which could include:

- Work in supervision, with your peer group, or in therapy with parts that may have been active to allow more space for Self's presence.
- Speak for any parts present and getting in the way of the client('s) with an apology or a request that the client(s) let you know if they sense the presence of that part in future.
- Decide on any changes you wish to make in how you are with certain clients and compare later videos to see whether you have achieved those changes.

c) Review normally using sound and visual and noticing both/all parties

- What did you do or say that you would rather not have done or said?
- What would you rather have said or done?
- What problems or risks might there be if you did or said the above?
- Who do you think the client sees/hears when they see/hear you?
- Are you reminded of anything or anyone from the past?
- Do you have any images or associations in relation to the session you are watching? (CSTD, 2009)

Notes

1 See Chapter 3, especially Endnote 3.

2 This is a general principle and differentiation may be needed for different clinical populations and individuals, please use your professional judgment. Tamala Floyd writes about working with the BIPOC population and the regular appearance of storytelling parts (2023, p. 90): "When attempts are made to have this part step back in this population, it tends to resist. It wants to share its stories. I find that engaging the storyteller builds trust within the system of which it is part."

3 Although it is important that we still study the classic texts and hold in high esteem the psychotherapy heroes of the past, neurobiology is shedding new light on old theories. For example, during an online conference (2021), Dan Hughes, founder and developer of Dyadic Developmental Psychotherapy (DDP) shared research findings from co-author, clinical psychologist and specialist in neurobiology, Dr Baylin that suggest it is not possible to have empathy for someone who is angry with you.

4 See also Schwartz and Sweezy, 2020, p. 116 regarding some of the nuances between *feeling for*, *feeling with* and the ability to offer both when parts and Self are in relationship and parts feel cared for.

5 In her podcast interview (Henriques & Shull, 2021) IFS therapist and educator Alexia Rothman lists six considerations for the IFS therapist and practitioner to hold in mind when letting their empathy flow to client parts and how that might or might not facilitate the client's Self-to-part connection. Lead trainer and trauma specialist Dr Frank Anderson (2021, pp. 38–41) includes interesting material on when to use compassion and when to use empathy.

6 Autonomy is an ethical principle defined by my professional body the British Association for Counselling and Psychotherapy (BACP, 2018, pp. 9 and 15) as "respect for the client's right to be self-governing". As a therapist, I aspire to "work with issues of identity in open-minded ways that respect the client's autonomy and be sensitive to whether this is viewed as individual or relational autonomy". From the IFS viewpoint of multiplicity of mind, (Schwartz & Sweezy, 2020, p. 30) "parts are discrete, autonomous, mental systems, each with their own idiosyncratic range of emotion, style of expression, abilities, desires, and views of the world". The autonomy of parts is not at odds with Self-leadership (see Schwartz, 2021, pp. 86–146). Rather, parts are *invited* constantly to trust in Self's leadership and Self's desire to be in relationship with each unique, autonomous part.

7 If you are not a trained therapist, you may *not* need to reconsider your approach to empathising as your parts may not be attached to the concept and practice.

8 I often think of an external family in which the parents are Self-led and therefore able to respond well to and embrace difference among their children, acknowledging the individuality, unique needs and contributions of each member of the family.

9 See Chapter 3, "Creating safety is crucial and includes giving safety updates".

10 See Chapter 2.

11 See Schwartz and Sweezy, 2020, pp. 16–19 under the headings "Cora" and "New Data" for Schwartz's discovery of the inner leader we now know of as *Self*.

12 If you are interested in the neuroscience of memory, see Afford, 2020.

13 See "The Question of Memories", Ch. 3 of Goulding and Schwartz, 2002.

14 Part of why I have written this book is to help highlight some of the gaps in knowledge and experience of those of you wanting to work as IFS therapists without a foundational counselling, psychotherapy, social work, or human services training, so that you may begin to fill them if you wish and are able to.

15 Ch 6. of Schwartz and Sweezy (2020) focuses on The Role of the Therapist in IFS in which they write about establishing a co-therapy relationship between the client's Self and the therapist's Self.

16 Frank Anderson (2021) suggests (p. 25) that he does not complete a formal intake assessment even with clients with complex trauma. Instead, he hopes, as exiles show themselves, to make a list of wounds from which he can determine an order of healing. This may work well for someone as experienced and confident as Anderson, who can trust that he will handle whatever and whoever shows up. I suggest that this not be considered the ideal template for working with clients suffering complex trauma when one is learning IFS or practising therapeutically using IFS for the first time.

17 Schwartz regularly teaches and writes that Self has a huge window of tolerance (Appendix II, Endnote 19).

18 When working with clients with dissociating parts, you may want to attend more closely than usual to client parts' feelings of safety and threat. For ideas of how to work with such clients, see the chapter by Twombly (2013).

19 Schwartz is not unusual in advocating this, see Erskine et al. (2012) and Yalom the famous existential psychiatrist and author (2001, p. 26–29) urges us to let our patients matter to us, enter our minds, influence and change us. He writes that therapist disclosure brings about patient disclosure.

20 As of the time of writing, the ability to assess external constraints is the third item on the list of IFS competencies to be rated as part of an application for IFS certification.

21 See Chapter 3 and the idea of building rapport with parts and negotiating with them, and Chapter 2, working counteractively vs transformatively.

Part III
Barriers to transitioning
Fear, loss and frustration

6
Embracing direct access and freeing Self to lead

Introduction

This is the first of three chapters (6, 7, 8) in Part III highlighting that fear, loss and frustration can occur naturally as part of the learning process and need not become barriers to fully embracing IFS (however you then implement it in your context).

Direct access is complicated. I encourage you to commit to becoming fluent at both implicit and explicit direct access by mastering a range of processes which this chapter covers:

- working with your own parts who put up barriers to freeing Self to lead direct access conversations
- your parts coming to understand the purpose and importance of direct access
- practising both implicit and explicit versions and differentiating between the different types of conversations

What is direct access?

I suggest reading the glossary entries in either of the Sweezy and Ziskind books (2013, 2017) and the second edition of *Internal Family Systems Therapy* (Schwartz & Sweezy, 2020). Meanwhile, here is my take on it: direct access is a conversation led by the Self of the IFS professional who is consciously, with awareness and using their ability to parts-detect, choosing to speak directly to a part. Direct access can take two forms: either the part can be openly invited to converse and respond directly (explicit direct access); or the IFS professional who is seeking to get to know a part – and be known by it – will just converse with the part without explicitly asking it for permission

DOI: 10.4324/9781003243571-10

or saying to the client (or the part) that this is what they are doing (implicit direct access).

The main goal of direct access (both explicit and implicit)

The main purpose of direct access is to create a validating, safe relationship with the other person's/client's blended part so that in time it becomes willing to give space, i.e., unblend and come into relationship with the Self of the person's system; to do that the IFS professional will need to access their own Self-energy. It is important a therapist or practitioner working therapeutically becomes confident with direct access as it enables the client's part to unblend and create a Self-and-part relationship inside the client's system (Pastor & Gauvain, 2020, p. 72), which ultimately brings that part (if an exile) or any part it protects (if a protector) closer to moving through the steps of healing.

Jeanne Catanzaro is a licensed clinical psychologist specialising in working with eating and trauma-related issues. She has recently had published a chapter, "Trusting Self to Heal: Removing Constraints to Therapists' Self-Energy Transforms Their Treatment of Eating Disordered Clients" (2023). Writing about supervisee Sarah role-playing her client Caroline's depressed part, Catanzaro details a great example of using implicit direct access and moving seamlessly into explicit direct access. Catanzaro explains to Sarah that a goal of direct access is to connect with a part, listen to its concerns and build a relationship of trust so the part can feel safe enough to separate from the client.

Reasons to use direct access

Drawing from Schwartz and Sweezy, 2020, pp. 83, 112–121 and the IFS Level 1 manual (Pastor & Gauvain) times to use explicit direct access include:

- when a part is blended and the client's Self is unavailable (in-sight is not therefore possible);
- to get to know and build a trusting relationship with a protector, enabling it to vet for safety, or get to know the IFS professional;
- to help the protector fully express, and/or embody, their feelings and thoughts;
- to help defuse the threat of a part the system is afraid of (a part holding a lot of anger, or urge to end the pain through suicide for example);
- if a part won't talk with the Self of the client;

- when parts are becoming or are extreme (such as a part threatening suicide, harm or neglect to another, or polarisations are dominating the system blocking access to Self);
- responding directly to a part can often help to regulate extreme emotion – for example, if an exile blends spontaneously or unexpectedly.

Naturally, one size does not fit all and there can be disadvantages to using direct access (see Schwartz & Sweezy, 2020, p. 116).

When to use implicit direct access

You can use implicit direct access for all the above reasons, and particularly at the following times:

- at the start of working with a new client not familiar with IFS, when it can be helpful just to notice which parts are there;
- getting to know a client's dominant protector for whom it might, initially, be too much of a leap to suggest that it is not "all there is" inside the client;
- working with a part who rejects the idea it is a part (or one that is likely to reject that idea);
- working with a client whose parts have not felt welcomed;
- in play therapy with a child who might demonstrate or enact inner world experience using toys or figures;[1]
- when IFS is a new modality for you and your client, and they currently understand therapy as blending with exiles for you to soothe;
- when other avenues have been blocked or not succeeded (in-sight, explicit direct access) implicit direct access offers a way forward rather than falling back on non-IFS ways of working.

However, don't let the intricacies between explicit and implicit direct access put you off from trying it. These are not "absolutes" nor "rules". Direct access comes through practising and experience rather than through head knowledge. Pamela Krause (2013, p. 46) makes it very clear that there is no one right way to respond when using direct access (implicit or explicit). The key for the IFS therapist or practitioner is to have their parts unblend so they can access Self, who is more than capable of handling it. It can help if, while lightly bearing in mind what you are trying to achieve, you are able to really buy into the part as an actual personality and just talk to and respond to it naturally, as you would to a person or more usually to a child.

In my practice, I make very little distinction between explicit and implicit direct access – the main difference being at the outset, where I ask for permission for explicit but not for implicit. Another difference is in the pacing of the relationship. With explicit direct access and a part willing to talk to me directly, I will cut to the chase faster than if I am using implicit direct access with a part who may not know it's a part. In the latter instance, I may patiently build trust with the part before then asking about its relationship to the client – the implication being "you are not the client, how are you trying to help her?" See the example below with supervisee Laney playing a part of her client Bethan.

Get to know and work with your parts

Parts putting up barriers to learning how to do direct access

Understandably, partly because it is such a significant aspect of the IFS model, and because it can seem so different to what we are used to, our parts can be fearful of the process. Responses I have come across, in my role as supervisor, from therapists and practitioners not attempting or persisting with direct access include the following:

> "They didn't teach it enough on my Level 1"
>
> "I don't know what to do"
>
> "I've never done it before"
>
> "The client can't do it"
>
> "I'll look silly"
>
> "What if the part won't agree to it?"
>
> "I'll lose control"
>
> "It gets us nowhere"
>
> "It doesn't work"
>
> "It's so frustrating"
>
> "I won't know who I'm speaking to"
>
> "The client doesn't stay speaking from the one part and I give up"
>
> "I might get it wrong"[2]

Each fear is understandable, can be validated, and addressed (see the next section for a couple of examples of this). "I've never done it before" was my number one "reason" for not doing direct access. A part of me that I value greatly, can get triggered in learning situations when it feels like it is being watched. It is also unwilling for me to do something new "on a client" (this is how it thinks of protocols) unless the client knows I'm in training or understands that I am fully trained and learning a new way of doing something.

Addressing our parts' fears

It can be all too easy to become frustrated with a so-called "uncooperative" client, thus leading with a part, which will only make it harder for the client to unblend from their own parts. In the second edition of *Internal Family Systems Therapy* (2020) implicit direct access gets little coverage but it does appear in the Glossary (p. 281 my highlighting):

> ... **when the client rejects the idea of parts**, or says, "That's not a part, that's me," we can speak to the part *implicitly*, without using the word part.

It is understandable that parts might get frustrated or fear rejection. Have them note the text in bold above, the client is rejecting *the idea of parts*, the client is *not rejecting you*, their therapist or practitioner (although it may feel like that to some parts). Even if they are rejecting you or part of you, the rejection is coming from a *part* not the whole of the client and that part will have ample reason for taking that position. Interestingly also, in my experience, as my system has released some of the feelings of shame and worthlessness, I'm more able to remain present for rejecting, angry, dismissive parts in clients, and I suspect it is like that for most IFS professionals (which is why we do our own personal work). My parts don't react with as much heat or extremity as they used to. I can more easily believe: like the Mafia, its business, it's not personal.

For parts who consider the relationship all important and struggle with a protocol, remember that both versions of direct access are relational. Yes, it may be a technique to be learned, it is also grounded in relationship. Mary Steege, author of *The Spirit-Led Life* (2010, p. 37) writes of IFS:

> There is a methodology, but the model itself is not mechanistic. It's much more organic and flows from a family systems framework, which means that it adapts to the needs of a particular relationship. IFS can help people address specific behavioral issues and specific life problems, but these problems are considered in the light of relationship.

Somewhat paradoxically, the more we know our clients, the easier direct access becomes; and the more implicit and explicit direct access we do, the more we get to know our clients.

Professional/therapist parts may be invested in leading and fear letting Self lead

More significantly perhaps, parts may be unwilling to embrace direct access because it means them "taking a back seat" (and relinquishing the role of expert) and letting Self take the lead. Here are some parts I have met (and some I would expect to meet) in working with professionals transforming their work with IFS:

- Psychodynamic therapists may have parts who don't like the idea of Self as the client's inner attachment figure. Such parts may be invested in them or the therapist being the reparative parent figure or the good parent. Direct access would not serve such part's needs therefore as it calls forth Self in the other.
- CBT therapists may discover parts who feel unsafe around strong emotion in others and unsafe with personal vulnerability (see Chapter 7); direct access may feel very risky.
- Despite being used to having access to Self-energy, bodyworkers may have parts who struggle to conceive of Self as a *relational* healing agent who can direct a conversation and verbally negotiate with a part.
- Bodyworkers and person-centred therapists may have parts who struggle with IFS because they believe they must follow the client rather than introduce a protocol (such as direct access).
- Art/creative/drama therapists may have active parts used to "directing" the other perhaps with the use of props or with an outcome in mind (moving through the hero's journey, for example). Such parts may fear the intimacy or exposure of having a direct access conversation with the open-ended curiosity that requires.
- All helping professions may have rescuer parts who think the way out of victimhood and to redemption is by rescuing the other to make their pain stop/go away/get fixed. These parts may fear redundancy or annihilation on first hearing of Self's existence, leadership role and powers of healing and transformation.
- Helping professionals' parts used to a triangular relationship (therapist + client + art material/light bar/worksheets for example) may feel exposed in and unsure of a direct relationship with the client without the "third party" materials.

- Any of us may have parts who struggle with not knowing, not being the expert, not being the one with all the answers; direct access comes from a place of curiosity of *asking* to get to know who a part is and how it functions in the system etc.
- Those of you without a prior therapy training (psychological or physical) may have parts who feel they have something to prove, or who feel unequal to the task of being an IFS therapist and who may resist attempting direct access for fear of failing at it.
- Busy health professionals may not invest the time and money in having their own IFS therapy (or not find a therapist with availability). and their parts may not experience direct access for themselves (whether implicit or explicit). This may affect their parts' willingness to allow space to give direct access a chance for others. Also, direct access asks a lot of therapists and practitioners; parts ask us *hard questions*, such as "where was Self back then when I was a child?" and "so, if I have to 'make space', is it my fault Self isn't here?" We need to "know in our bones" the answer to such questions, and/or trust that under that spotlight Self's clarity, confidence and courage will come forward so we can respond. Reading about and personally experiencing the laws of inner physics as well as working with our parts takes time and commitment.

Exercise 3 at the end of this chapter is designed to introduce you to any parts who may feel invested in the status quo professionally.

Negotiating with parts who don't want to do IFS

As we know, there are no bad parts (Schwartz, 2021), and protectors have positive intentions for the system although they often get or create the opposite of what they intend.[3] Along your journey transitioning to IFS fluency, there will be times when parts get in the way of the work and will need to meet and learn to trust your Self and Self's choice of IFS, (including choosing or offering direct access when relevant). Below is an example (used with permission) of what I mean.

Transition reflection

"I find my 'fall-back parts' so interesting. They are still active as I work for a public agency where my responsibilities include providing both individual and group therapy in other modalities alongside transitioning to IFS." (Sarah Murphy, Clinical Counsellor)

I'm working with Fiona and it's our fifth supervision session. Fiona has taken on a new client, a senior male psychologist referred to her by another mental health professional. She reports that feelings of imposter syndrome are coming up. She is judging herself as having failed at parts-detecting, and as lacking the nerve to do direct access while struggling to help the client do in-sight. So big were these feelings that Fiona experienced severe chest pain and got herself checked out medically. Naturally, Fiona is curious about what parts might be active and she tells me she has become aware of a male part's involvement. What follows is a reconstruction of a supervision session in which this part becomes the target part:

> *Supervisee:* "He makes me fall back on my Person-Centred therapy (PCT)."
>
> *Supervisor:* "Okay, would you like to spend some time now meeting with him?" (*She nods.*)
>
> *Supervisee:* "He's in my chest and I'm curious."
>
> *Supervisor:* "Great, ask him how he's trying to help you."
>
> *Supervisee:* "The part says he can tell I'm surer of PCT ways of being with a client than I am with IFS at the moment. This part thinks it's important I stay with what I'm sure about it."
>
> *Supervisor:* "That makes sense to me, does it to you?"
>
> *Supervisee:* "Yes, it does. (*Pausing as she listens inside.*) The part says it gets on edge and anxious when the client can't do what I'm asking (*i.e.*, 'something IFS')".
>
> *Supervisor:* (*Sensing a change in tone.*) "Fiona, how do you feel towards the part as you hear that and feel some of the part's anxiety?"
>
> *Supervisee:* "I don't like it being there in my chest, it's getting in the way of my work with clients. ... And I'll ask that critical part to give me some space, I get what it's saying but ..."
>
> *Supervisor:* "That's great. It's stepped back? (*She nods.*) How do you feel towards the part who has the anxiety around your lack of ease with IFS compared to PCT?"
>
> *Supervisee:* "Calm and connected. He can feel I'm back with him."
>
> *Supervisor:* "Ask this part what he wants for you."
>
> *Supervisee:* "He wants to make me look good at my job."
>
> *Supervisor:* "Ask the part if that's working out at present."
>
> *Supervisee:* "No, no it's not."
>
> *Supervisor:* "Fiona, is there anything you want to say to the part on this?"

Supervisee: "I'm letting him know that if he doesn't ease off then we're not going to get the best for the client."

Supervisor: "See how he responds."

Supervisee: "Flustered that I'm not on board with what he wants, which is to revert to his old PCT ways."

Supervisor: "And you're still feeling connected and open-hearted towards him?"

Supervisee: "Yes. ... I'm asking if he'll trust me, give IFS a go and keep watch. (*Listening inside.*) He says the next client will be a test. I'm saying it will be better if he helps me and assists me with the IFS. (*Smiling*) The part's pleased I'm not trying to abandon him. I'm telling him that I want to use everything I know which includes IFS and if the part gives me space, he can see for himself how great IFS is. (*Pausing inside.*) That feels complete for now."

Supervisor: "Just before you come out, can you send some appreciation from us both to this part? (*Fiona nods.*) And, in your imagination, just think of this senior male psychologist client again (*She nods.*) and how do you feel towards him?"

Supervisee: "Hmm, more confident and my heart's not guarded against him. (*Rubbing and opening her eyes.*) I think I'll move on now ... I'd like to share some of the successes I've had with IFS clients recently."

Make use of supervision to familiarise yourself with using direct access

Understandably, beginners in IFS can feel nervous about doing explicit or implicit direct access with clients (I know I was at first). Supervision can be a great place in which to practise and see direct access (implicit and explicit) and have it modelled. See Table 6.1 for the different possibilities available in individual supervision.

Table 6.1 Possibilities for practising direct access in individual supervision

1. Supervisee	plays therapist	supervisor	role-plays blended part of client
2. Supervisee	plays therapist	supervisor	blends with own part
3. Supervisor	models therapist role	supervisee	role-plays blended part of the client
4. Supervisor	models therapist role	supervisee	blends with own part

I enjoy supervisees role-playing a client's part with me speaking to it directly (No 3, Table 6.1) and it can be a powerful experience for the supervisee. Eliza was experiencing some frustration with a young client who had been sent to therapy by the grownups and was struggling to use the space and relax into the relationship. Eliza played the client and I enjoyed being curious, playful and accepting towards her which on the receiving end felt really good. In our next supervision session, Eliza tells me the role-play "really helped, it was much easier to be with the client because you had been *so* curious with me". This makes some sense as I am one step removed from her client and there is no pressure on my parts to succeed therapeutically so they can relax. The more I do direct access with supervisees, the more I can trust that what needs to happen will happen. After direct access with another supervisee playing a client's part, I asked if he got what he needed. Ivan tells me it was a "beautiful experience, it felt so spacious and with a real lack of agenda" (which is what he wants and was struggling to offer his clients, and which involves his parts giving more space).

I also like to help supervisees practise direct access as therapist while I play their client's part (No 1, Table 6.1). This can be a rich experience for a therapist who is willing and feels safe enough to get instant feedback from me on their interventions. Also, it can be remarkable what can be picked up "from the field" or from the right hemisphere's open/global attention (Afford, 2020) and fed back to the therapist while playing someone I've never met. In group supervision, the possibilities are even richer as participants can role-play with each other, be coached by another member of the group and/or the supervisor.

Explicit direct access with a don't know part

One of my supervisees, who I will call Hestor, has difficulty with a client's don't know part. Understandably, a part arises in the therapist that is attached to the client knowing, or, in other words, answering the therapist's questions. Hestor's initial psychotherapy training is Integrative, and she has been taught to ask questions and elicit answers as part of both the healing process and the creation of a healing therapeutic relationship. Hestor says she has already tried a reframe with the client, "If you did know, what might you say?" Don't know parts are often triggering for those new to IFS and I offer Hestor various options for our supervision time together:

- Work with parts in Hestor who get so upset and blend when the client answers "I don't know".

- Have Hestor play the client's part while I play the therapist and use explicit direct access.
- Review together theoretically the steps involved in direct access.

Hestor chooses the theory option, and I share, in outline, what works for me (see the box immediately below).

Direct access

1. Have parts relax (especially any holding frustration or hopelessness) and trust Self to lead. Appreciate their willingness. (If parts aren't willing to step back, consider not attempting direct access except in a practice situation until your parts give more space).
2. Greet the client's part from Self (out loud for explicit or inside the head/in imagination for implicit).
3. Help the part feel seen and heard.
4. Validate the part, so it feels understood and valued.
5. Find out and address the part's concerns/fears and foster safety (including updating).
6. Hope-merchant to the part re its individual, specific concerns.
7. Offer to introduce the client's Self (if their system allows).
8. Broker the introduction to Self or pass the baton as Schwartz calls it.

Hestor reflects and realises she gets the theory; lack of understanding or knowledge of the process is not the issue. She then opts for us to do a role-play with her playing the client, Mary's don't know part, and me playing the therapist using explicit direct access. Below is a reconstructed account of that, linked to the eight-point process above, which is what I am modelling to Hestor.

(*Feeling warm and open* [1] *towards the supervisee and curious to meet the client's part.*)

Emma, supervisor, as therapist: "Welcome, I Don't Know part." [2]

Hestor as Mary's don't know part: "Hello."

Therapist: "I hear from Hestor that you have an important role in Mary's life – is that right?" [3 and 4]

Client: "I don't know."

Therapist: "Ah, I wonder, is that your job in Mary's system, to not know?" (*Silence*)

(*Self's clarity is strongly present even with so little being given away by the part played by the supervisee. It feels like I "know" the part.* [3])

Therapist contd: "I've heard from Hestor that you step up and reply whenever Hestor asks Mary how she feels about something."

Client: "Yes."

Therapist: "And I get that. It's not your job to know about feelings, is it?" [3 and 4]

Client: "No."

Therapist: "I wonder. Is it your job to stop Mary feeling her feelings?"

(*Although this is more about getting to know the part's job than finding out its fears if it didn't do what it does. In hindsight, I could have explicitly asked what it's afraid would happen if it didn't stop the client from feeling her feelings.* [5])

Client: "Yes."

Therapist: "And I wonder if you know the answer to this question, you might not and that's okay: how long have you been doing this job?"

(*Validating the part's not knowing and its service to the system.* [4])

Client: "I don't know."

Therapist: "That's okay. But it's your job to protect her from uncomfortable or difficult feelings coming up?" (*Supervisee nods.*)

(*I'm putting words in the part's mouth and the supervisee seems to think they are accurate enough.* [5])

Client: "Yes."

Therapist: "I see, and I remember now that Hestor told me about something awful that happened to some of Mary's relatives. Maybe you've been very active since then because the feelings got more or got worse around then?"

Client: "Yes. Lots of overwhelming things happened at once."

Therapist: "Ah, and that's when you started working extra hard for Mary? (*Supervisee is nodding.*) Do you like your job?"

Client: "I don't know."

Therapist: "That's okay. I'm going to let you know something I think you might not know: Mary is in therapy with Hestor to help her feel better after all those awful things happened."

(*Taking responsibility for sharing information, including an update that might help the part feel safer in the present with Hestor. If the part/supervisee doesn't like me sharing this, they can let me know.* [5])

Client: "I didn't know that."

Therapist: "No. And part of that therapy is helping Mary's Self be with the hurting parts which helps them let go of their hurt. Then you might not have to work so hard."

(*Hope-merchanting to what I imagine are the part's fears* [6]; *introducing the concept of Self to the part.* [7])

Client: "Oh."

Therapist: "I'm guessing that you might not know Self yet, might not have met."

Client: "No."

Therapist: "Would you be willing to meet with Self do you think?"

(*Offering to make an introduction between this part and Self.* [7])

Client: "I don't know how to do that."

Therapist: "That's okay … if you just have the intention to give some space inside then it will happen. If you make space, I can ask Hestor's Self to come and say hello."

We stop the role-play there as Hestor is confident with passing the baton (8) to Self. In the debrief after the exercise, Hestor shares that she feels warmer towards her client (her anti-don't know parts feel less threatened perhaps) and can imagine bringing Self's curiosity to that part in future sessions.

Implicit direct access with an angry part

Pamela Krause (Pastor & Gauvain, 2020, pp. 75–76) states in her Direct Access Decision Tree that all sessions generally begin with implicit direct access. The person we are relating to at the start of each conversation and each therapy, coaching, or other form of session or interaction is probably speaking from one main part or speaking from several parts, while as the IFS professional, we hopefully attain and maintain Self-presence and leadership[4] and are able to detect the part/s we are hearing from.

Here is an example from my supervision practice of role-playing the start of a therapy session with the supervisee, Laney, playing one of her clients:

Emma playing therapist: Welcome, Bethan, how have you and things been since last week?"

Laney playing client Bethan: "I did it again, I lost my rag with him. It was 10pm Sunday night and he'd not done his homework and I knew it had to be in first thing on Monday."

Therapist: "You got angry with him and …?"

(*Talking directly and implicitly to the angry part.*)

Client: "Yes, and I knew I shouldn't, and I was yelling but I kept right on going."

Therapist: "You felt bad about doing it, but the anger kept on coming out."

(*Signs here of a critical part who doesn't want her to be angry. I continue to focus on the angry energy and don't get side-tracked. I could have been more explicit and said, "Part of you felt bad about doing it …"*)

Client: "Yes, and … I … don't … can't … ggrrhh!"

(*The supervisee is doing well and sticking with the angry energy.*)

Therapist: "And how is this anger helpful[5] to you and your son, any thoughts on that?"

(*I could also have been more explicit and asked, "How are you trying to help Bethan by being angry?"*)

Client still played by Laney the supervisee: "Well, I can't bear the thought of him failing at school and being a loser like I was. It took me until I was in my forties to get my qualifications so I could get a decent job. I do *not* want that for him, he's really bright."

(*Here we are beginning to get a hint of the exile(s) beneath or behind the angry protector.*)

Therapist still played by me, the supervisor: "Makes sense, doesn't it? You want to protect your son from making the same mistakes you made. And, how else is the anger trying to help?"

Client: "I will *not* be a failure of a mother, like mine was with me. She didn't give a damn what I did, with whom, at whatever time of the day or night. Anything could have happened to me, and it did, and she'll never know about any of that."

Therapist: "Absolutely, and how do you feel towards this angry protecting part of you now as you learn how hard it is trying to prevent both you and your son from failing?"

(*At this point, I decide to role-play taking the risk of using the 4th F to see if the angry part can unblend. In an ideal IFS session, the client would now be able to get some separation, to differentiate[6] Self from part and might say something like: "I feel warm and appreciative towards it."*)

Supervisee: "That was powerful. I feel really warm towards that angry part of the client. Bethan's terrified of failing as a mother, I know that."

(*Laney comes out of the role play, back into the supervisory space and talks to me as a supervisee/therapist about her client and the client's part.*)

Supervisor: "Great, so in role playing her angry protector you now have a possible sense of how it is trying to help her system. Any thoughts on the exiles it might be protecting – and we both know you'll need to ask to directly find out from Bethan's system too?"

Supervisee: "Sure, she's really been failed – neglected or abandoned – by her own mother so there will be exiles carrying the pain of that, I guess. And, as a mother, there will be parts carrying the pain of failing her son too perhaps."

Supervisor: "Yes, quite possibly. Also, did you notice how it was pretty much like normal therapy and I was asking the angry part how it was helping without explicitly saying 'Angry part how are you trying to help'? I wasn't even using 'you' each time; I was being curious towards the function of the anger in the system."

Supervisee: "I do, yes, I'll need to let that sink in some more ..."

Supervisor: "Sure, and remind yourself of the material by Toni Herbine-Blank and Pamela Krause[7] on direct access in the IFS Level 1 Manual (Pastor & Gauvain, 2020, pp. 75–76) which includes an example of implicit direct access with an angry part."

Transition reflection

"Roleplaying direct access in supervision has really helped me go for it. I recommend trying it out, don't worry about saying exactly the right words. Even if the client isn't ready to go with it, trying it is unlikely to have negative consequences." (GJ, psychotherapist with two years' experience of IFS work)

Implicit direct access in business

The management consultant I mentioned in Chapter 1, Helen Telford, describes (2021) how she got to know her parts activated while she was up on stage doing her consultancy group work. She describes one part who is uber professional and who used to, before IFS, manage down any conflict in the room. With her transformation to IFS, Helen tells us how she now soothes her parts, helps them be less anxious and has them trust her to do the work of being Self to the group she works with. As such, she thinks of these groups as a single system (in the way that one person has a system of parts). As she interacts with her audience, she is doing implicit direct access, hearing from the managers, firefighters, and exiles present all of whom need to have a voice in the process she is orchestrating as part of reaching an agreement.

Another time, Helen arrives late to a meeting with a group of healthcare professionals having mistakenly been at the wrong venue and the surgeons are not present. All voices in the system cannot therefore be heard which is activating for those who are present. A woman in the auditorium blends with her angry protector and "lets rip" verbally. Helen sets some tasks for the rest of the group to perform and has a private conversation with the woman, asking, "Where's all this anger coming from?" The woman's distress, her exile energy, blends, and she starts crying. Helen, accessing her Self-energy, then continues the conversation which, in IFS terms, could be called implicit direct access with an exile. The part feels seen, heard, validated, and receives Helen's empathy and compassion and unblends. (Bear in mind that speaking directly with an exile is not the same as "doing IFS" with an exile, which in addition to accessing your own Self-energy and being trained in IFS implies following the IFS healing protocols.)

Being with exiles

In an ideal process, the client's Self would speak to the client's exiles, but this is not always how it happens in real life, in business or in therapy spaces. If an exile appears, it is important that you can access your own Self-energy and be a compassionate, connecting presence for the wounded part. Don't forget, Self isn't fazed by extreme emotions and beliefs. (See Schwartz & Sweezy, 2020, p. 271); if you are feeling scared, ask that part to give you space to be there for it and the client.

Also, it is worth bearing in mind the different levels at which we can work with exiles and whether you are trained adequately and feel confident enough to work at each level. In the Helen Telford example, we see her being with an exile which enabled it to feel heard and welcomed enough to unblend. Had she been in a one-to-one space, she might have worked at a richer level of IFS with that part, which might have wanted to leave a distressing scene in the past and relocate in time to the present. In therapy, systems might allow exiles to go through all of the IFS healing steps. It is important to work within your competence (or scope of practice). If you have read an IFS book or two, you may have the confidence, Self-presence, and skills to witness and validate, perhaps even to retrieve, while not offering anything further. If that is the case and you are already trained as a therapist, then you might do deeper exile work using a different modality that you have more confidence using. If you are a practitioner without another therapy training to fall back on or utilise, you may need to develop the skills to refer clients on for deeper IFS therapeutic work. Alternatively, you may be Self-led and proficient enough to offer all of the IFS healing steps yourself.

Exercises

1) You and direct access: a review

- What are the situations given in training for when to use direct access with clients? What are the benefits of practising direct access in supervision? What are your thoughts and what do you recall from the start of this chapter?
- If you are already accomplished at this IFS skill, do you remember the first time you used it professionally, perhaps in an office or therapy space? How did it go? What did you learn from the experience? How did your parts respond before, during and afterwards?

2) Direct access and your parts

In a quiet, reflective place where you won't be disturbed, perhaps with journalling materials or paints, pencils, and art materials for you to record what your parts share or for parts to use to draw, paint and generally express themselves, get yourself into a receptive and open-hearted place inside. If you can do this without my help jump in at the questions, otherwise, see if you can use the following to quieten your system ready for parts to share with you their reactions to and thoughts about using direct access (implicit and explicit)

- Notice your surroundings using as many senses as you can/wish (touch, taste, smell, sight, hearing).
- Be mindful of a few breath cycles.
- Create some sort of imaginary meeting place (board room, kitchen table, campfire, teleconference, etc.).
- Issue a general invitation to professional/therapist/coach/supervisor/ practitioner parts to come to the meeting place for a meeting of a set time.
- When they arrive, ask yourself "How do I feel towards my parts?" If the answer reveals some Self-energy, then proceed; if not, ask any parts to give you space or to go elsewhere. If the part(s) won't unblend, enquire

about and address concerns until you have more spaciousness. If you need to get assistance from someone, do so.

- From a place of Self-energy, ask for individual part's responses, one at a time, to questions like the following: "Do you understand the reasons for doing direct access?" "Who is onboard with trying this?" "If you aren't onboard, what are you afraid would happen if you gave me space to speak directly with the client's part?"
- Listen to each part, appreciate, and validate its concerns and, together, agree a way forward (this might involve further study, experimenting, practising with peers, having supervision, etc.).
- Appreciate the parts for coming, speaking, and contributing to your system and if necessary, schedule another meeting.

In addition, or as well as, you might want to ask this question: "What are you concerned about if you don't get to talk to the client (i.e., their part/s) like you normally/used to do?" (Substitute, for "talk to", words appropriate to your non-IFS practices, for example:

- Reflect back, summarise
- Coach
- Challenge the cognitions of
- Interpret for
- Do resourcing
- Free up the patient's body
- Do breathing techniques
- Pray with
- Supervise … and so on.

3) Freeing Self to lead; discovering parts invested in the status quo

- You might like to do this with a peer or peers, in supervision, with a colleague or on your own
- If you wish, use writing or art materials, or sand tray/small world items
- Set aside some time(s) to explore, express, plot answers to the following questions for which I have included some phrases to prime your awareness (try and be as honest as possible, remember there are no bad parts).

> Q: What aspects of being a non-IFS professional, coach, therapist, practitioner, supervisor, etc., do I enjoy?
>
> A: ??

Example answers include:

> *I love teaching*
> *Narrative work*
> *It helps me feel good about myself*
> *I like the variety and stimulation*
> *I like having answers for people*
> *Making a difference*
> *Seeing people grow and heal*
> *Always being there for someone*
> *Being the one person they have to rely on*
> *The power/sense of control*
> *The fun and creativity*
> *Having an impact*
> *Seeing results*
> *Being important to someone*
> *Connection*
> *Hearing people's stories*
> *Being close to other's suffering*
> *Being able to hold it all*

Your answers to the above may give you clues as to protector parts of you who have yet to meet Self and may be invested in current ways of being and doing. You could dialogue with these parts using the next part of the exercise.

If you are doing this in pairs (adapt for a group as appropriate):

- Choose who is Person A and who is Person B.
- Person A goes first and shares their answers with Person B.
- Person B helps Person A parts detect and choose a target protector with whom to begin a conversation.
- Person B helps Person A using in-sight or direct access to befriend the target part using the 6 Fs and standard interview-the-protector questions.
- A and B swap and do the same for the other.

If you are working on your own:

- Once you have answers from this question, from an open-hearted, welcoming place, invite each part (or group of parts) who gave an answer to have a conversation and get to know and be known by Self around what this part likes about how things are now professionally.

- See if you can express appreciation and understanding for what your parts share.
- Perhaps enquire if the part knows about the IFS training or the plans to train and have a dialogue about any concerns it may have, particularly about Self taking the lead.
- If necessary, reassure parts that no parts can be ejected from their system or made to change by other parts nor by Self and that Self wants what is best for your system and is open to going at the pace of the most cautious of parts and earning parts' trust.
- If it's relevant, send appreciation to all the parts. If it feels right, remind them that they are valuable both inside your system and outside in the world. We can't function without our parts and wouldn't want to and those who are burdened and extreme can be helped, in time, if they are willing, to unburden and be less extreme.
- Check with your system and if it feels right, let parts know, if now is not the time to spend longer with each one, that you will be back to continue the conversation.

4) Freeing Self to lead; discovering parts invested in the future

- You might like to do this with a peer or peers, in supervision, with a colleague or on your own.
- If you wish, use writing or art materials, or sand tray/small world items.
- Set aside some time(s) to explore, express, plot answers to the following questions (try and be as honest as possible, remember there are no bad parts). (I have included a couple of phrases to prime your awareness.)

> **Q:** What aspects of being the professional, coach, therapist, practitioner, or supervisor I am now am I *not* enjoying?
>
> **A:** ??

Example answers include:

> *There's just not enough progress with the more complex cases*
>
> *I need a change, it's been too many years of the same thing*
>
> **Q:** What aspects of being an IFS professional, therapist, practitioner, coach, or supervisor am I excited by?
>
> **A:** ??

Example answers include:

> *It reaches parts other therapies don't reach*

Your answers to the above may give you clues as to protector parts of you who are invested in the future and may be willing to cede leadership to Self.

If you are doing this in pairs (adapt for a group as appropriate):

- Choose who is Person A and who is Person B
- Person A goes first and shares their answers with Person B
- Person B helps Person A parts detect and chose a target protector with whom to begin a conversation
- Person B helps Person A using in-sight or direct access to befriend the target part using the 6 Fs and standard interview-the-protector questions
- A and B swap and do the same for the other

If you are working on your own:

- Once you have answers from this question, from an open-hearted, welcoming place, invite each part (or group of parts) who wrote one of the answers to have a conversation and get to know and be known by Self around what this part likes about IFS or is hoping for from the training and transitioning.
- See if you can express appreciation and understanding for what your parts share.
- Perhaps enquire if the part knows about the IFS training or plans to train and have a dialogue about any concerns it may have, particularly about Self taking the lead.
- If necessary, reassure parts that no parts can be ejected from their system or made to change by other parts or by Self and that when Self leads, harmony and co-operation on the inside flourish.
- Check with your system and if it feels right, let parts know if now is not the time to spend longer with each one that you will be back to continue the conversation.

Notes

1   See Krause's chapter "IFS with Children and Adolescents" (2013) in which we meet Ellie who is playing with a raptor and a brown horse. At first, Krause speaks directly to the raptor about its treatment of the horse.

2   My system's fear of "getting it wrong" continues to reduce as more healing from trauma occurs. Understanding how important making mistakes can be in learning and creating something has also helped. See *Black Box Thinking* (Syed, 2015).

3   I first heard this from IFS lead trainer Mike Elkin and knowing this has been immensely helpful in negotiating with and hope-merchanting to protectors.

4   It would be understandable if at the start of a session an IFS therapist or practitioner might be blended with various parts: a nervous one, a pushy one perhaps or even one who is used to short-term working and may be panicking *We've only got four sessions left*. Hopefully, as you develop your ability to make Self-to-part connections on the inside, you are or will be able to soothe these parts and help them relax and let the You who is not a part lead.

5   If the response is something like "What do you mean the anger is helpful?" or "It's not, anger never helps" then I suggest the speaker has shifted from embodying and speaking from the target part. Another part is making itself known. If this happens, I might address the part briefly, "I can hear you have some confusion/ concerns about anger and you don't have to understand or agree that anger is helpful. However, I would appreciate it if, for now, you would give space so I can continue talking with the part holding the anger." This, would, of course, move us into explicit direct access.

6   For more on differentiation, see Chapter 3, Endnote 3.

7   See also Krause's chapter "IFS with Children and Adolescents" (2013) and her IFS Continuity Program with the same title.

7
Being with triggering parts and helping them be with you

Introduction

Issues covered here include:

- An exploration of vulnerability and values (see the exercise at the end)
- Ways to respond to being triggered
- The role of the supervisor
- Working with parts of clients that novice IFS therapists and practitioners working as therapists find challenging
- Therapist and professional authority

Vulnerability isn't what you think

We all get triggered. Just this morning (January 2, 2021, during the global pandemic and between lockdowns), I have woken feeling anxious and tense. This is partly because for the first time in many weeks, I will be in direct contact with someone not in my household: my hairdresser. As I turn inwards towards the nervousness, I realise that underneath, I am also angry. About what? The anger is protecting me from feeling fear about catching the coronavirus. Also, it comes from watching episodes of a TV series last night in which a person in a position of power bullies and dominates others, including those who are vulnerable[1], and no one gets angry. No one challenges the bully directly or gets in his face as he's too "valuable". In addition, I also witnessed yesterday what parts see as an absence of appropriate vulnerability[2] in authority figures when there "should" have been some. You probably know how it goes when someone talks about their ACEs (adverse childhood experiences) and they do it in a cheery, robust kind of way: "If it weren't for what happened to me, I wouldn't be here now …" I imagine

DOI: 10.4324/9781003243571-11

we've all done it; I know I have. Ouch, my exiles are feeling triggered, and my tired protectors are activated.

Why am I telling you this? Because it highlights a way in which I like to respond to triggered parts, when I can, which is to:

- Turn towards them
- Listen to them
- Allow them airtime and space
- Look for complexity (more than one feeling/part may be active)

In other words, I try and *be with* my parts. "I'm here," I tell them, "You're not alone."

Vulnerability is also a key value of mine and something I welcome in relationships. By vulnerable and vulnerability, I do not mean the standard definitions as referenced in Endnotes 1 and 2, nor do I refer to the popular usage (usually by protectors) suggesting "weak", "stupid", "unfixable", etc. Nor do I refer to one of the uses I have noticed in the IFS community, in which vulnerability is equated with exile energy or woundedness. Instead, I suggest a new concept of "appropriate" or "complex vulnerability" which I understand currently and define from a more rounded IFS perspective as:

> Self-led professionals who are appropriately vulnerable, possess a work-able, live perspective whereby they know, act from, and are aware of their own simultaneous woundedness and healing, while also relating to others as being the same way: whole, wounded, and protected all at the same time. Vulnerability also contains an ability to not have to know, do, and control, but to be, be with and welcome alternate or multiple realities.

To me, welcoming vulnerability is holding awareness of the pain, the protection, and the Self in each of us. This is what we invite our clients into, implicitly or explicitly, encouraging them to bravely turn to face their wounds, painful past, fallibility, and to accept and welcome emotions, even the difficult, so-called "negative" ones. The cheery robustness I mentioned earlier, I sense as coming more from protectors than from Self. Here is an example from fiction of a protector inside the young President Snow as characterised by Suzanne Collins in her book *The Ballad of Songbirds and Snakes* (2020, p. 516). Snow is remembering his first love, Lucy Gray Baird, the winner of the 10th annual Hunger Games, who fled from him fearing for her life:

> Sometimes he would remember a moment of sweetness and almost wish things had ended differently. But it would never have worked out

between them, even if he'd stayed. They were simply too different. And he didn't like love, the way it had made him feel stupid and vulnerable. If he ever married, he'd choose someone incapable of swaying his heart. Someone he hated, even, so they could never manipulate him ... never make him feel ... weak.

Not only do our protectors have important jobs to do in keeping exiles locked away, they also don't like to feel and be with anyone or anything that evokes feeling what Snow considers "vulnerable" i.e., weak, wounded, or broken. This means that they often fight against love, against Self. In this chapter, I will be offering ideas and igniting hope for how to work and be with extreme protectors. Remaining in contact with and aware of your own complex vulnerability is one of the things I recommend, and it will, seemingly paradoxically, help you maintain Self-energy.

Ways to respond to being triggered

In addition to the U-turning or turning towards as mentioned above, the Room Technique (Anderson et al., 2017) or Fire Drill (Schwartz, 2021) are designed to help you get to know parts that are triggered by certain people, have them unblend and let you approach or be with the other from a more Self-led place. These techniques can be used before going in to work and between sessions to invite parts to give space and let Self be present to handle the work. In addition, negotiation can take place so that parts can phone in or share information as they watch from somewhere nearby, without taking over.[3] I remember Barb Cargill, IFS lead trainer, now retired, mentioning how she would handle a busy day, packed with clients, by offering parts the option to play in a nearby park for the day from where she would stop by and pick them up after work. Those parts that wanted to play could be together, leaving Self and therapist parts/consultants to be with her as she worked with her clients.

Working with challenging parts and challenging situations

One of the analogies for supervision that appeals to me is that of a third person being with the therapeutic dyad to support it, as a partner supports and helps contain the parent/caregiver and child dyad. Being in regular supervision can be invaluable as a novice IFS professional finds their feet, their competence and their authority.

As of the time of writing, the IFS Institute makes no stipulation about the nature, frequency, and amount of supervision a non-certified IFS therapist or practitioner must have. It only stipulates the amount of consultation needed to become certified and remain certified. My sense is there is an awareness that, at times, all of us will get stuck (Schwartz & Redfern, 2023) and if we are not already in supervision, we will then turn to an experienced colleague for support to unblend, for information, and challenge as necessary. In the following I share some of my knowledge and experience as well as that of Schwartz and other experienced IFS therapists and consultants to provide some holding and containment for readers. I hope that sharing these accounts here inspires you as much as they have inspired me, and I highly recommend joining the IFS Continuity Program. This section, like this book, is not intended to replace a supervisory relationship or experience. It touches on parts or groups of parts that novice IFS therapists often find challenging. (Don't forget, all parts are more than their shorthand labels, and it would be more accurate to write "a part who becomes angry" or "a part that has the role of thinker".)

- Angry parts
- Parts caught in the cycle of addiction
- Parts and depression
- Suicidal parts
- Parts labelled as "psychotic"
- Dissociating parts
- Intellectual parts
- Parts who move the body and make themselves known physically

Angry parts

I offer my own reflections on four areas to consider:

1) Your system's different reactions to anger
2) Things to remind your parts of in the moment
3) How to respond to the angry part of your client (pupil, colleague, etc.)
4) When someone might want you angry

1) I have a different set of inner responses depending on who is being angry with me – whether they are a client, a supervisee, my husband or an authority figure. Generally, anger directed towards us can trigger shame and we might respond from parts using any of three general tendencies: to move against (go on the attack); to move away from (stonewall, leave the room, dissociate); to move towards (join with a

compliant or fawning way perhaps or by making an alliance to "attack" another). I will also have inner reactions going on preceding or coming after the external response to the other. If we have experienced a lot of trauma, our parts may redirect the anger that it would be appropriate to direct outward or express in some way by turning it inwards (verbally beating oneself up, physical self-harm, for example). It can be helpful to reflect on the range of reactions you have experienced in the past when faced with anger so that next time, in the moment, you might be more able to slow things down or spot something helpful (a body movement, a breath pattern) that will help your parts remember that You are there too, they are not alone and do not need to hijack or flood you so quickly or so fully.

2) To reassure my parts, I tell them things inside my head like: "I'm here. ... Yes, they are angry. ... They have the right to their feelings. ... It doesn't mean we've done anything wrong. ... We don't have to agree with them. ... This is important. ... The angry one isn't the whole of him/her/them; it's probably a child part who might be hurt and scared. ... What they are feeling is mostly about them not us. ... We don't have to get angry too (I can tell some of you want to, but let me be here), nor do we have to be scared. ... Feel my energy, can you feel I'm bigger than the angry part(s)?"

3) As you respond to an angry part in the other, hold your seat: be curious and welcoming, non-shaming and non-judgmental. Validate the response if it makes sense to you; if it doesn't, perhaps you could ask for more information. Being curious generally may be useful and help repair the rupture in connection. If it feels right, apologise for any hurt their parts have experienced – even if it doesn't feel right to apologise for what you did, said or were, that angered them.

4) To parts of supervisees who get angry with clients, I may say things like: "My sense is your parts are feeling controlled by parts of the client which your parts don't like. It's possible that part(s) of the client are trying to control you by making you feel angry. When they say things like 'IFS doesn't work' or 'This is so slow' it doesn't mean those things are true. Their parts can believe those things; your parts don't have to. How would it be if, in the moment, you ask your parts to feel what they feel (including anger) at a distance from you (and the client). Appreciate them for letting you handle things with Self's perspective that multiple realities (the client's parts, and your parts, and Self in each) can safely co-exist."

Parts caught in the cycle of addiction[4]

Everyone, not just those with a label (alcoholic, addict, etc.), exists somewhere along a continuum from abstinence through using to abusing. Certainly, I have had and still have parts with addictive tendencies. Particularly, I recognise the inner Drama Triangle cluster of rescuer, victim, and persecutor parts as having a distinct addictive edge to them (Redfern, 2021). Since training in IFS, I more clearly see the systemic and cyclical nature of addiction which we work with in the usual IFS ways. I want to speak to that here, drawing on the teaching of Cece Sykes and Frank Anderson in month one of the IFS Continuity Program Trauma and the Addictive Process (Schwartz et al., 2021).

An addiction and trauma specialist, Sykes points out that *all* categories of parts (managers, firefighters, and exiles) are involved in an addictive cycle. Typically, a manager continues to be in a long-term polarity or conflict with a firefighter which heaps pain, shame, and isolation on the exile(s) the polarisation protects. Sykes contracts and works with multiplicity in mind. She doesn't side with the manager(s) to get the firefighters to change, she doesn't just target the exiles for unburdening, she doesn't just try and focus on the using. Instead, she advocates using IFS therapy to create Self-to-part relationships on the inside for *all* the parts involved. In addition, she works on creating new part-to-part relationships so that parts that were locked in conflict can come to see that they are on the same side and can ease back on opposing each other. The potential being that a healthy Self-led system can figure out how to maintain balance and harmony without resorting to the addictive cycles of the past, when parts dominated.

Anderson responds by speaking for therapists' relief at this, that we don't have to hold the agenda to fix and take the problem behaviour away. What we do is work to heal the complicated and damaged relationships and help Self take more leadership.

Note the absence of a counteractive approach (see Chapter 2) in the IFS understanding of the addictive cycle. In IFS, it is about building internal Self-to-part relationships and having Self befriend the parts involved. Also, as with getting to know any polarity of parts, it can be life-changing for the client when the parts realise that they each have a positive intention for the inner system to which they belong and what that is. Sykes speaks to how significant it is to help people unblend from managers and help those managers see that things and parts are more complex than they seem on the surface.

Another aspect of befriending the system is to ask about the fears of the protectors, as we would with any client. Some parts will be afraid of what will happen if they don't do what they do, and others will be afraid of what will happen if other parts continue to do what they do.

As IFS therapists, we know that Self-to-part relationship is healing; parts that are scared and acting out of fear can find safety and comfort in Self's presence, compassion, and connection and all the other Cs and Ps. Anderson speaks to the huge impact of the relational healing and repairs that can happen between Self and parts, and Sykes reminds us that connection is the antithesis to addiction not abstention.

I want to end this section by briefly considering protector parts that may be activated in therapists when working with client's systems around addiction. These include protectors who feel hopeless, deskilled, in need of rescue (possibly by the supervisor), robbed of all agency, hypercritical and overly-caring. Also, protectors who believe the reality of whichever part of the client is speaking; those who get seduced by the client's addicted parts or hopeless parts. Other therapist protectors may take too much control; collude with the critical manager(s) and abstainers; and/or polarise with parts of the client.

Your own exiles may also be triggered, especially if, in the past, you the therapist suffered at the hands of someone with an addiction or have struggled with your own addictive processes.

In my view, it is helpful when working with this client group to remain true to IFS, its laws of inner physics and its teaching on how to work with the addictive cycle.[5] More than ever, monitor your own Self-energy, and parts-detecting, perhaps by asking yourself the following:

- How do I feel towards the client?
- How do I feel towards this part of the client?
- Who is driving my inner psychic bus if I don't have a critical mass of Self?
- Who am I speaking to in the client? ... And now who am I speaking to?
- Am I polarising with a part of the client?
- I know who is speaking in the client now. Is there a polarised part we need to speak with or a part we're missing?
- Am I using IFS or am I falling back on old ways of working?
- Who in me needs attention to unblend?

Parts and depression

I feel fortunate that I've not had to unlearn professional ways of working with depression. Before training in IFS, I rarely if ever contracted to work with someone specifically "on" their depression, though relief from depressive symptoms was often an outcome of or by-product of our work together. I also have learning from my own personal experience of depression and being on SSRIs in my early 30s. This was long before I knew of IFS but even so, I had a sense of inner multiplicity which I now understand as managers seeking medical assistance to keep exiles at bay because suicidal firefighters were lurking with a more radical solution.

It is important to approach every client in an ecologically sensitive[6] way. Every system and each part is unique, and yet, patterns of feelings, beliefs, and behaviour between parts, and across systems can be noticed and held lightly in mind as we work with and encounter each individual part and every individual system or level of a system. Ande Anderson, co-mentor and founder with iKE ALLEN of AVAIYA University interviews Schwartz as part of AVAIYA University's online summit Overcoming Depression and Anxiety (November, 2020). Schwartz shares his wisdom accumulated from working with many depressed or depressing parts:

- Some clients have protector-based depression to keep them shut down/ numbed (as I did);
- Another common protector-based depression is to keep clients small, passive, or lacking in confidence so they don't take risks;
- Some depressing protectors may create feelings of despair or futility to stop the client from getting their hopes up only to be disappointed;
- Some depression results from parts being polarised with strong inner critic or shamer activity;
- Depressing parts may be anti-feeling good parts for fear that the contrast between feeling good about life/oneself and the feeling when that changes/stops will be too painful; and
- Other depressing parts may try to counter/polarise with extreme firefighter activity that they believe is putting the system at risk.

Helping clients befriend the protectors doing the depressing is important. Managing your own parts in the face of their tenacity is also key. In the same interview, Schwartz offered encouragement by reminding us:

1) Protectors are young, over-promoted children trying to run the client's life; they need Self's leadership.

2) These are not their natural roles.
3) The tenacity of the protector is directly related to the extremity of the parts they are protecting.
4) Protectors (like exiles) are frozen in time and don't know life has moved on, that things have changed, and more resources are now available.

As is usual with protectors, updating is helpful. Depressing protectors will probably think the client is still a child, as the interviewer, Ande, discovers when doing in-sight guided by Schwartz. Her protector thinks she is seven years old, and Schwartz encourages Ande to update the part about how old she is, who she is now and how life now is different. This brings a lot of relief inside and Schwartz moves to sowing seeds of hope by asking what the part might like to do if it didn't have to do this any longer and can stop "victimising" Ande's whole system. Also, he offers hope that once the exile it protects goes through the IFS steps of healing the depressing protector will be able to relax more fully.

Schwartz also speaks about acute depression, which is when exiles storm the gates and flood the system with feelings of worthlessness, not being loved or mattering. In other words, the exiles either bypass the protective system or the protectors' usual mechanisms of keeping on the go, gaining valid-ation, success and accolades, etc., are abruptly interrupted by events outside of their control such as illness, redundancy, the global pandemic, and so on. As therapists, it is important we are curious towards the client's system as the depression may come from protector activity or exile activity and our responses will be ecologically sensitive.

Suicidal parts

In month one of the IFS Continuity Program's module on Self-led Sexuality, Schwartz demonstrates doing direct access with a so-called[7] suicidal part (Schwartz & Rich, 2020). The client's system is experiencing backlash from this part who says it wants to hurt and kill the client. Schwartz is persistent and uncovers that the part is furious with the client for showing vulnerability (which it thinks of as weakness) in therapy.

Here are some pointers about how to work with suicidal parts modelled on Schwartz and from my own experience and understanding:

• Use explicit direct access with such parts
• Stay curious, access your own Self-energy and presence; and help your scared parts to trust you and give you space.

- Remain non-patholohising (some of you may have been taught only to focus on the threat posed by such parts and to see them as "endangering the therapy").
- Hold to the IFS principle that *all* parts have positive intentions for their systems and there are no bad parts; validate the part's attempts at protection.
- Think systemically: a firefighter suicidal part may well be reacting to another part's activity and they may ease back a little if you negotiate with that other part to ease back a little (polarisation work may be needed).
- Exile feelings and beliefs will be strong and may relate to life when the client was a child and to more recent traumatic times to do with past suicide attempts (hospitalisation, medication, abandonment, and shaming, even incarceration); you may need to be the hope-merchant that *change on the inside* is possible even in relation to what's already happened.
- Update the part, it may not know the client is now more resourced, no longer in past scenes or relationships; differentiate between how life is now (improved and with more options) and how life was.
- Negotiate with the part on how to proceed.
- Bring in the client's Self to meet, appreciate and get to know the suicidal part.

Pamela Krause, senior IFS trainer and co-developer of the Online Circle with Toni Herbine-Blank, is a specialist in working with children, young people and families and consulting to therapists who do the same. She shares a powerful case study (Krause et al., 2017) about working with Laura. Laura is a young woman of 20 with a recent experience of hospitalisation after a suicide attempt. The suicidal part shows up in therapy as a revolver and they get to know it together using explicit direct access. It explains that killing Laura is to stop the pain of the nothing – empty feelings that neither therapy nor medication have been able to help before. Krause explains that she – with the part's help – *can* help those feelings (she's being the hope-merchant), and she requests two things from the part: that it steps back so She and Laura can work with the part that feels empty; and that it agrees to Laura staying alive for a period of time to do the therapeutic work (which is extendable if needed and if the part is seeing progress).

Transition reflection

"This is a very nuanced conversation. I really value suicidal protectors in clients, and I've witnessed that they can have a hard time stepping back (for good reason). Sometimes change needs to happen on the inside and the outside for the client to remain safe." (Sarah Murphy, Clinical Counsellor)

Additionally, there are cases when a system blocks access to a suicidal part due to other parts fearing it. If this is the case, then it is important to be curious towards these scared parts and address their specific fears. If the parts won't respond, practise persistence and see if you can address the fears anyway, perhaps using both implicit and explicit direct access. Here are some examples:

- "I can understand how you and other parts are frightened of the suicidal part and that's why you block access to it. I'm aware that parts of you may still be carrying a lot of distress and trauma from past suicide attempts and if you allow access to those parts, we can help them let go of those burdens."
- "I understand you are frightened to let me speak with the suicidal part and I can assure you that speaking with it won't give it more power. In my experience when parts feel heard and validated, they become less extreme."
- "It makes sense to me how scared of the suicidal part you are, and I'm wondering if you can really look at me and see/sense that I'm not scared of this part. If you like, you could ask around inside and see if any parts in there can vouch for who I am and how I've already helped other parts with extreme roles."
- "I get how scared of this suicidal part you are, and I'd like to introduce you to the Aidan who isn't a part and see how calm, courageous and safe he feels. My guess is that the Aidan who isn't a part may not have been available in the past, but he is now. Would you be willing to meet with him?" (Have that safety update[8] happen and continue to request access to the suicidal part). "Aidan, ask this part if it's ready now to let you speak to the suicidal part and if not, see if it could pass on a message" (and proceed accordingly).

It can also help reduce protectors' fears to mention that parts can choose whether or not they overwhelm a person. As IFS professionals we offer to negotiate with parts to not overwhelm, which can be reassuring enough to allow us access to them. Similarly, while we talk to a part that is feared in the system, it can be contained in a secure room, off-planet or beneath the ocean, etc., if necessary (and it agrees). Parts can also be contacted by phone or videocall, which gives distance and reduces parts' fears of allowing access.

Lastly, there is no shame in asking for help in some way. The IFS professional and the client with whom he had been working for a couple of years already had an existing three-way relationship with Schwartz. The certified practitioner recognised and responded to his own fearful parts by asking Schwartz to give the client a session. Some professionals who are just starting out, or new to IFS, may take care of their own parts by screening out clients who have complex histories, including past suicide attempts or a history of suicidal ideation. Other professionals may work in an organisation with strict protocols about what needs to happen, regardless of therapist orientation.

Working with parts labelled "psychotic"

Subscribers to the IFS Continuity Program generally receive three webinars each month for four months related to a specialist topic. In addition, Schwartz currently alternates showing a video of himself working with a client one month and providing live online consultation to therapists and practitioners on the alternate month. Schwartz teaches an IFS therapist how to respond after her client has had a serious and scary psychotic episode of considerable duration (month four of Healing Cultural Trauma with Internal Family Systems, Schwartz & Young, 2020). Here are my takeaways:

- What the world/your client labels "psychosis" is parts activity; these parts are probably just doing whatever they can to be met and heard.
- Work with your system's fear that being with these parts is dangerous.
- Access your own curiosity.
- Help your client access their Self.
- Help your client to be curious towards these parts, what scared them, why they showed up.
- Work with the client to re-establish her system's trust in her Self-leadership, which may have been knocked.
- As therapist, work to re-establish trust if you've lost any with her system.
- Keep accessing your own Self-energy and leadership.
- Do not buy-in to any messages that amount to exiling these parts once more.

Dissociating or dissociative parts

I have a great fondness and appreciation for dissociating parts – the blankers, the I don't knows, the hiders, the numb-ers, the deniers, the buffers and blockers, for example. This is partly because as a child my system relied heavily on the protection of dissociating to manage physical pain, shame and fear that continually threatened to overwhelm my system. I had no other means of self-regulating (and co-regulating was rarely available) and have had to learn over the years in therapy to allow Self to be there for my parts, which is the ultimate in self-regulation. Looking back, I don't believe I would have made it this far without such dedicated protectors.

Professionally, a couple of experiences in my IFS training helped reduce the fear or frustration my therapist parts might have had at being faced with dissociation in a client. During Level 1 training in a practice group, it was my turn in the client seat, and I was "taken out" by a protector. However, for what felt like the first time ever, I not only had warning that I was going to be taken out and could ask my colleagues, "keep talking to me"; but while "taken over" I was also aware that I was taken over or "gone"; and other parts didn't come in and "cover" for my absence. Crucially, although the practice group may not have responded in a fully IFS way, I believe they retained access to Self-energy and at no point was I/the part shamed or criticised. This was a powerful and positive experience for which I continue to be grateful. A few years later during a Level 3 training I was fortunate to witness and learn from Schwartz's response (using direct access) to a participant taken over by a part that could be termed dissociative.[9]

A clinical case example involves a supervisee whose core training is psychodynamic. He regularly brings a client (whose pronouns are they/them) to supervision, and I regularly fail to recall the client without a lot of prompting which is very unusual for me but gradually made more sense.

Like many therapists, the supervisee thinks of "dissociation" as something other people have and even when thinking in terms of parts, tells me "I don't have any of those, I scored low on the DES (Dissociative Experiences Scale)". In line with his culture and psychotherapy training and like many therapists, he had come to fear dissociation. When I asked him about his fears around his client blending with a dissociative part, he replied:

- "I'm concerned they'll stay gone a long time."
- "They might harm themself while they are gone."

- "I'm concerned I don't know enough; I've not had specialist trauma training."
- "I'll feel like I've done something wrong, pushed them too hard."
- "I might dissociate too."

Transition reflection

"Before IFS a client completely 'tuning out' would have freaked me out. Now my parts know it's parts' activity it's no big thing." (Volunteer counsellor)

I spend some time validating the parts' frustrations and addressing their fears. Gaining some perspective, the supervisee realises the fears don't relate directly to the reality of this client who always comes back and has parts who do want to connect with their therapist. Also, the supervisee knows about Self and Self's fearlessness. In addition, I sing the praises of dissociative parts and how I wouldn't have survived to be here today without mine and how I value their presence in me and in others. Like all parts, they have a positive intention for the system and are only trying to help. This intrigues the supervisee, and he feels excitement rather than fear or frustration.

Before the supervision session ends, we do a mini role-play with me as therapist to the supervisee role-playing their client's dissociative[10] part. I bring lots of curiosity, appreciation and welcoming to the part for all their hard work. The supervisee as the part lets me know they don't like all that "breathing stuff" the therapist makes the client do (grounding and breathwork). I get this and let them know that my parts don't like having to do all that in therapy either.

Coming out of the role-play, the supervisee asks: "What do you mean? I do that with this client all the time, I did it yesterday."

Inside I think: *Yes, and you do that because a part of you is afraid the client is going to feel overwhelmed, and a dissociative part will take her out which will scare you further.* On the outside, I ask: "Shall we look to see who is driving your inner psychic bus?" In the moment, the supervisee detects these parts:

- Not good enough therapist
- Wanting to be a good enough, reparative parent figure
- Rescuer

- Frustrated
- His own wounded part
- Being "the other" or "different" part
- Empathiser
- Educate the ill-equipped therapist part

We negotiate with all but one of them to go sit at the back of the supervisee's inner psychic bus and let Self drive. The not good enough therapist part is suffering from feeling judged and found wanting in a previous professional encounter and needs more attention. Using more of the healing steps of the IFS protocol, this part is able to let go of the burdens it has been carrying from that relationship.

Then I suggest the supervisee brings the client to mind in imagination:

> *Supervisor:*   "How do you feel towards the client now?"
>
> *Supervisee:*   "Empathy."
>
> *Supervisor (Sensing a lack of Self-energy):*   "And do you recall how old your empathy part is?"
>
> *Supervisee:*   "(*Playfully*) Yes, I do. You've made the point she shouldn't be driving the bus either. I get it! What do you think of the client as I played them?"
>
> (*The supervisee's curiosity is returning.*)
>
> *Supervisor:*   "I have a soft spot for dissociative parts."
>
> *Supervisee:*   "I can tell, you really seemed to warm to the client."
>
> *Supervisor:*   "Yes, the client has come alive for me like they haven't before."

Interestingly, when I next saw the supervisee, he said that in their following session together this client revealed, for the first time, their awareness of a strongly dissociating part in their system.

Intellectual parts

It's common to meet parts, in both therapist and client, that want to keep the work "on the surface" at a cognitive or "talking therapy" level. Schwartz did some interesting work during a live consultation session with a therapist who had a female client with a life-threatening illness (month four's live call, Schwartz & Young, 2020). The client has a history of developmental or childhood relational trauma during which her protectors learned to be very logical, rational and process the facts. Emotions were ignored, denied and exiled so that the client would appear calm to the outside world. Many of us have experience of systems like this – our own and/or those of others – and I would see in some of my supervisees parts that are afraid to let them go inside and turn towards their emotions.

The therapist explains to Schwartz that initially she decided to partner with the client's cognitive parts by offering cognitive behavioural therapy. This worked to a point. Next the therapist wondered about offering a form of meditation but sensed this would not help the client access her feelings. She reports feeling under time pressure due to the client's illness. Here are some nuggets I took from watching Schwartz explaining how to use explicit direct access with such a dominant thinking part:

- As therapist, negotiate for more space in session from your parts (including thinking parts and those who may have concerns about offering and using IFS)
- Recognise the ubiquitous presence of avoidance (yours and the client's) so, don't wait for an invitation and ask to speak to the intellectual or thinking part directly.
- Appreciate that part for all it has brought to the client's system
- Have the client externalise the part if that's easier (maybe the client could move to a different chair or place in the room, or choose an object to represent the part).
- Explain the process of direct access while cutting off at the pass any overthinking about the process, for e.g. "I know you can do this: I ask questions, you answer them spontaneously, and we take it from there."
- Be prepared for the part to drop out of direct access, maybe with a concern or two which you can address ("It seems real enough to me", "Don't worry I'm not judging your performance").
- Get to know this part and work to earn its trust in you and the IFS process.
- If you think you've already been doing all the above and feel it hasn't got anywhere, then spend more time with your own parts.
- Don't give up on the part, keep relating to it each session so all its fears (including fear of loss of control) are addressed, it comes to feel appreciated and understands that it has something to gain by giving space for the client's Self to lead – at least during the therapy hour.
- Trust the process – if you offer IFS and your Self in relationship but the part doesn't go for it and the client leaves, then you did what you could.[11]

Parts who want to use the body[12] or who show up in the body[13]

If you are a bodyworker, dramatherapist, psychodramatist or run action/ active groups, then you may already be comfortable with clients who want to embody their parts or otherwise use their bodies in therapy, whether for expression, release, distraction etc. For others who are new to giving therapy or have parts invested in "talking" therapy, then clients who move can be triggering.

First, see if you can build a Self-to-part relationship with the parts of you who are triggered. Find out what their concerns are and see if you can address them, helping them trust you enough to give you space to welcome whatever might want or need to happen physically. It would be understandable if intellectual or analysing parts that like to know become concerned. After all, it is relatively rare that someone in an IFS demo or practice group starts moving their body or getting up and doing things mid-session. Your parts may value some context and reassurance around what's okay. I hope they find some of that in what follows.

I agree with Schwartz that IFS is a body-based psychotherapy. Trailheads are often physical in nature: "I feel sick in my stomach"; "There's this tension in the back of my head." The very practice of asking parts to "give space" or "step back" and the therapist asking, "how close are you to the part?" all suggest physicality and energetic presence, they recognise, include and invite in the somatic. Also, the idea of a mind-body split has been debunked. Mind/brain and body (in all their physical, electrical, hormonal, and so on multiplicity) are inextricably connected, impacting each other and interacting perpetually. True or real psychological transformation happens on many levels, including the visceral, spiritual, hormonal, and intellectual (Afford, 2020).

Transition reflection

"Parts are inherently somatic. When working with a part, you are also inevitably working with and affecting the body, sometimes with startling results." (IFS psychotherapist, Gayle Williamson)

I wonder if one of the reasons people suggest that IFS is not a body-based psychotherapy is because such people may themselves be dominated by intellectual parts who eschew the body. Also, for those of us who visualise our parts very clearly inside (whether as people, shapes or colours, etc.), this may distract and detract from what is happening and there to be felt in our bodies. Offering clients a more overtly physically embodied IFS process at any stage can be empowering for all involved. Remember occasionally to check Self's presence with the part as it does what it does, or, if the part is fully blended and you are the Self to the other's system, you might want at some point to have the part give space for the client's Self to come and make contact. Also, allow plenty of time, it might not be ideal to invite a part feeling very angry or judgmental to fully blend and stomp around the room if the end of the session is approaching.

In terms of the steps of healing, see Table 7.1 for some examples of how the body has been actively involved and included in individual IFS sessions at different places in the model. Also, remember that imagining or visualising doing something physical is not distinguished by the brain from physically doing the thing. David R. Hamilton (2014) writer and speaker with a PhD in organic chemistry, reminds us that what we imagine to be happening is actually happening as far as our brains are concerned. So that imaginary hug between Self and part feels real and wonderful, *and* our clients can give themselves a butterfly hug as well, or squeeze a cushion, if they wish.

Group IFS

If therapist parts feel unskilled, consider training in Somatic IFS with Susan McConnell and her team. Alternatively, attend a workshop that combines IFS and dramatherapy, so that you can have fun and feel some liberation. I attended such a workshop and found it very powerful. The group held the expression of strong emotion and was fun and freeing! We learnt about clients with eating disorders being encouraged in their group therapy to play their eating disorder part and taking it in turns in the spotlight; we saw and took part in sculpts whereby a client would use other group members to play different parts of their inner world; individuals pretended to be a machine making a sequence of movements and sounds to express, which we then mirrored. I was also fortunate in training and PA-ing with Barb Cargill, who was very creative and embodied in the way she taught IFS. In demos, she demonstrated externalising using scarfs, objects, or even writing the individual parts on pieces of paper and then placing them in relation to each other. Another memorable experience was when our staff team created a circle divided into different areas for Self, managers, firefighters, and exiles. The students then moved between the areas, physically enrolling

Table 7.1 Movement and use of the body

6 Fs – client differentiating and orienting themselves to parts[a]	• Turning one's head to face a part on the left or right • Bending over to look down at a part on the ground, or looking up to a part in a tree • Placing a hand on a physical sensation in the body • Embodying the part as it shows its posture, walk, speed, etc.
Self-to-part connecting – How do you feel towards the part?	• Suggest the part *feel* Self's presence, safety, calm, etc. • Suggest the part notices the difference between how *they* feel and how *Self* feels; can they feel both at once?
Inviting the part to inhabit the body fully – use direct access as the part does so	Client moves around the room, speaks, and interacts as the part
Witnessing using in-sight – body movements to connect and reassure	• Putting a hand on where in the body the part is experienced • Rocking, smiling, hugging the body
Redo – physically doing what needs doing back then but was curtailed	• Punching or pushing with the arms, kicking with the legs • Moving the body in a way that the body wants to move • Banging a drum, punching a cushion, making noise
Unburdening – releasing or ritualised movements	• Physically (and consciously) blowing with the mouth and lips • Bodily reactions (involuntary) such as tummy gurgles, laughing, yawning • Moving the arms as if undressing and dressing again, or throwing something

[a] Lead with your curiosity. Don't assume that all sensations come from one part as its experience unfolds, nor that each sensation is a reaction to the previous one (i.e., multiple parts) – ask.

as individual parts and embodying Self while the PAs and trainer held and offered Self-energy from outside the circle.

In consultation, Schwartz offers therapists loans of his confidence (Schwartz & Redfern, 2023) and experience so that they might embody more presence and authority in working with and welcoming all parts. Meanwhile, here are some thoughts on professional authority and identity.

Professional identity and authority

From my experience as a (serial) trainee, and as an IFS supervisor, I am aware that one of the areas challenging to beginning IFS therapists and practitioners is establishing professional identity and owning the professional authority that goes with that. I don't recall this subject featuring on the syllabus of my own foundational training or any of my post-qualifying therapy trainings (including IFS). However, it did feature as part of my supervision training. In watching a recording of myself in session and from feedback, it became clear that at that time, I lacked authority in the role of supervisor. This was indicated in my voice, body postures, and in seeming to be younger than my chronological age. Now, many years after that supervision training, having experienced much successful trauma therapy including IFS, I believe I hold and exercise more authority as a therapist and as a supervisor. I will explain what this means to me briefly and trust this provokes some reflection of your own (see also Figure 7.1 Circle of professional authority).

I think of my professional authority (which supports my professional identity) as coming from what "holds me" professionally. In Figure 7.1, which looks a little like a compass or ship's wheel, I am held by four things (forming an outer ring):

1.   Skills I have developed through training, professional and life experience, reflection, writing and training others.
2.   Values I hold to, and which parts in my system identify with.
3.   My professional ethical framework and affiliations, including my "home base" of the British Association for Counselling and Psychotherapy.
4.   Ethical boundaries of the profession I hold to, which help me differentiate and manage complexity with less fear.

Within this outer professional holding, Figure 7.1 depicts an experiential process of holding:

• Self relates to protectors enabling them and exiles to heal, transform, and rest.
• This brings more spaciousness to my system and self-acceptance, which means I show up more easily and incrementally more fully in the world.
• This in turn leads to more Self-energy, and so a virtuous cycle continues.

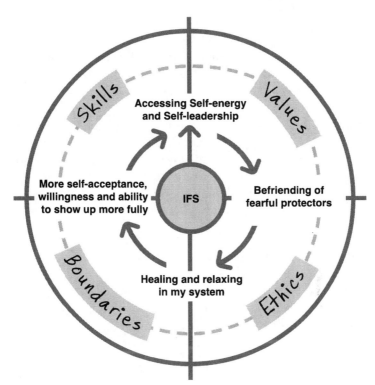

Figure 7.1 Circle of professional authority

At the centre of this circle of professional authority is IFS, my spiritual and philosophical home.

If you were to draw, create a collage, or sculpt your professional identity and authority, it would look different to mine. Perhaps you have some discomfort with your current professional "home", and you are seeking a new professional affiliation. Together, as a natural part of the supervisory process and relationship, supervisees and I sometimes explore the following key concepts and continuums:

- Power
- Autonomy
- Expertise
- Vulnerability
- Healing
- Truth

A supervisee once memorably called me "ruthless", hastily adding that this wasn't quite the word he was searching for. I kind of grasped what he was getting at and by the end of our supervision session, I had come up with my own translation of what I think he meant: that I sometimes "cut to the chase" more than he does and others to whom he relates. By this, I mean that although I validate the beliefs of a client's part, I don't let them become *my* beliefs. I retain my autonomy, and my belief in the laws of inner physics taught in IFS. This supervisee's practitioner parts, on the other hand, can sometimes buy into clients' non-IFS concepts and beliefs and this is constraining for him. He is a novice, and this is understandable especially when the client is an experienced therapist. As his supervisor, I choose not to be constrained by, for example, his therapist/client protector's belief that it has the power/expertise/truth/ability, etc. to already know what the exile(s) need and want even before the client has "gone inside" and met them.

Parts that constrain professional authority

See if you recognise any of your parts in the following. If not, try writing out some of the sentences and see what and who comes up and spend time with them (and any parts they are polarised with):

I don't know enough …
I have to read every book on trauma before I can work with a client who has a trauma history
If I … I will hurt the client
If I don't … the client will leave
I mustn't take the lead, I must follow the client
Following the client for 10 years doesn't seem to have worked so far, but it will
I must believe the client's truth
The client is the expert
I don't want to be the expert
I must stay small, it's safer
Hiding and staying silent and not voicing any difference works best
Therapists need to be gentle not tough
They are paying me so if they want CBT, I give them CBT even though I don't believe it works in the long term
I mustn't show any vulnerability, it's weak
I'll have failed if I make the client cry
The client will think IFS is weird when I ask them to go inside
I can't afford to alienate any clients, if they don't take to IFS immediately, I'm not going to persist nor offer it again

If you are transitioning to becoming an IFS practitioner and don't already have a foundation in psychotherapy, your system may need extra support in building a new sense of professional authority. You may find parts triggered by what they think they should know or feel they've missed out on:

I don't know if I'm supposed to … (fill in the blank)
I have a part terrified I'll hurt my client if I …
I didn't know I wasn't supposed to …
I feel about 12 when I'm with this client, is that normal?
Nobody will tell me the rules everyone but me knows

I believe a significant way to grow in authority as an IFS professional is through enabling fearful protective parts to trust Self to lead. Also, the more healing of your system you achieve, the less reactivity will be present, and the fewer young parts may be activated. IFS assistant trainer Dan Reed, writes (2019, p. 62):

> Psychotherapists, just like their clients, have parts that can react to situations and strongly influence or take over the psychotherapists with their fear-driven agenda or overwhelming feelings. Since the psychotherapist is in the higher power position and being hired to facilitate the psychotherapy process, they bear the responsibility of working with their reactivity and for opening Self space in the room.

Lastly, let's return our awareness to our clients and what their parts need from us IFS professionals in the words of Richard Schwartz (2013, pp. 12-13):

> It is one of life's great inequities that so many people who get hurt as children are reinjured throughout their lives because the original hurt left them so raw and reactive. They deserve to be close to someone who, after initially being triggered, can regain *perspective* and see behind the client's explosive rage, icy withdrawal or manipulative controlling, to the pain that drives those behaviours. The ability to regain compassionate *presence* in the face of a client's extreme protectors or exiles is the *sine qua non* of a good IFS therapist.[14]

Exercise

Values

An exercise I and others have enjoyed and found useful is to pair up with a colleague and help each other explore our values. You can find an eResource on this book's product page: (http://www.routledge.com/9781032153094). Once there, click on "support materials" and you will find a table of values for you to use if you wish to explore which values you hold in life and bring to your therapeutic, coaching, professional and supervisory relationships. Also, see if you recognise the probable values held by those with whom you relate.

- Choose who goes first (person A) and who goes second (person B).
- The person going first reads the values and chooses 10 of them as their own core values and shares these with their partner.
- Person B accesses their curiosity and connectedness to help person A explore those 10, then pick five of the 10 and finally pick one key value.

Swap partners and do the above.

If you have time and wish to explore further, you could choose values you would like a supervisor, colleague, intimate partner, friend and so on to hold.

Lastly, consider how the concept of values fits within an IFS framework, if you think it does.[15] Does your final value align with Self qualities? How might knowing your values help you relate to your clients, customers, and colleagues and their parts?

Notes

1   The standard (i.e., non-psychotherapeutic) dictionary definitions of the word "vulnerable" as being "exposed to the possibility of being attacked or harmed, either physically or emotionally" or "someone needing special care, support, or protection because of their age, disability, or because they are at risk of abuse or neglect" apply in this context.

2   "Vulnerability" comes from the Latin for "wound", *vulnus*, and is the state of being open to injury or appearing as if you are. Therapists sometimes display their past wounding as a badge of honour, having triumphed over their adversity. Alternatively, therapists may worry about their client's level of vulnerability in the sense that they may be "too damaged" to work with. I am advocating in this chapter for a different understanding by IFS professionals of the concept of "appropriate" or "complex" vulnerability.

3   For reactive parts as consultants, see Chapter 1 and Redfern, 2023.

4   Helpful reading includes lead trainer Cece Sykes' chapter "An IFS lens on addiction" (2017, pp. 29–48) and certified therapist and presenter on the IFS Continuity Program Nancy Wonder's chapter on pornography addiction (2013, pp. 159–165).

5   During a live call with a consultee (month two, Schwartz et al., 2021) Schwartz tells the therapist asking about how best to support an addict recently out of

residential treatment, to maintain and hold to the IFS frame, even in the face of opposition. Schwartz suggests that the belief that an addict needs intensive treatment by a team of professionals is more to do with the treatment style of fighting or counteracting firefighters than due to the addict's own needs. If in true IFS style the therapist does not polarise with the firefighters, that highly-peopled style of treatment may not be required. Schwartz suggests that IFS's compassionate rather than polarising approach may reduce the need for a multi-agency or multi-disciplinary approach. (I am aware that other IFS lead trainers may have a different view, and you will need to determine what sits right with your Self-led system and with each of your clients.)

6 Schwartz and Sweezy (2020, p. 42) explain: "To be ecologically sensitive we drop the interpretive stance of the expert and, in a spirit of humble curiosity, collaborate with the client's parts to map their inner relationships. Once we have a preliminary map, we are guided by it in a spirit of respect and the willingness to keep learning."

7 I use the term "so-called suicidal part" – which may seem less harsh – as this helps me remember that the desire to die or kill the client and the term "suicidal" does not provide an accurate nor complete picture of what is going on for this part and inside the system.

8 See the section headed "Creating safety is crucial and includes giving safety updates" in Chapter 3.

9 Certified IFS Practitioner and psychotherapist Stephanie Mitchell in Australia specialises in working with non-ordinary states of consciousness (what is diagnosed as psychosis by psychiatric services) and runs trainings for professionals. See stephaniemitchell.com.au

10 Schwartz in a Continuity Program live call (month two, Schwartz & Rich, 2020) consults with Anna whose client has a dissociative/don't know part. He explains that when he meets such a part, he doesn't expect the part to talk. Instead, he will talk and give what he calls his "patter" as he hangs out with the part who is checking him out to know whether or not he's safe. In his patter, Schwartz conveys particular messages to extreme parts like this: 1) empathy or validation for why they do what they do; 2) a promise that he and the client won't go to more wounded parts without this one's permission; 3) a guarantee that he and the client can help this, and other parts trapped in horrible places in the past and get them out of there so they can be free to be happy children – potentially; 4) the part has the right to set the pace of the therapy process and not feel pressured.

11 See the chapter on consulting to therapists with a serious illness for a further example of when such difficult circumstances may make it virtually impossible for protectors to relax and give space for Self to be present and lead (Omin, 2022).

12 See Ch. 5, "IFS and the Body" in Schwartz & Sweezy, 2020.

13 Parts' activity can also affect a person's body as attested to in an article by Shadick et al., 2013. The authors engineered and took part in a Randomised

Controlled Trial (RCT) formed of a 36-week IFS-based rheumatoid arthritis intervention which was completed by 82 per cent of those enrolled. One year later, self-assessed joint pain, self-compassion, and depressive symptoms remained improved. At that time the overall pain and function occurring at the end of the trial was not sustained and there was merely a trend toward reduced anxiety.

14 From The Therapist–Client Relationship and the Transformative Power of Self, pp. 12–13, by Richard C. Schwartz. In *Internal Family Systems: New Dimensions* edited by Martha Sweezy and Ellen L. Ziskind, copyright 2013 by Taylor & Francis. Reproduced by permission of Taylor & Francis Group.

15 A therapist who is not IFS-trained works with values to good effect with some of her clients. By using a chart such as this, she asks her clients to choose a handful of core values. Often, it becomes apparent that the client is experiencing stress or upset in life because they are not living in alignment with and may even be living against one or more of their core values. In IFS terms, I might consider such a client as having parts in conflict and seek permission to work with inner polarisations.

8
Working with Self-like parts and clients with "no Self-energy"

Introduction

As well as featuring a section on hope-merchanting[1] to parts for buy-in to therapy, this chapter focuses on working with clients when a Self-like part (or series of Self-like parts) is in the driving seat of the client's inner psychic bus.

This includes looking at the following problem areas:

- Fear of shaming a client by suggesting you think a Self-like part is in the lead.
- Thinking you, the therapist/practitioner, are in Self when one or more of your own Self-like parts is trying to help.
- Supervisee concerns of guiding a client all the way through the steps of healing with a Self-like part in place of Self.

Parts who are nervous about "outing" a Self-like part

Use different terminology

I find that mentally changing the label "Self-like part" helps reduce my parts' reactivity. I prefer to think of Self-like parts as "parts who believe they are Self" or "parts who believe they lead the system". See how your system reacts to each of the following sentences. Try reading the sentences below one at a time:

- *My client has a Self-like part*

Now read the next sentence:

DOI: 10.4324/9781003243571-12

- My client has "*a part that thinks it is Self*" or "*that* wants *to be Self and is used to running things*"

Did you notice any difference in your responses to the two sentences? My system responded to the first as if it described a problem. I could almost hear an internal "Oh no!" and my Self-energy felt constrained. When I think of someone I am working with (either as a training course PA, as a therapist or supervisor) and I think that they have Self-like parts active, my stomach drops. Fearful parts come up whispering: *Now what? How are you going to handle telling them? They'll be offended and think you're saying they are doing it wrong.* If the person is an IFS trainee or another therapist, I hear inside: *They might take it personally and ask if I think they are a useless therapist!*

My response to the second statement was freer and I could almost hear an inner "Yes, so?" Recalling that I have some clients (both therapists and non-therapists) with parts who believe they are Self or *want* to be Self and do all the healing needed in the system themselves, doesn't feel so problematic for me. My breathing doesn't tighten up and I even sighed as I typed and read the second statement. My feelings of competence return, and I hear inside: *I'm trained in IFS, I know how to validate and befriend managers and address parts' fears. I know what Self feels like in my body and I'm getting better at recognising it in others. I know that nothing on the inside can hurt me if I have no fear of it (i.e., access to my Self-energy and Self-leadership).*

The putting of the word "part" at the start of my preferred phrase – 'a part that thinks it is/wants to be Self' – helps me instantly recall two key things about parts such as these: they act out of fear and are responding to fear of their own and/or fear in the system; and they have a positive intention for the system.

Parts who want to lead

Another phrase I might use instead of "Self-like parts" is "parts who want to lead/be in charge". The usual term seems to relate to the client's identity or being, which can fuel the concern about shaming our clients – *she'll feel like she is in the wrong if I challenge her.* A term like "a part who wants to be in charge, have control, lead" relates more to the part's function and that can give us more leverage and take us out of shame territory. For example: "AJ, I know you said you felt compassion towards the target part, but I just wonder if there's a part trying to take the lead here – which would make complete sense and doesn't mean a part is doing anything wrong. Just check and see if that fits at all."

Parts who are trying to help

Also, instead of "Self-like part", which links the part to the ideal leader of the system (the Self), I prefer to think of these parts as "parts who are trying to help because no one was there for them when the client was young". Schwartz regularly reminds us that parts are just little kids. Let's bear in mind the name of the therapy: Internal *Family* Systems therapy. Through parental neglect or abuse (and absence of Self-energy from and in parents and caregivers), a child is likely to become parentified (Schwartz & Sweezy, 2020), and takes on too much impossible responsibility to keep themselves and their various family systems safe.

Transition reflection

"If I collude now with the part who thinks it is Self, it might get more entrenched. I'd rather welcome it early than late." (Ellen Bush, somatic IFS therapist, level 3)

Self-like managers or "parentified child parts who think they have to lead" need to have Self befriend them. That way, they can begin to relax a little and trust Self to handle difficulties in the outside world, therapy work, etc.; and to go to the exiles in the inside world who need Self's healing presence. If, because our parts have concerns, we don't ask the parts who think they are Self to get to know Self so they can step aside, then we are allowing on the inside the equivalent of a parentified child in the outside world running the household, looking after the younger kids, etc., while the real caregiver, guardian or parent is constrained and unable to help. Ideally, we wouldn't do that on the outside, so why would we let it happen on the inside? For example: "Connor, how do you feel towards the part? And just ask any parts trying to help to relax; and if they won't, let me know. They may not know Self yet."

Parts who think they are Self can feel shamed; Self cannot

I've also found that the term "Self-like part" can put some therapists off. One supervisee recently raised with me their concerns that a client had gone a long way down the IFS steps of healing and he was not sure there was a critical mass of Self in the client (nor in himself). As part of exploring what he could have done differently or could do differently in future, I enquired as to why he had not in some way "challenged" the client, or rather, challenged the part of the client who was trying to do Self's work. The supervisee responded, "Who am I to judge another's spiritual experience?"

Such a statement arises, I think at least in part, because of the term, "Self-like". It is as if we think that to challenge such a part, we are challenging Self, saying the equivalent of, "Hey, Self, are you sure it's you? Are you sure you're up to the job?" Instead, I suggest that we imagine arriving at a house, ringing the doorbell and a child opens the door dressed in her mother's black patent work shoes, blouse with the ruffles and a string of pearls. "Hello is the head of the household in?" we ask, "Yes, that's me," the child responds, and we continue as if she is the head of the household with matching capacity for clarity, confidence, curiosity, etc. Would we do such a thing in the outer reality? No, I think not. With our own playful presence to the fore, we can ask the child to step aside and let us speak to the appropriate person. Sure, the child may not respond well if we are terse and unkind as we do this, but we do not need to feel threatened by or go along with the child's desire to be thought of as the one in charge.

Also, if, say, a part blends with me suddenly adding their nervousness to the mix and I clumsily enquire of the client's bona fide Self-energy, "Just check and have any parts trying to help give as much space as they can," then I doubt Self will be in the least bit bothered. No offence will have been caused. If inside the client they hear, (or say out loud) *Look clever clogs therapist, you don't always get it right, of course I'm Self!* then this provides important information, as that response suggests a part is present and needs attention in order to relax when it is ready and has good reason to do so.

As part of the IFS Continuity Program, and in trainings, Schwartz regularly teaches that direct access with these parts is the way to go and asks to speak to the part himself. Even if he's told, "No, it's not a part, it's me", he will persist and ask to show the part that it's not who it thinks it is (or would like to be). Although it may sound argumentative on paper, in person it is more like a difference of opinion. I've done this myself successfully and would describe my Self-energy at those times as calm, confident, clear, and non-attached or neutral with a sense of offering something new rather than telling. Oftentimes, the part almost seems relieved it's been rumbled and glad there's "a grown-up in the house" taking charge.

For the founder of the model who has been developing and doing IFS for coming up 40 years, it is going to be relatively easy to stay in Self and to know when a client or supervisee is not accessing a critical mass of Self.

However, the professionals who consult with me, do not find it easy to be confident in their own level of Self-energy, often because they have therapist parts trying to work things out and get things right. This, in turn, makes it harder to have clarity and confidence about the level of Self in clients.[2] Ideas for how to discern Self and parts in clients and in oneself follow later in the chapter.

Being the hope merchant

IFS places particular emphasis on therapists being the hope merchant (Malamud Smith, 2017), or as I call it now "hope-merchanting". In its broadest sense, it is sharing the certainty that feelings can change, and exiles can heal. In the first edition of *Internal Family Systems Therapy* (1995, p. 99), Schwartz counters the managerial belief that the pain needs to be kept away because what's done is done and can't be undone, by reassuring that:

> The parts that hold your pain and fear can change if they are taken care of. Their extreme state is the result of being stuck in the past and of having been exiled. Once retrieved and cared for, they will let go of their extreme feelings and will be valuable, enjoyable parts, and you (the managers) will not have to stay in this extreme role of trying to keep them out.

Personalised hope-merchanting

The nature of the hope we offer to parts depends on the individual part's role or circumstances. For example, we might hope-merchant that healing exiles will make a protector's life, or protectors' lives, easier. Senior lead trainer and author, Krause (2017) shares a case study of Harry and his hardworking part who is polarised with his pot-smoking part – both of whom take action to prevent Harry's feelings of worthlessness from surfacing. Krause helps Harry become the hope merchant to the pair of protectors, telling them that they won't have to work so hard if they grant access to the exiled part and allow it to be healed by Self.

At other times, we might hope-merchant by negotiating with another protector on behalf of one being deeply affected by its actions. For example, a protector who wants to "end it all" – by which it means "bring peace" to the system – may be reacting to a slave driver, overworker or compliant part who is overextending the system in ways that are frightening to the "suicidal one". Our message of hope might then be "we can help that over-working part be less extreme and get to know what drives you both and heal what's there, if you are interested".

> ## Transition reflection
>
> "In my initial training, I was taught not to give any form of guarantee, not to lead, just to 'be with' and not to explain any of the processes involved in therapy. It's not like that now, and it's great to have the confidence to be able to hopemerchant that parts can 'lay down their stuff'." (GJ, psychotherapist with two years' experience of IFS work)

Here is an amalgamated example from my supervision experience working with Integratively trained therapists who later learn IFS. I am calling the supervisee Drury, and I'm hope-merchanting or negotiating space for Self with one of his parts who thinks he is Self.

Supervisor: "As you recall the session working with the client when you were not sure the client had sufficient Self present, how do you feel towards the client?"

Supervisee: "Yes, she definitely wasn't in Self, I see it now."

Supervisor: "How do you feel towards her as you see her in your mind's eye?"

(*Attempting in-sight work*)

Supervisee: "I just wish I could help her be more in Self?"

(*Sensing the supervisee is blended with this part I move into implicit direct access with it*)

Supervisor: "It sounds like we could work really hard in supervision and come up with all manner of ways for you to determine how much Self-energy this client has…"

Supervisee: "Yes, that would be great."

Supervisor: "Absolutely … and then what?"

Supervisee: "What do you mean?"

(*Moving into explicit direct access to see if the part will go for being a part.*)

Supervisor: "Well, if you help Drury do all that working out, how does that help him help the client?"

(*Beginning to explore the part's role and positive intention*)

Supervisee: "Well, it's part of my job to make sure they do it right."

Supervisor: "Ah, I see. What are you concerned might happen if Drury doesn't get it right and can't help the client get it right?"

(*Here, I'm exploring the fears of Drury's part as per the sixth F*)

Supervisee: "Well, if the client does it wrong then Drury will feel bad, like he's failed, and my job is to prevent him feeling any shame or like a failure."

Supervisor: "Ouch, that's a big job you have!" (*Validating the part.*)

Supervisee: "Sure, it is, and there I am trying to help the client get more Self and all I can hear inside is, *She's not in Self*. But I can push that away. I can't have them thinking they are getting something wrong."

Supervisor: "So, you work hard "on the outside" trying to protect Drury and the client from failing and feeling shamed. Do you also work hard on the inside protecting little ones who are already carrying lots of shame?"

Supervisee: "I do yes ... it's tiring."

Supervisor: "I can believe that. And how old do you think Drury is? Just say the number that comes to mind without trying to work it out... Well, no wonder you want to help him if you think he's only nine. The thing is, Drury grew up without you knowing it – which is completely normal by the way, that's just how life happens. He's in his 40s now with grown-up children and no longer lives with the people who used to shame him so badly and for whom he had to get everything right first time, stuff *they* couldn't even get right."

Supervisee: "Huh?"

(*The supervisee's jaw has dropped slightly.*)

Supervisor: "Yes, he's in his 40s, and the Drury who is there now, unlike when he was nine, has many, many resources, and qualities to bring to his work and to you."

Supervisee: "How do you mean?"

(*The part's curiosity is piqued.*)

Supervisor: "Well, that Self you want for Drury's clients all the time? Drury has that too. If you would like to, you can get to meet Drury's Self and speak together about how you can help Self to help the client."

Supervisee: "Okay, if you put it like that. What do I do?"

(*I ask the part to unblend so I can introduce him to Drury and help them get to know each other.*)

Supervisee: "I'm letting the part know that I'm also in IFS therapy and, in time, the exiles he protects can be healed and then he will feel much freer. He likes that. (*Smiling*) He's also pointing out that if he can't have control in sessions, then other parts shouldn't either."

Supervisor: "He has a point there. Do you have a response to that?"

(*Allowing the supervisee's Self to lead in responding to the supervisee's part*)

Supervisee: "I'm reassuring him that this isn't personal. It's not about replacing him with another part and if other parts try and take the lead, I'll work with them as well. If he wants to help me parts-detect inside me and the clients, I welcome that, and he can do that from the side-lines."

Supervisor: "Great, how would it be for this part if you ended it there for now, and, if it feels appropriate, arrange another time to get to know him more."

(*Drury nods and closes it up with the part for now.*)

Getting to know your own parts who want to lead/help

As part of the IFS Level 1 training, time is spent helping participants become aware of common therapist parts. The new Internal Family Systems Institute Level 1 Training Manual by Pastor and Gauvain lists examples (2020, pp. 137–138) such as striving or hardworking managers. When I did my Level 1 training and was program assistant on Level 1s in pre-pandemic days, one of the PAs might be asked to record on flipchart sheets the therapist parts called out by attendees. These included parts like the rescuer, blamer, frustrated part, educator, caretaker, perfectionist, sceptic and so on.

Any, and all, of these parts might be triggered when working with clients. Also, for those therapists already trained in a different modality, there will be managers attached to the old ways of working in which they might have been skilled and "in charge" of the therapy. Moving to IFS is often seen as threatening to such a part's status or control, especially when these parts feel they've been doing a good job and getting results (see Pastor & Gauvain, 2020, p. 137). Since I have been supervising therapists, I would add the following therapist parts to those mentioned above:

- Over-giver
- Got to make a difference/make change happen
- Working extra hard/pushing on to get results/get it right
- Giving away my Self-energy to such difficult clients is so tiring (victim)

It is helpful making such lists in training, but awareness of a part in the abstract will have less effect than being in relationship with the part in reality. Our parts need befriending either during IFS therapy or in supervision. As I went through the IFS certification process, this was one of the most helpful aspects of the process. At the time of writing, certification applicants write a detailed self-assessment of their Self-energy and the parts active in the therapy session they have recorded for submission. In my self-assessment, I described how I maintained Self-energy and how I worked with therapist parts that were triggered, which included:

- You need to show the client you understand
- Trust the client's Self
- I need to know
- Anti-too much content
- Parts polarised around giving/withholding tissues
- Frightened of doing it wrong
- Sympathetic
- Hurry-up

These are some of the ways in which I worked with some of these parts:

- Anticipating the presence of my frightened of doing it wrong part, I remind this one beforehand that IFS is a robust therapy, and with sufficient Self present it is hard to "get it wrong". During the session itself, when the part becomes active at something it perceives I have done wrong, I let it know, "It's OK, we've not done anything wrong. I'm here, let's trust the process." My part relaxes and further relaxes when the client's Self responds by making a choice and directs the session beautifully.
- During the session, I check in on my body posture and face (at one point I noticed forward movement in my head and seriousness on my face suggesting the presence of parts with pity/sympathy rather than or in addition to Self's compassion). I physically adjust and let my parts know "I'm here" and they don't need to make themselves known to the client, she is doing just great without them, *and* she has her eyes closed and can't see them.
- Later in the session, sensing a hurry-up part, I physically smile in greeting and say out loud "and there's no rush". I figured speaking that message out loud couldn't hurt and might help more than just my part!

Getting to know what therapist parts think of Self

Interestingly, not only can therapist parts who like to be in charge in the therapy room feel threatened by the idea of Self leading the inner system, these parts often have a limited and distorted view of who and what Self is. (Parts may project onto Self their own qualities but "bigger" or project onto Self their opposite.) Recently, I've become openly curious about this, and parts have suggested that Self is:

- useless
- without a brain and can't think
- a passive observer
- another tool to learn
- the enemy out to make me redundant or get rid of me
- beyond me: I can't "do Self"

As with any part's beliefs, these will make sense; I can respond to or address each individually. "No wonder you aren't interested in meeting Self if you think it's just a blob" or "I know using your brain and thinking is important and helpful to the system, and Self has a different form of thinking, a wisdom or clarity. Both ways are valuable." "Yes, I get that, and Self isn't something parts have to learn, Self is someone parts get to meet." It is introducing these parts to Self so they can come to know/feel/sense/experience Self personally and directly that is so important in building Self-leadership.

Remember, the goal of IFS isn't to get rid of parts. I often tell supervisees and their parts, "It's not either/or, it's both/and… It's Self *and* parts. Self is available as a resource." Also, it may take a while to get to know your key therapist parts or parts who want to be Self/lead/help/run the therapy, so being gentle with oneself is important as you transition to doing or using IFS and being an IFS professional. Something that might be helpful, and is recommended by Toni Herbine-Blank and Pamela Krause on the IFS Online Circle, is to remember to be curious. Asking yourself "How do I feel towards this client/the target part/my part?" And if something other than one of the 8 Cs is present, make a request or invitation, "Let me be curious. I'm not asking you to stop feeling what you are feeling or thinking what you are thinking, … just let me be curious." In this way, there is no agenda to have the part change, there is no shaming of the part for feeling and thinking what it does and being as it is. Though there is a request to allow curiosity.

Getting to know client parts who don't yet trust Self

For those of you who may not yet feel confident in trusting your sense that a "part who wants to be Self" is in the client's driving seat, here are some ideas:

Look out for feeling controlled

As I look up this subject in the index of *Internal Family Systems Therapy 2nd Edition*, I notice the preferred term is "Self-like managers" about whom the authors write (Schwartz & Sweezy, 2020, pp. 134–135):

> There is a certain kind of manager who is caretaking and solicitous. …
> It is important to remember that the agenda of a Self-like part is, no less than any other manager, to control other parts.

It can be helpful to notice inside yourself whether the work with the client is feeling collaborative and has flow or if you feel subtly controlled. In my experience, clients who are overly "controlled" or "contained" are likely to have parts (sometimes quite a few) who wish to control other parts in their own system. These "managers who don't yet trust Self" may also wish to control parts in *your* (my) system, for example:

Therapist: "I'm aware after last session that I'd like us to spend more time getting to know your protective system."

Client: "What do you mean? No, we made contact with that exile for a few moments before the sceptical one came in, I think we should press on."

(*Here I have a choice point. Accept this as a wholly reasonable client-led choice for the session; or explore, using implicit direct access, any parts wanting to push ahead. I choose the latter option.*)

Therapist: "What are you afraid would happen if we didn't press on towards that exile today?"

(*I use a typical protector question to gauge the presence, or not, of a part.*)

Client: "I'm never going to get past this (physical) pain. The pain definitely eased when we made contact with the exile."

(*The response suggests desperation and agenda, which are signs of parts activity. I begin the process of differentiating the part for a relationship with Self.*)

Therapist: "And how do you feel towards this part who so wants you to be free of pain?"

Check for an agenda

One of the ways of spotting when Self is not in the driving seat is to notice whether there is a significant agenda. In the above example, it seems clear that there is a part wanting to get therapy done and gain pain relief. A beginning therapist might think that this desire to reconnect to the exile and heal it is coming from Self, which is why I've listed some ways to check this out below. Also, I recommend you read Ch. 1, "Getting Unstuck" (Sweezy & Ziskind, 2017), especially the section headed "When a Self-Like Part Steps in for the Self".

Assess how the target part responds to the client's Self-energy

As you already know, the key differentiating question in IFS is how do you feel towards the part? If the answer is one of the 8 C qualities or the like, this tells us whether Self is present or not. So, the client may say they feel "open," "warm" or "sad *for* it". But if there are any indicators that there isn't sufficient Self, I can ask the client to extend that warmth and openness, or suggest, "let the part know you feel sorry for it", before checking, "How does the part respond?" This provides more information to clarify whether it is the client's Self that is present or not (see Chapter 3, "The 4th F").

Ideally, if the hook-up between Self and part (see Chapter 3) has begun, you will hear answers like:

- I can feel the part's relief
- He's moved closer to me
- She's looking at me now
- She's still turned away from me, but I know she's listening
- It's so moving (the client is tearing up or crying), it's like the part has been waiting for me to be here for so long

Ask the part who it sees when it looks at the client[3]

Saying to your client, "Ask the part who it sees when it looks at you" is another useful question. Sometimes this reveals another part: "she thinks I look like my mother" or "she senses some anger", or "he sees a child". We can then have the parts who have been identified by the target part to make space for Self to be more fully present. If the answer then shifts to "she sees me as I am now", I might then check, "and what does she notice about you now?" I'm looking here for answers like "she's surprised by how strong/calm/grown-up I am now". I could also ask: "And how is it for this part that you are here?" These latter questions will hopefully assist the Self-to-part connection or indicate the continued presence of a part or parts.

Ask if the client sees themselves

This is the easiest "tell". If the client can see themselves in their mind's eye, then a part is trying to do Self's job and we can ask it to make space for Self to be present too – or instead, depending on the part's willingness. Alternatively, the part trying to help can become the target part.

Notice the senses and the body

As I mentioned in Chapter 1, Reed and Wooten (2023) offer a check-list of markers to help determine the presence of one's own and another's Self-energy. Amongst other things, they list somatic aspects to check for blending, including voice, body tension, posture, breath, eyes and energy consumption. Let's look at a couple of these in more detail:

Voice

In her book *Somatic Internal Family Systems Therapy*, McConnell states (2020, p. 108) that nothing reveals parts like voice tone (by which she refers to the therapist, but this applies equally to our clients). We can gauge by voice tone, pitch, volume, and rhythm whether the client is experiencing a ventral vagal state of social engagement or whether the ANS (the autonomic nervous system, which controls the fight or flight response) is activated. Those of us who have been privileged to watch demos by Schwartz himself, know that one of the signs for him (as it is for others) that he is accessing Self-energy is how relatively few words he speaks. Thus, we can also tell the presence of Self by the quantity and quality of what is said.

Breath

The practice of conscious breathing, about which McConnell writes (2020, p. 109), highlights the importance of noticing our clients' breathing patterns. "Our breathing pattern can reveal our degree of Self-energy, and changing it can increase it." I have noticed that when parts of me concentrate in a "heady way" it is as if I am holding my breath. When with a client, I consciously breathe into my abdomen, pushing it out, which helps me feel my spine and opens up space for Self. As a client, before coming across IFS, I worked with a body psychotherapist and we noticed that I struggled to exhale fully. For me, McConnell's words (2020, p. 111) sum up what was going on implicitly in my system: "Parts that restrict the exhale may have fears of letting go, fear of dying, or a deep desire to give up and never breathe in again." If I am struggling to exhale, that's a clue a part might be active – one that I may need to acknowledge/reassure in some way.

Body

McConnell (2020, p. 155) gives an example of how she uses her own body and senses and assesses her client Helen's Self-energy as absent. In addition, although the client declares she feels compassion towards her part – which she has chosen a blanket to represent – there don't seem to be corroborating markers for that in her either. McConnell uses a body-based question to further determine the absence or presence of Self in the client.

> When I ask Helen to feel the blanket, to hold it, to find out how she feels toward it, she answers, "Compassionate." I don't sense compassion when I look at and listen to Helen. I wonder if she is really in touch with this quality or if she had just learned from her reading that this is the "right" answer.
>
> Susan: "Where in your body do you feel this compassion?"
>
> Helen: "I actually feel blank toward it."
>
> This tells me the blank part is blended with her.

Remember, differentiation is a key skill to develop in IFS and it takes intention and practice to determine who is doing what. Initially, it may not be easy to sense whether the calm regulation you or someone else feels comes from Self's presence or from protectors working hard to dampen or blunt sympathetic arousal through dissociation, or from soothing using an external substance or process.

When the tracking is unclear or if the IFS professional would like to verify the level of Self-leadership, they can also ask the client, "Instinctively, as a percentage, how much Self-energy do you sense you have?" or "Just spontaneously, how high is your Self-energy out of 10, with 10 being a lot?"

"The client has no Self-energy"[4]

Supervisees often make this plaintive cry in IFS supervision (in Integrative supervision the plaintive cry is more often phrased along the lines of "the client is incapable of changing"). Thankfully, my parts usually don't buy into these ideas. Self is innate, undamaged, and whole and exists beneath the surface of parts. And, like death, and taxes, change is a certainty in life. Yes, Self can be obstructed by parts as the clouds can "hide" the sun. However, the sun is still there in the background.

There are many ways in which to respond to supervisees holding this belief. My first move is to recall that it is a part or parts of the supervisee speaking (Self does not make such pronouncements). Usually, the part sharing in supervision is scared. This may show up as frustration or the supervisee may be feeling victim to a "difficult client", or fear being persecuted by me as being bad at IFS, having no Self-energy themselves and so on. I also bear in mind that Self attracts Self, and parts attract parts. If the client has little access to Self-energy this is likely to have activated parts in the therapist or it may have been parts in the therapist who activated parts in the client, or both.

As the reader may be aware, using direct access, implicit or explicit, is helpful in having parts unblend. Below is a reconstructed piece of direct access with a supervisee who was feeling held back by self-consciousness and unable to use direct access with a client with whom he has been working for some time using another form of psychotherapy. The client is, as yet, unable to access their own Self-energy. The supervisee is an IFS novice, and we began to work together during his Level 1 training. My lightly held aims in doing this piece of work were to:

- initiate a Self-to-part relationship so that the therapist's part can be less dominant in sessions with the client;
- model doing explicit direct access; and
- help the supervisee get a sense that direct access can be both useful and enjoyable.

> *Supervisor:* "Hello, am I speaking with the part of Peter who isn't comfortable about Peter using direct access with this client?"
>
> *Peter speaking as his part:* "Yes. It's just that we've been working together for so long and the client's happy talking to me like he does. I'm happy talking like we do."

Supervisor: "I get that. It's hard doing something new. Are there other parts there who are excited about using IFS and want to be free to use all aspects of it?"

Supervisee: "Yes, and there's all this talk about healing, as if what we've been doing together previously doesn't count."

Supervisor: "It makes sense to me that you might be feeling discounted, and I apologise if my work with Peter has contributed to that. It's just that doing direct access with clients as complex as this one who struggle to access Self-energy, can be beneficial."

Supervisee: "Yes, I get this direct access is meant to help the work go better, but it seems so stupid, like some role-play game."

Supervisor: "Ah, is that what concerns you that you might look stupid or be thought childish if you use it with this client? I seem to remember he has some intellectual parts."

Supervisee: "There is that. And, what if the client says something and I don't know how to respond?"

Supervisor: "Well, that concern makes sense to me, too. You think it's all a bit unpredictable and might be too spontaneous? (*Peter is nodding*) What are you concerned would happen if you relaxed back and let the Peter who's not a part lead the direct access with the client's parts?"

Supervisee: "If I lose control, I might never get it back … who knows what might come out of Peter if I move out of the driving seat."

Supervisor: "Ah, I see. You have concerns about letting go of the power and control you have in Peter's system? (*Supervisee is nodding*) And how has this been for you to talk with me like this?"

Supervisee: "Okay. Yes, it's felt safe enough and nothing embarrassing has happened."

Supervisor: "Well, I appreciate you speaking with me in this way, and I'm guessing the Peter who's not a part has been listening, too. I'm sensing he'd like to speak with you if you are willing. And I think you might like him. Would you be open to meeting? If not, that's fine, too. I am aware that Peter is in therapy and he and you can get to know each other there if you'd prefer."

(*Speaking from the part still*)

Supervisee: "Yes, I've got therapy tomorrow, but I'll meet this Peter you're talking about, just briefly."

Supervisor: "That's great. So, just allow some space for Self to be there. (*After a pause*) Is that you Peter? (*He nods*) Do you have a sense of this part?"

Supervisee: "Yes, I see it there. It's quite stern looking."

Supervisor: "As you see it there, how do you feel towards it?"

Supervisee: "I'm curious and open to hearing from it, and letting it know that I'm here."

Supervisor: "Great, let the part know; and if it feels right, commit to getting to know it better in your individual therapy."

We left it there.

How far to go with a client's part-who-wants-to-be-Self in the lead?

You may recall from earlier when the supervisee did not want to challenge the client's Self-like part? Unfortunately, and fortunately (depending on your perspective), it is part of an IFS therapist's job to ascertain, as best they can, how much Self-energy a client has available. As I mentioned in Chapter 1, when using in-sight with clients, I prefer *not* to proceed far along the healing steps without the presence of the client's Self. However, other IFS professionals may choose to go all the way with the client's part in the lead, saying, "after all, parts have Self too, and it does seem to help the client unblend". Others may not realise until the end of a session or afterwards that perhaps a Self-like part was stepping into Self's role in the healing steps. Whatever the circumstances, parts do not deserve either to be feared or vilified for trying to help. And we can negotiate with them in the hope and expectation that, in time, they will free Self to lead the client's system. Raising this with IFS senior lead trainer, Chris Burris, he offered reassurance suggesting that at worst this was a form of rehearsal (personal communication, July 31, 2020). HCPC-registered dramatherapist and certified IFS therapist, Martin Redfern, said something with a similar feel: "If it's a part running the show, then that's probably what it was – a show, a performance or an attempt to make something real" (personal communication, April 11, 2022). Such work may bring some benefits to the system. Yet, the part's activity or "performance" will not bring the depth of transformation that being in the healing presence of Self will.

Equally important is the question: "How far do I go with a client's part when Self is not leading in *my* system?" I hope this chapter and the rest of the book proves helpful on your journey of transitioning to Self-leadership.

Exercise

Which part says: "The client has no Self-energy"?

You can either do this on your own, perhaps using a journal, or with another person who can hold Self-energy and ask the questions below. I give instructions for both versions.

On your own

Think of the last time you said to yourself (or to your supervisor): "The client has no Self-energy." Allow yourself to recall that occasion, the person about whom you said or thought this. Blend with the part who believes this. You can ask the part to write the words down, adding any underlining or emphasis it wishes. Alternatively, you can fully embody or enact the part, allowing it full use of your body for gestures and body movements that go with the words.

As you are blending in whichever way you choose, see if you are also able to be a curious observer and take the stance of a "visiting anthropologist" towards this part's expression. In other words, see if you can have the dual awareness[5] or dual attention needed for Self-to-part relationship, i.e., awareness of being both Self and part at the same time.

Ask yourself: "How do I feel towards the part that holds this belief?" If your response evidences C and P qualities, then from your own curiosity and/or using any of the prompts below, continue to hear from this part. Have it express and/or embody its experience or write its responses to the following questions:

- What/who do you think Self is?"
- "Yes, the client has no Self-energy… how is that a problem for you?"
- "Yes, the client has no Self-energy… do you believe that says something about you?"
- "Yes, the client has no Self-energy… what are you telling yourself about your work together?"
- "Yes, the client has no Self-energy… what do you tell yourself about how your supervisor will respond to you around that?"
- "Yes, the client has no Self-energy… what do you want to happen in supervision?"
- "Yes, the client has no Self-energy… what do you want to be different/change?"

There may be more that is not expressed, so ask "is there more?" or "what else?" until it feels like you can ask, "Is that it for now?" Validate the part's concerns in writing, verbally, physically, mentally in your head or a combination.

Negotiate around what needs to happen next. This might be to get some supervision, to work with the activated part in therapy, or to come up with a plan together so that this part isn't present in future sessions with this client.

If parts come in with opposing views such as "of course the client has Self-energy ..." ask the parts to wait for now and come back to them later. If they're not willing to relax, then switch target part.

With another or in a group

Have a colleague use direct access to ask the above questions or any that their curiosity brings to the part holding the belief "the client has no Self-energy". Ask the colleague to validate the part's concerns and to ask what it wants to happen next. Ask your facilitator to broker an introduction between your part and your Self and help that relationship build.

Notes

1 I highly recommend reading Schwartz and Sweezy, 2020, on the concept of hope-merchanting.

2 Schwartz tells us in month two's live call of the Continuity Program (Schwartz et al., 2021) that although Self-like parts can be hard to spot, they can be detected either because they have an agenda, are resisting, protecting, or promoting something (or a combination of all of these).

3 This is different to the technique "See yourself through my eyes" developed by IFS senior lead trainer and expert negotiator with parts, Mike Elkin, which is well worth making part of your IFS practice.

4 See Schwartz and Sweezy (2020, p. 144) for an interesting aspect of this related to exile burdens of neglect and abandonment. See also p. 151 for a beautiful metaphor re Self's absence being like an eclipse of the sun, which IFS therapy can bring to an end.

5 See Schwartz & Sweezy (2020, p. 265) where Schwartz writes of his early experience of clients dropping into a seeming alternate universe inside such that they "accessed a remarkable state of dual awareness, feeling as if they were here and there, inside and outside, at once". This is one form of dual awareness in IFS, another is being aware of being both Self and part(s) at the same time, another is the awareness of existing both in the past and in the present at the same time.

Part IV
Barriers to transitioning
Professional isolation
and loneliness

9
Being in IFS supervision

Introducing the chapter

This is the first of three chapters, 9, 10, and 11, forming Part IV of the book, which focus on professional isolation and loneliness. Respectively, the chapters focus on, making use of supervision and having a professional "home"; engaging in IFS therapy; and creating connection with others journeying with IFS.

For your information and to pique your interest, this chapter highlights different elements of IFS supervision. Exercises ask you to reflect on your own supervision experience, do some research and explore your own or your group's reactions to contracting.

What professional affiliation do you call "home"?

By now in your reading of this book and along your IFS journey, you may be feeling "at home" to some degree in the IFS community. It took many years before this was true for me but as my sense of belonging and contributing to the IFS community grew, (through attending Levels 2 and 3, PA-ing and writing), I had, and still have, my professional "homebase" of the BACP (the British Association for Counselling and Psychotherapy). It can be hard to be adrift professionally, and it is possible that as a practitioner you may be somewhat alone in not already having a professional body or home you feel you belong to. The IFS Institute and international partners do remarkably well in creating a sense of an IFS community, but at the time of writing, the institute does not function as a standalone professional homebase.

Currently, if you are applying for certification, you will be expected to indicate the number of years you have been a member of, or affiliated with,

DOI: 10.4324/9781003243571-14

your professional body. An example of such a body in the US would be the American Association for Marriage and Family Therapy (AAMFT). As a therapist living in the UK, I indicated my affiliation with the BACP, which has been my base for over 20 years now. My sense is that this is a quality-control measure, as applicants are openly stating the professional body whose code of conduct, complaints procedures and ethics, etc., they stand by. However, you may not already be affiliated to a relevant body or may wish to leave your existing one. In this case, you might want to consider joining a relevant professional body – which may involve retraining – to provide the necessary holding and professional accountability. As for practitioners, you would indicate your coaching or bodywork organisation, etc., as applicants from a diversity of professional backgrounds are currently (January 2022) welcomed.

Variety is the spice of life

If you are a professional learning IFS or newly using it, it is likely that someone further ahead on their IFS journey who is offering supervision, mentoring or coaching might be helpful, supportive, and challenging in your ongoing learning experience. As you may know, there is no official IFS supervision training (as of the time of writing) and no official requirement from the IFS Institute regarding hours of supervision/consultation. If you are applying for or are already certified with the institute, a certain number of hours of IFS Continuing Education (CEs) must be proved – half of which may be consultation/supervision.

Also, there is no one universal term for the processes of supervision and the range of supervisory relationships in existence. In America, it is usual only to use the term supervision for the oversight of trainees or interns who are not yet licensed to hold clinical responsibility for their caseloads. In this case, I believe the supervisor may be employed by an agency or training institution and have an evaluation and safeguarding role in regard to the supervisee's progression to qualified status. Once qualified and fully licensed, the professional gains autonomy and clinical oversight of their caseload. As such, they may only drop in for occasional consultation.

In the UK, for example, the term supervision tends to be used whether the supervisee is in training, qualified or accredited. This partly reflects the cultural emphasis on the ongoing and lifelong nature of a therapist or practitioner's learning. It also reflects the situation that most supervisors do not take clinical responsibility for the work of qualified professionals, who – if they are self-employed – are expected to take out their own indemnity insurance and abide by their professional body's code of ethics and so on. The exception to this is when a counsellor is in training and clinical responsibility may be held jointly by a placement supervisor and the training institution, for example. For a neat description of the difference between "supervision" and "consultation" in America, see that by Cooper and Corey, in their chapter "Serving Those Who Served: Providing IFS-Informed Supervision and Consultation to Clinicians Treating Military Veterans" (2023).

Not only does the terminology differ, but there is also a cornucopia of different IFS supervision and consultation offerings available. Below is an overview of the range I am currently aware of (drawn from the IFS Continuity Program; and the multi-author book, Redfern, 2023).

- Drop-in style (à la individual sessions with Schwartz as part of the IFS Continuity Program)
- Crisis consultations or one-offs for qualified professionals (more prevalent in the US)
- Long-term, monthly session to meet basic professional requirements (more likely in the UK)
- Long-term, weekly or fortnightly sessions to meet professional requirements while learning or qualified and managing a big or diverse caseload
- Open-ended groups for professional development and personal support
- Time-limited groups for certification purposes and perhaps as a first experience of IFS consultation/supervision
- Individual certification consultation at whatever frequency works for the supervisory dyad
- Various peer supervisory arrangements

In addition to considering which of the above you might prefer or be able to access, you will also want to consider whether you want a supervisor or consultant who is a generalist or someone who specialises in working with a specific clinical population or age group. If you are a practitioner, say a business coach, using IFS, then you may wish to find a seasoned IFS coach to support and mentor you, rather than an IFS therapist. Additionally, as so many of us, whether therapist or practitioner, are qualified in multiple modalities, you will need to consider whether you wish to continue with any existing supervision or mentoring arrangements and add an IFS supervisor, or search for someone who can supervise all your client work. Naturally, any requirements of your insurer and your professional bodies will need to be met.

> **Transition reflection**
>
> "Last supervision session was really helpful. Realising part of me feared parts of my client stopped our dance of taking one step forward, two steps back. I've seen a real shift in our work." (ED – transformational mentor and IFS practitioner)

What might IFS supervision include?

Anyone who subscribes to the IFS Institute's Continuity Program is able to watch videos of the founder of IFS, Richard Schwartz, giving consultation sessions to IFS professionals who are stuck in their clinical work. Table 9.1 lists in alphabetical order some of the interventions and foci of supervision I have noticed from watching many of these consultation sessions, together with reflecting on my own practice and knowledge of the way other consultants and supervisors work. (Naturally, the list is not exhaustive; and to avoid repetition and because this book is primarily for those transitioning to Internal Family Systems *therapy* rather than to IFS *supervision*, I will not explore all the items listed. For a more detailed dive into the work of 16 IFS consultants and supervisors (including Richard Schwartz), see *Internal Family Systems therapy: Supervision and consultation* (Redfern, 2023).

Attending to fear and safety

One of the draws for me of IFS is the respectful, insistent focus on both fear (which drives protector behaviours, roles and choices) and its antithesis: Self. In the IFS Institute trainings, attendees are made aware of the importance of accessing Self. I'm not sure all attendees pick up on the significance of attending to and looking out for fear in themselves, their clients and colleagues. Figure 9.1 shows several radiating waves potentially impacting the client (or supervisee, pupil, mentee, etc.) who is represented by a head in profile on the right. The radiating waves moving from the left represent sources of potential fear or safety (or both simultaneously) which include:

- the IFS professional and professional relationship
- therapy and the therapeutic relationship
- the IFS model and processes
- Self

Table 9.1 Aspects of IFS supervision

A	B	C
Attending to fear and safety	Boundaries	• Case conceptualisation • Co-creating a mutually satisfying relationship including fit • Contracting • Cultural humility
D • Demonstrations • Diversity, equity and inclusion – awareness, training and resourcing	**E** • Encouraging embracing one's learning edges • Ethical awareness and decision-making • Evaluating	**F** • Feedback • Fire drill exercise, etc.
G • Gatekeeping • Group dynamics	**H** Hope-merchanting	**I** • Informed consent • Integrating • Inner work with therapist/practitioner parts
L Loaning Self-energy	**M** • Modelling compassionate confrontation • Models of supervision and consultation	**P** • Parts as consultants to the work • Parts-detecting • Practising skills
R • Reflective practice • Reviewing recordings • Role-playing (also called real-playing)	**S** • Self-awareness • Skills • Speaking for parts • Sharing from experience • Supervising of non-IFS professionals • Supervisory relationship	**T** • Teaching and learning • Themes and parallels • Transitioning to IFS
U • Unblending for increased Self-energy • Updating skills and knowledge	**V** • Validating and "going for the gold" • Values	

- change
- the wider community

The IFS professional

Having been supervising for 12 years now, I have noticed that many supervisees expect clients to feel safe with them and without fear. Therapists have reported telling a new client something like "You are safe with me" or "I'm safe". I understand that this comes from a desire to co-create a safe enough relationship and to communicate "I am trustworthy". Yet, I am not sure that these therapists understand that both danger and safety already exist inside the client, regardless of how safe the therapy room and therapeutic relationship may feel at any moment. Though it will have some impact, safety in the outside world does not negate, cancel out, nor in-and-of-itself heal danger being experienced in the inside world (represented in Figure 9.1 by radiating waves within the head of the client).

Also, with our IFS lens, we know that professionals may have parts who use anger, sarcasm, and criticism, for example. IFS professionals are humans and make mistakes – we have burdened parts and biased parts, just like clients. Part of transitioning to IFS is to tend to your inner world, which includes letting parts who become fearful in the presence of others' extreme parts know that You are there and can handle things, and debrief with them later. It also involves unburdening, ethical practice, working within one's competence with transparency and accountability.

Change

Supervisees who bring their struggles in transitioning to IFS from another way of working often presume the difficulties they're experiencing with

Figure 9.1 Origins of potential impacts

clients lie purely at a practical or skills-based level. I often wonder otherwise. Introducing a new modality is to bring in change, which can ignite fear of failure and performance anxiety (in client and therapist). It also introduces the unknown, which can feel destabilising and scary. And it can amp up inter-relational concerns as clients may struggle with whether or how to voice their inner responses: *I don't like this new way of working but if I say anything he might drop me.*

Therapy and the therapeutic relationship

Many of our clients are adult survivors of emotional neglect and abuse. As a child their distress may have been ignored or invalidated and they may have been attacked for having distress or expressing any emotion; they may not know how to ask for and receive support. They may also be suffering from having taken on legacy and cultural burdens. If, for example, a client's system is organised around an exiled core belief "I am not allowed to be distressed/emotional", then being in therapy and doing IFS is likely to feel scary and unsafe at times. As supervisor, I find myself reminding professionals that what their frustrated therapist parts may think of as resistance, ambivalence or ineptitude may be the reactions of fearful parts in the client whose fears need to be addressed, patiently and persistently. I encourage working with client parts for buy-in to using IFS to relate to distress, while recognising that therapy itself is *not* a stress- or risk-free endeavour (Afford, 2020, p. 4):

> Empathy and compassion work their magic in the background, creating a relationship conducive to neuroplasticity and supportive of the client in tolerating the stress required for neural re-organisation. (Cozolino 2010)

I advocate going towards the fear in the therapy space and having Self come alongside fearful parts (in client and therapist). It's not possible anyway to do away with risk, in my view, as risk is part of relationship. Peter Afford, therapist, trainer in focusing and neuroscience and author (2020, p. 85), writes: "The client needs to feel safe enough, and so does the therapist." Notice, he doesn't say "safe" but "safe enough". Most ethical professionals commit to doing their own inner work (with clients' parts as helpful *tor-mentors*). It can be helpful to ask ourselves and our clients how safe they feel with us, how we feel towards parts of the client and who in us needs Self's calm attention.

The IFS model and processes

I have mentioned how introducing IFS to clients (new and existing) can be destablising, and how therapy itself can be frightening to client parts. But, of course, we therapists have fearful parts, too, and IFS supervision can be a space to attend to our scared parts. Especially if you are new to IFS, you may have parts fearful in relation to the processes of IFS (including fearing the unknown, not having control, failing, looking stupid, not getting it right, forgetting what's been said, not knowing what to do next, etc.) and in relation to specific clients and their parts.

Self

Parts can be distrusting of Self and fearful of letting Self lead. They fear loss of influence or control, they fear change (both internally and externally), and they may fear being abandoned once again. Some clients may have suffered abuse as children when they revealed Self-energy, so being invited in therapy to manifest Self may feel very threatening. Similarly, for clients (which includes IFS professionals, don't forget) whose systems made them cut off from their body for survival reasons, asking them to feel and notice embodied Self-energy in sessions can initially be very scary. Also, as Schwartz points out (Goulding & Schwartz, 2002), in cases of extreme abuse, scared parts may have hidden or even expelled Self from the system. This can be unsettling for therapists, whose parts may believe such clients have no Self. Equally therapy can be daunting for these clients, as it involves rebuilding trust between parts and Self.

The wider community

Also, at the time of writing, divisions within the IFS community and lack of clarity from the IFS Institute can be the source of unease for beginning IFS professionals. A "hot potato" for some in the IFS community is that non-therapists can attend and complete all three levels of IFS training where trainers demonstrate amazing unburdenings of exiles and protectors; where they will practise how to facilitate other attendees in potentially moving through *all* the IFS steps of healing; and they may hopefully experience their own unburdenings. Yet, these same IFS practitioners, which includes coaches for example, may receive the message during Level 1 training "you must not work with exiles; it's not safe"; and "you need to refer deep inner work out to an IFS therapist". However, if these IFS practitioners then wish to certify, which they are eligible to do (at the time of writing), they are expected to demonstrate Self-leadership and IFS skills, including an exile unburdening – potentially without having been able to gain clinical experience in this skill; and there are many certified IFS practitioners who work successfully and safely as therapists by a different name. Thankfully, this does not apply to me. I can imagine if it did how burdened with fear my parts would be by such mixed messages. They would fear:

- hurting potential clients
- breaking the rules
- being unethical
- getting caught

I can imagine good girl parts vigilantly and fearfully looking out for exiles – to avoid them or shut them down. I can imagine desperate practitioner parts resorting to lying and manipulation telling their supervisor no exiles were worked with even if they were (or bypassing supervision and accountability altogether). None of which is conducive to Self-leadership, using IFS well and the making of informed choices by clients. (I believe this is something the IFS Institute is looking to review.)

Co-creating a mutually satisfying relationship – including fit

For longer-term supervision or consultation relationships, rather than "drop-in" or "one-off" style consultation, there are relational elements to attend to and consider. Just as a therapist and client may or may not be a good fit for the work they intend to do together, it is important that supervisors and consultants and those coming to them for their services assess whether they are a good enough match or fit. Ideally, a trained supervisor/consultant will be able to tailor their use and presentation of the IFS model for the supervisee in front of them, in terms of their respective stages of development and experiences whether as coaches, teachers, bodyworkers, or therapists. However, some of us work better in some circumstances than others. For example, I infrequently offer group supervision (IFS or otherwise) whereas many certified IFS therapists in America specialise in this. Some consultants prefer to work with those who have completed at least Level 1 training, others are willing to work with trainees or those who have not attended a Level 1 IFSI training. Some supervisors prefer to work with supervisees who have separate individual IFS therapy.

A colleague and the first IFS lead trainer in the UK, Liz Martins (2023), has written a chapter "Facilitating Flow: Developing a Framework for Integrating IFS and Supervision in Private Practice in the UK". In it, she writes of coming into partnership with the IFS model as she realises that

IFS can be her modality as a supervisor whatever the supervisee's approach. For those not trained in IFS, she employs more implicit direct access, uses less IFS terminology and parts language and less going inside. For example, when supervising non-IFS informed student therapists, she encouraged them (in a way that made sense from their frames of reference) to let go of being helpers and to bring curiosity and compassion to their clients. In this way, they would be offering a potentially powerful reparative experience for their clients. (In IFS parlance, we might describe Martins' intervention as encouraging therapist parts to relax, thus enabling greater access to Self-energy; but this would not have made much sense to her non-IFS supervisees.)

Ideally, both supervisee and supervisor (or mentee and mentor, whatever your language) will spend some time establishing and openly working on creating a mutually satisfying relationship, which will be reviewed periodically. This may include attending to aspects listed elsewhere in the book:

- Exploring personal values and expectations of the relationship and each other
- Getting to know each other, exploring power dynamics
- Understanding where each comes from, noticing and attending to difference
- Contracting for the work, including discussing reviews and handling of ruptures or conflict
- Considering whether certification is on the horizon, and if so, the near or far horizon

For example, in her chapter "Bias: How IFS Consultation Can Increase Awareness and Reduce Harm", Kate Lingren (2023), co-creator with Percy Ballard of Bigotry From the Outside In (BFOI), shares that from the outset, she intentionally contracts with consultees to work with parts holding biased beliefs. She makes explicit that these parts are to be expected and welcomed and requests the consultee's permission to bring attention to these parts as they emerge and are noticed.

Following, or partnering with the IFS model

Encouraging supervisees to do and be "the IFS way" in service of the client's well-being and transformation certainly forms part of my supervision offering. This can be important as oftentimes the therapist has been trained to not do things or be certain ways. For example, following the client and waiting for a part to show up rather than initiating "could we speak to that part …?"; or nervously working hard at keeping the client in their window of tolerance instead of asking exiles not to overwhelm – when these are necessary in doing IFS and being an IFS therapist.

Many a time, Schwartz explains to consultees that spending weeks listening to and joining with a manager keen to keep things on the surface will be of less value (financially and therapeutically) than gaining permission from the part to "go inside" or "be curious" in a more actively and recognisably IFS way.

Similarly, in IFS supervision and consultation, elements of the IFS model itself are applied and made use of (Redfern, 2023).

Hope-merchanting

In my experience, an important part of being an IFS supervisor, is being the hope merchant for supervisees and encouraging them to be hope merchants with those to whom they take IFS. I write about this in more detail in Chapter 8, so will merely introduce a few additional ideas here:

- If you are already trained as a therapist, your prior training may leave you feeling uncomfortable about this aspect of IFS as being too salesperson-like or "too invested and setting up the other to push back" – don't forget, hope-merchanting from Self-energy will feel different to doing it from a part trying to make something happen.
- It can feel uncomfortable as it involves you holding to your version of reality and allowing the other's part its version of reality without needing one to win out over the other; both realities can co-exist alongside each other for a period.
- Don't rush, if you can't personally offer genuine hope or optimism about an aspect of the IFS model, then wait until you can; these will come once your system allows you to buy into IFS more fully.
- Our personal experiences of having IFS and meeting Self bring relief to our exiles and hard-working protectors, enhancing our ability to be the hope merchant (Malmud Smith, 2017).
- Hope-merchanting is relevant for or involved in many different aspects of the IFS process – for example, the no-overwhelm contract when we might ask a protector "If I assure you we can have the exile not over-whelm the system, would you allow us access"?

- Hope-merchanting is best personalised to the part with whom you are speaking – for example, Schwartz will often (e.g. Schwartz & Sweezy, 2020, p. 139) tell a part it's the boss and in charge of the pace of the process. Sometimes, I hope-merchant from a slightly different angle, saying to young and overwhelmed parts, not that they have the power to stop the work, but that "You have the power to let this happen. I know you may not have 'stepped back' before, but all parts can do it in their own way, and you can find yours, if you want to."

Inner work with therapist/practitioner parts

It is usual to enquire about parts in the therapist who may be getting in the way (stuckness in the work being due to parts' activity in either the client, the therapist or both) and sometimes contracting to work there and then with a protector or even an exile to have the part unblend. Some supervisory dyads contract that deeper, inner work with exiles takes place in therapy not in consultation (see the example of consultee named "Mary" in Wonder, 2023), while others contract to work with exiles as part of the consultation contract (see Booth, 2023).

If work is done with the therapist or practitioner's parts in consultation, an enquiry might be made about how the therapist now feels about working with the client next time they meet to see what constraints have been lifted in the therapist's system; the goal being to increase Self-energy, Self's presence and leadership. IFS lead trainer and clinical consultant, Fran Booth, describes in her chapter "IFS Consultation: Fostering the Self-Led Therapist" (2023, p. 204) the therapeutic work she and a consultee she called "Jane" contracted for in her consultation. After unburdening parts activated by the therapeutic work, Jane found her relationship to the client had shifted: "I feel connected to her and to her pain, but not responsible. My urgency to help is gone."

Parts as consultants to the work

I mention this in Chapter 1 and merely wish to share here IFS lead trainer and author Pamela Krause's words on this (2023, pp. 50–51). Although this is from the perspective of a consultant and therapist specialising in working with children, young people and their families, it applies also to the therapist/practitioner, and indeed to anyone willing to listen to what their parts are sharing with them.

The Self-led internal system functions well because the Self and parts have mutual respect. The Self leads and parts give their input. No one is expendable, everyone is necessary, and neither parts nor Self is better or worse than the other. They are different and essential for our functioning. ... With Self-leadership we feel our parts and know them well, even when they are activated. They communicate with us constantly. Our Self is a resource for our parts and vice versa. When consulting, I have the opportunity to practice this way of being. I listen to my parts and learn from them, and they do the same. Their views and reactivity inform my consultations in crucial ways. For example, if my parts react to something the therapist says, it's likely that at least one other system (the child's, parents', or therapist's) has parts who are reacting in the same way.

Reviewing recordings

Ann Drouilhet (2023), couples and family therapist specialising in IFIO (Intimacy From the Inside Out), the IFS version of couples therapy recognises that self-reporting therapeutic work is going to be limited by protectors in the presenter as well as be limiting to the consultant responding. She writes eloquently of the value of recording consultation sessions:

- She and the consultee can examine the pros and cons of different interventions at choice-points in their session's role play;
- the consultant's willingness to be recorded can strengthen the relationship; and
- being recorded can itself prove a tor-mentor, revealing parts of consultees who would benefit from attention.

Although reviewing a recording is not the same as the live supervision, Terry Real enthuses about (Winter, 2021, p. 23), I believe the potential benefits include those he cites: therapists learning not to take themselves so seriously; a reduction in shame at not making the perfect intervention; and learning "to let go of a certain preciousness".

Role-playing (also called real-playing)

This refers to the acting out or performing of a part of the client by one member of the supervisory dyad or group. The other person in the dyad or another group member plays the IFS professional relating to the other in an IFS way. The benefits of this are many depending on the configuration of roles: the supervisor is modelling good practice; the supervisee or learner is practising a technique (which can help anxious parts to relax); the supervisee often experiences more clarity about the client, their work together, or the model; playfulness might be present, which can be enjoyable and aids unblending; and there can be greater access to compassion and curiosity toward the client in reflecting on the exercise afterwards.

Another aspect of role- or real-play is the fire drill. This is when one person is coached to play a part that triggers the practising professional, who then notices and gets to know which parts become activated in relation to the triggering part being role-played. Negotiations can then take place asking the parts for more space when working with the person, or trailheads marked for future therapeutic work.

Themes and parallels

It can be helpful to notice themes across the work (or patterns, Taibbi, 2021). This might reveal practitioner/therapist blind spots or learning edges to attend to. In a group, it may be that more than one member's work highlights something in common with others. Noticing and exploring such phenomena together can bring clarity.

Attending to supervisor parts (mode six of the seven-eyed model of supervision according to Hawkins and Shohet, 2012; and facet four of The 8 Facets of IFS Supervision, Redfern, 2023) and supervisee parts (mode four and facet three) is important also. Here are a couple of examples from my practice:

Projective identification

A supervisee is using the space to feel and voice her anger. I notice that this isn't like her and that it seems important in a way that is beyond just her. My system feels like it is waiting for something. The supervisee then gets more focused in her rage about the to-ing and fro-ing for "where the [expletive] pain went" when she was facilitating the client in an externalising exercise. Suddenly I feel strongly tearful and "realise" that the supervisee has been feeling what the client has been unable to feel – homicidal rage at her abusers, who she experienced as annihilating. Meanwhile, I wonder if I am feeling what might lie exiled beyond the anger – the pain and wounding. I voice this and instantly the supervisee is no longer in the vice grip of the rage, I am no longer tearful. It is as if the supervisee's system and mine have antennae picking up communications from the client's system that, as yet, are beyond her awareness or her capacity to "own" or tolerate.

Parallel process

Training in the seven-eyed model of supervision (Hawkins & Shohet, 2012) and in IFS has helped me become sensitive to occurrences of paralleling or mirroring, as it is sometimes called. This can be of feelings and interpersonal interactions. A common parallel to look out for is the occurrence of feeling like a victim, feelings of frustration and helplessness, or hopelessness. It's as if these are contagious and the client passes it to the professional who passes it up to the supervisor (who hopefully spots the hot potato and interrupts the process). However, the "infection" can start up or down the line – a "victim" supervisor can be mirrored to the client via the supervisee.

IFS supervision that favours stuckness (see, for example, "An Interview with Richard C. Schwartz", Schwartz and Redfern, 2023; and "Facilitating Flow: Developing a Framework for Integrating IFS and Supervision in Private Practice in the UK", Martins, 2023) and accesses patience and persistence can notice and interrupt these processes, which results in unblending and more Self-energy becoming available.

Validating and "going for the gold"

Schwartz often models validating the therapist's commitment and effort as well as acknowledging for how long therapists sometimes must be the Self to the system when working with some clients. He also models highlighting what seems to be going well in the work presented. In a supervision session this morning, the therapist told me about a client who has sought therapy due to panic attacks. We noticed the positive shift in the client's nervous system by the end of sessions, and how this would last some days. I took the opportunity to voice my noticing of the client's ability to sense the presence of calm in his system as being a positive sign for IFS therapy. I also shared my sense of how grounded and in calm Self-energy the therapist was for this to have happened.

"Going for the gold" is often easier said than done. Perhaps due to cultural influences and burdens, many supervisees come to supervision in the UK with a noticeable problem focus. Such professionals seem to want to focus on what they are doing wrong, on how the client can't do IFS, and expect me somehow to fix things or offer solutions. If this is familiar, consider explicitly using a supervisory question or focus which may help curiosity and creativity get back in the driving seat. Chesner and Zografou (2014, pp. 71–85) give examples of supervisees using Chesner's six-shape supervision structure (a creative and reflective method) together with the supervisee's initial questions concerning how to go forward and how to manage the boundaries of the work. These help the supervisees to access their own "knowings". See Ch. 14, Redfern, 2023, for further examples of supervisory questions and foci in IFS supervision.

Contracting for a piece of therapy in supervision

If you are a UK reader, you may have noticed an aspect of IFS supervision that is different to the type of supervision you are used to. Because we all have parts and Self (clients, supervisees, and supervisors/consultants), IFS therapy principles and protocols can be applied in the supervisory relationship as they are in the therapeutic relationship. Thus, as an IFS therapist or practitioner guides the internal attachment of Self with parts of the client and proceeds through the healing steps as needed and agreed between them, so an IFS supervisor/consultant might do the same for and with their supervisee/consultee. What occurs will therefore look, sound, and be like therapy (see Booth, 2023). Usually in the UK, non-IFS supervision is less likely to include such moments or may do so occasionally, with a cultural preference being to keep therapy and supervision separate.

However, as of the time of writing, IFS therapists with space on their books are rare. Many clients find that IFS therapy becomes a way of life rather than a short-term intervention through one of life's rough patches and this can cause a log-jam in professionals' practices. Thus, some supervisees will not have a therapist to whom they can take their personal work. It can make sense, therefore, to make full use of supervision to include working therapeutically with parts. Personally, I like to do this and will contract on an individual basis with supervisees about whether this is something we wish to include in the relationship and whether they are amenable to working only with the protective layer or also with exiles. However, I am also a firm believer in maintaining a difference between IFS therapy and IFS supervision as I explain below.

Therapy-style supervision – is it for you?

Some IFS consultants, particularly in America where the cultures and practices of consultation and supervision are different to those in the UK, are of the opinion that any personal work in supervision will benefit the client and they will therefore give supervision "therapy style" as I call it. I agree that working therapeutically with parts in supervision can assist supervisees in establishing Self-to-part relationships for the first time if this did not happen during Level 1 training. Also, such work, which includes establishing a therapeutic relationship, can be a form of modelling for the supervisee to take back into their own therapeutic work.

However, having this style of IFS supervision exclusively does not meet all supervisory needs and has drawbacks. Meeting monthly (and in the UK this is usual) and using reactions to client work as a trailhead to go inside to whoever needs attention makes sense, but it can leave a lot of pieces of therapeutic work unresolved. If, for example, the next month different clients or personal circumstances are triggering and we follow those different trailheads inside, another piece of work might open and the previous one will be left hanging. Some IFS consultants overcome that difficulty by doing fortnightly or weekly consultation sessions for a time to complete the piece of therapeutic work (Booth, 2023).

Another drawback of doing exclusively therapy-style supervision is that the supervisee may then miss out on many aspects of IFS supervision. Having an IFS supervisor who only does therapy means that I do not have a more experienced professional of whom I can ask questions about technical aspects of practising the model, or who could help me with case conceptualisation, for example. As the *Ethical Framework* of my professional body the British Association for Counselling and Psychotherapy (BACP, 2018, p. 14, 21, 22) states, supervision (which in my professional practice encompasses IFS supervision), includes keeping skills and knowledge up to date and "Working to professional standards" by:

> 14d. reviewing our knowledge and skills in supervision or discussion with experienced practitioners

and

> 53. We will consider carefully in supervision how we work with clients.

Also,

Supervision

> 60 Supervision is essential to how practitioners sustain good practice throughout their working life. Supervision provides practitioners with regular and ongoing opportunities to reflect in depth about all aspects

of their practice in order to work as effectively, safely and ethically as possible.

Just as the therapy relationship is ideally unlike other relationships in the client's life, so the supervisory relationship can be unlike any other therapeutic relationship. The BACP *Ethical Framework* (2018, p. 22) states:

> 62 Supervision requires additional skills and knowledge to those used for providing services directly to clients. Therefore supervisors require adequate levels of expertise acquired through training and/or experience. Supervisors will also ensure that they work with appropriate professional support and their own supervision.

For me, it doesn't make sense to offer IFS supervision that is almost indistinguishable from IFS therapy; it is a needless duplication of a relationship. The supervisor/therapist misses out on so much, too. One of the reasons I am a supervisor as well as a therapist is because I like variety in my work. I do not want every professional relationship to be the equivalent of the therapist–client dyad. Here are some of the less "therapy style" aspects of supervision that I enjoy:

- Developing a collegial and mutual relationship;
- empowering supervisees to explore and establish their professional identities and ways of working and being in the therapy room;
- celebrating the supervisee's growth and development as a professional as well as celebrating their client's successes;
- encouraging and supporting the learning and understanding, which includes challenge, of novice therapists and practitioners, particularly around boundaries and contracting, for example;
- teaching – whether that is through sharing theory or my experience as client, therapist, PA, supervisor, etc., or through modelling experientially in our relationship;
- learning – supervising has been an immense time and source of learning for me;
- being playful with a colleague as we role-play, and they coach me in playing their "tor-mentor" of a client or they play the "tor-menting" client and I model being curious towards them;
- parts-detecting in myself, the consultee and the client and their interrelated systems; and
- helping trainees develop self-reflection and self-evaluation as we engage in mutual evaluation of and feedback re our work together and their work with clients.

Another reason that I am concerned about IFS supervision being too like IFS therapy is that it can be all too easy for an IFS therapist or practitioner to feel in a "one-down" position in need of personal work from a "one-up" therapist. Similarly, we each expect and desire a certain level of privacy and we have the right to choose the level to which we will allow access to our inside worlds (Reed & Wooten, 2023). Some of us may not want to work with our supervisors at the exile level; some of us may be happy to do so or come to this in time as trust in the relationship grows. The BACP *Ethical Framework* speaks to this:

> 61 Good supervision is much more than case management. It includes working in depth on the relationship between practitioner and client in order to work towards desired outcomes and positive effects. This requires adequate levels of privacy, safety and containment for the supervisee to undertake this work.

Making conscious and informed choices

In summary, I urge you, the reader, to make conscious choices with your IFS supervisor/consultant/peer(s) about the nature of your work together and the depth to which you will share. This will be informed by the code of ethics of your professional membership body and your original therapy/practitioner training if you have one. I urge you to dialogue and explore together and draw up a written contract that you can review and update as needed over time. (If you choose not to work at depth in supervision, then you may want to secure an IFS therapy relationship.) My hope is that such decisions are made jointly and consciously as informed choices rather than being motivated by ignorance (not knowing how else to do something), incompetence (not giving it any thought or presuming everyone is on the same page/wavelength), or the desire to escape accountability (information is power and some people prefer an uneven playing field).

I am aware that some supervisors go light on the contracting at the start of a supervisory relationship and at times I have let this stage slip, only to regret it later. (See Ann Drouilhet's chapter "Consultation for the IFIO Therapist", 2023, pp. 67–68.) However, over the years, as a supervisor and supervisee, I have come to value contracting as a process and the contract as a baseline and point of reference.

Transition reflection

"This first supervision session felt really important, like our systems introduced themselves to each other." (Anon)

I like to think my supervisory style is characterised by certain values:

• Vulnerability
• Personal authority/potency
• Responsiveness (to myself and the other)
• Transparency
• Collaboration
• Permission
• Choice
• Accountability
• Responsibility
• Growth
• Learning
• Development
• Integrity

Some of these values are reflected in the inclusion of the choice/informed consent process shown in Table 9.2 which is quoted from my typical (at the time of writing) contracting for Consultative IFS Supervision.

This is designed to give supervisees choices and to consider how vulnerable they wish to be with me in supervision. If we agree to use most of the IFS practices, that frees me up to model how to do various aspects of IFS. While doing so, it potentially helps us both more accurately evaluate where the supervisees' strengths and weaknesses lie; and it helps us work towards freeing Self-energy in both of us. We may also get to befriend some of the supervisee's main protectors. Although I pride myself on my desire to meet supervisees where they are, I like to be explicit about how I work as an IFS supervisor. If we have an IFS supervision contract, I will make use of IFS concepts and practices and I will expect the supervisee to use IFS concepts and practices in their work if they are characterising themselves as an IFS therapist or IFS practitioner. I will also, with permission, expect us to work with any of their "fall-back" parts who might be blocking their transition to using IFS to the fullest.

Table 9.2 Choosing IFS practices for supervision

Contracting for IFS supervision for Self-led practice

IFS practices may form part of IFS supervision by prior agreement, supervisee to indicate preferences: Yes, No, or P for possibly (agreement in the moment will additionally be sought):

IFS practices   *Yes/no/possibly?*
• parts-detecting (supervisor to supervisee):
• parts-detecting (supervisee to supervisor):
• supervisor enabling supervisee to unblend from protectors
  using in-sight, direct access, the room technique, leading a
  meditation, etc.
• practising speaking *for* not from parts in our relationship:
• role-playing with supervisee playing client or therapist:
• role-playing with supervisor playing client or therapist:
• facilitating supervisee's use of in-sight with own exiles:

Supervisee goal(s) for supervision and means of evaluating progress towards these (to be agreed with supervisor):

Conclusion

I refer the reader to Reed and Wooten's writing about IFS-informed supervision (2023) and concur with them that the most significant difference between IFS as it is applied to supervision/consultation and to psychotherapy is the intention. Though the goals of both may appear identical (supporting personal development, well-being, and healing), the scope of supervision and consultation is more tightly focused on supporting the professional development and efficacy of the therapist within the sphere of their work. Any inner work or support of parts in IFS supervision/consultation is related back to the therapist's clinical work and development as a professional.

Exercises

1) Reflecting on supervision

Either with a partner, in a group, or on your own, give yourself some time and uninterrupted space in which to reflect on all that you've read in this chapter. If you wish, review the list of elements of IFS supervision in Table 9.1 and bring some curiosity towards your existing supervision practice (as supervisee or supervisor). If you do not want or think you need IFS supervision, do you have a mentoring or line-management relationship that might benefit from some attention? You may want to ask yourself the following questions. See who answers and be aware that parts may not all respond alike. Give yourself time and move through at your own system's pace if possible, making your own pauses and timeouts as needed.

- How satisfying is my current supervision arrangement?
- How satisfying is my current supervision relationship?
- Does anything need to change?
- Does anybody want to make a change?
- Do you notice any strong reactions to any of the potential elements of IFS supervision?
- Have any memories of past supervision arrangements or relationships been stirred up?

Ask yourself how you feel towards whatever has shown up. Extend Self-energy to any parts that wish to receive it, let them know you are here. See who, if anyone, wants a stronger connection with you and see if it is okay with your system to witness their sharing in more depth. Welcome any responses to supervision that they wish to share with you. Just be curious, and patient and present. Do any parts need anything on the inside or in the outside world? If so, how do you respond? Can you agree to meeting those needs or moving towards that? Do you need to make changes or have discussions with others? What needs to happen before you say goodbye for now?

2) Supervisee (and supervisor) research

Join with a colleague/peer or a group at a similar stage of transition to you (whether becoming an IFS therapist/practitioner or becoming an IFS supervisor/consultant). Collaborate in some research to find any additional elements of IFS supervision that aren't featured in this chapter, and share with each other what you might find. Sources of information might include:

- Your IFS reading, the IFS Level 1 Manual and any IFS supervision contracts/arrangements you have been part of.
- Asking colleagues for their experiences of IFS supervision.
- Asking your supervisor/consultant for their experiences.
- Reading Dan Reed's dissertation (Reed, 2019).

- Reading the multi-author book on supervision and consultation (Redfern, 2023).
- If you are a supervisor, you might have attended training on integrating IFS into Supervision with myself and my colleague, Liz Martins.

Finally, you might challenge yourselves to come up with one sentence each that sums up what IFS supervision means for your system (or for a particular part), for now.

3) Contracting – a creative exercise for more than one person

Contracting is a therapeutic and relational activity that contributes to creating clarity and a safe container for relationships – whether in supervision, psychotherapy, or in business. Transitioning to a new modality provides an opportunity to review this whole subject in a variety of relational contexts – with your therapist, your supervisor, your clients.

However, sometimes our parts may not be completely on board and open to the idea of contracting or recontracting to work in a new way with existing clients. If parts of you are open to it, you could perhaps get to know them and their views about contracts and contracting in a way that you may not have done previously.

As a group or a pair, I suggest you take time to read through the exercise initially before you start to work through it for the first time. Once you have done that, feel into your choices about who to do the exercise with, when and for how long, whether you will divide one session between you or have sessions each. (Allow yourselves plenty of time. It can also be helpful to appoint someone who is not doing the exercise to hold Self-energy for the group or pairing and keep the exercise on track.)

Now choose a means of stimulating a reaction:

- think about co-creating an IFS supervision contract with a supervisor, peer supervisor or supervision group
- imagine recontracting with one of your existing clients
- consider the possibility of contracting with a new IFS client
- recall a memory (or memories) of contracting with a person or group of people or a comment someone made about the process

- write down sentence stems to complete, for example, "Contracting is ..." and "Contracting isn't ..."
- use a visual or concrete example of a contract to assist you
- something else of your choice

Next, if possible, choose a single creative method to use this time round. You will be using this to express reactions to the above:

- Drawing or painting
- sculpting using plasticine or Play-Doh
- making marks, pictures, sculpts or scenes in a sand tray with or without small objects and figures
- using scarves, cushions, or pieces of material
- writing on different sizes and shapes of coloured or plain paper
- another method of your choice
- stream-of-consciousness writing
- writing in dialogue (part and Self)

Now you are all set either to begin parts mapping initially and then getting to hear from individual parts in more detail, or to blend sequentially with parts who react to the initial stimulus and to each other.

Each of you, using your chosen creative method, represent what comes up for you in response to your chosen stimulus. Allow time for this.

Next ask your partner or the group to hold space for you as you share your creativity with them in a way that feels right to your system or to each part that shares. You might blend with your artistic representation: "I am the purple swirly scarf, and I don't want to be tied to a contract. I like fluidity and lightness of touch." Or you can speak for the parts you have creatively mapped: "This circle of clay in the centre of the sand tray represents the part who feels really strongly that contracting helps contain the work in a positive way. ... This mouse half buried in the sand over here feels overwhelmed at the idea of recontracting with clients."

See if your parts can feel validated and receive some of the C and P qualities, either from your partner or the group if you are blending with parts, or from the you who isn't a part. Be curious if, any of your parts need anything to happen either on the inside or in the outside world. Perhaps you can agree to all or some of this, or to working towards something. Maybe you can agree to revisit with a part or parts about this.

4) Creative exercise around contracting for a supervision group

Use an active and playful, or creative way of enquiring into each group member's approach to contracting – the aim being to have the participants react spontaneously and without fear of being judged or having to be the same as the leader or peers.

a)   For example, if the supervision group is meeting in person, move the chairs to the edges of the room and create an open space the whole length of the floor, if possible. Walk to one end of that floor length and give it a position in relation to the concept of contracting. Walk to the other end of the room, and label that point with the opposite position. Ask group members to place themselves in a line in relation to the two points. For example:

Supervisor: "At this end we have 'I always initiate having a written contract or agreement for professional relationships.' At the other end we have 'I've never drawn up a written contract or agreement for a professional relationship.' Each of you line up in relation to each other and those two positions. ... Great, OK, take a look at where you each stand and let's do another one."

The next example could be chosen by the supervisor, or a group member can suggest something.

Supervisor: "At this end we have 'Written contracts are a waste of time' and at the other end 'Writing a contract together is a valuable experience.' Again, each of you position yourself in relation to each other and these two positions. ... Look at where you each stand, see if you are near the same people or ..."

See if you can have fun together and allow weird and wacky examples to be suggested. The idea being to encourage playfulness, perspective, curiosity. Then follow the group to what needs to happen next which could be any or all of the following or something else entirely:

- speaking for parts about past experiences in supervision around contracting/safety/vulnerability/having fun (or not)
- agreeing a soft/hard/interim/draft contract together
- using this method with another topic (beware of avoiding difficult material, but it may be that more play is needed at the outset, and you can always poll the group about which way to go next)

Additionally, while group members are lined up, consider tapping one or more on the shoulder (consecutively not at the same time) and have them verbally share their perspective from the place in which they are standing.

b)   For a supervision group meeting online using a secure platform, a fun exercise might go like this:

Supervisor: "How about we use the top and the bottom of the screen to show positioning so you each place your hand in relation to the top and bottom of the screen, then I'll ask you to speak (very briefly for now) for that position in relation to contracting?"

Jeni: "How do you mean ...like this?" (holding her hand out flat about a third of the way up her screen? Supervisor agrees)

Jason: "Yes, and I'll label the position at the bottom. (He gets up from his seat in front of the screen and goes and lies down further back in his room but still visible to the group.) From this place, I hate contracts, they aren't worth the paper they are written on."

Supervisor: "That's great Jason. Everyone, let's go with this if you can do so safely, position yourself in your own space in relation to your floor and your ceiling. I see that Mona is standing on a chair and reaching up to the ceiling. Mona what do you say from there?"

Mona: "I think drawing up an agreement together shows respect for myself and the other members of the group. I have a part that doesn't like surprises and it feels cared for when I engage with contracting with my own therapist. It's also a way to respect my clients and help them feel cared for and like I'm taking our work together seriously."

Supervisor: "Thank you, Mona. I see Gilly, you're standing in the middle of your room. Tell us what that position means for you."

Gilly: "I feel in the middle somehow between Jason and Mona. I think contracts are important, but I don't think a written one should be more important than the on-the-spot contracting and recontracting like we do in this group. Like when we decide who presents a case or how we divide up to do a role play. That can only be contracted for in the moment surely?"

Supervisor: "Great point, Gilly. I see that Jeni seems a bit frozen, and I don't mean by the technology. I'd like to end this experiment here and see what is coming up for Jeni. How would that be?"

10

Having IFS therapy and experiencing the laws of inner physics

Introduction

Potentially, there is a lot to go through on your journey with IFS and it can be helpful to have a professional alongside to help you care for and negotiate with your system, as well as from whom you may learn the intricacies of IFS. There are alternatives such as buddy systems, practice groups or IFS drop-ins which might also help you feel less alone and supported. I encourage you to find the external support you need and if you get disappointed, keep looking.

Personally, I have many parts who like to "go it alone" and are attracted to DIY therapies such as Emotional Freedom Technique, and self-development or spiritual activities such as meditation, and Qigong that *we can do on our own, thank you very much*. Indeed, one of the benefits and impacts of the IFS model is that we can build relationships and spend time with our parts outside therapy. However, for progressing through the steps of healing, I recommend you are accompanied; having another's Self-energy and experience to guide, hold and support is invaluable (as it is in my Qigong practice). If solo IFS continues to be your preferred modus operandi, then that might be a sign a hardworking manager could benefit from external companionship.

This chapter touches on the following:

- experiencing the laws of inner physics (Schwartz, 2021);
- experiencing other aspects of the model, such as protector fears and Self;
- letting your clients be your *tor-mentors*;[1]
- letting evaluation processes such as IFS certification[2] provide trailheads;[3]
- having IFS therapists/practitioners as clients;
- how IFS consultants/supervisors also benefit from therapy; and
- exploring beliefs about emotional and psychological pain.

DOI: 10.4324/9781003243571-15

Get yourself some IFS therapy

Urging readers to have IFS therapy themselves may be my favourite top tip – therapy junkies that parts of me are. In the UK, most if not all professional therapy trainings stipulate that students have a certain number of hours of therapy during training. The IFS Institute also values experiencing the model as client during the trainings and encourages peer groups to form to practise with each other. Some of the most profound learning comes from personal experience. Dr Schwartz began developing the model through listening to and enquiring about the experiences of his clients and then being with and being curious towards his own experience of parts and Self. However, at the time of writing, the IFSI does not stipulate hours of therapy as part of training or certification.

Also, being a trainee can be a lonely journey; having a therapist as part of your outer-world team can really help you last the course. Transitioning to IFS can be an isolated, even alienating, experience both professionally and personally. You may have had your worldview rocked by knowing about and experiencing parts and Self, but others in your world – colleagues, friends, and family – may not. Some may even be antagonistic, especially if you lead with evangelising parts: "You must try this parts work, I'm learning, it's …" It can be helpful to have the support of an IFS supervisor or supervision group, practice group or dyad where you can be with likeminded people who speak the same language. (For those for whom English is not their first language, it can be even more challenging to find a place in the world of IFS, though this is changing.) As you go further into your IFS journey, you may find that you seek colleagues to form partnerships in which you can contribute to knowledge about IFS (through articles, leading workshops, etc.), add to the IFS lexicon, and disseminate the practices and concepts.

Personal experience of the laws of inner physics

In 2016, Schwartz was the trainer on one of the weeks of my Level 2 IFS training. I drew the lucky playing card one day and got to be client in a demonstration session. Schwartz guided my system right the way through the healing steps of IFS in which a pre-verbal exile was witnessed and on through to unburdening and integration. Perhaps because of the nature of the experience and the Self-energy present in Schwartz himself and in the other students, I still think of this as my deepest encounter with Self to date (they say you never forget the first time!). I had what I've heard Schwartz call an "in your bones knowing" of Self. My system experienced in my whole being (not just intellectually) that Self:

- Is whole
- Does not need to develop
- Cannot be damaged
- Heals
- Is always there (parts don't have to feel alone any longer)

Although not corresponding exactly to any of the individual laws of inner physics as described in the final chapter of Schwartz and Sweezy's book (2020), my experience is in line with what I read there.

Now, when I work with a client who has deeply traumatised protectors who cannot contemplate changing roles or allowing Self access for healing, I can hope-merchant to those parts from my head knowledge (I read a lot) *and* from my mind-body-spirit experience that the safety they crave and strive to create in and for the system, is "already there in Self. And would they like me to make the introduction?"

A key law of inner physics that Schwartz and Sweezy write about and which I have personally experienced in therapy (as client and therapist) is this (2020, p. 278):

> ... the Self can handle anything in the inner world. When trauma survivors face a very scary part, I often tell them, 'Nothing inside has power over you when you are not afraid of it, and your Self will not be afraid.' This crucial law has never been violated in my decades of doing IFS.

Working with traumatised clients who may have unattached burdens and extreme parts, this is of fundamental significance in me "holding my seat"[4] as a therapist. Similarly, as a client I have been blessed with therapists who have also known "in their bones" that none of my scary inner world can hurt them if they are in Self.[5] Wanting to sit with clients (traumatised and otherwise) without fear has led me to train in therapies such as EMDR and IFS. Now that I have found IFS, I no longer have a need to pursue the next therapy training, and then the next after that, in the hope that it will finally give me what I'm missing; I truly am the one I have been waiting for both personally and professionally. Not that this means I excel at s/Self-therapy; many of my parts still don't like the idea of me paying attention inside of me.

Therapy is one of the best places in which to fully feel for yourself what it is to create a Self-to-part relationship inside, and to benefit from all that this brings. If you have supervision with a non-IFS supervisor or your supervisor is IFS trained but does not facilitate inner work in supervision at some level, then it is important you have the space in therapy with an IFS professional to experience this yourself.

Experiencing protector fears

In the interview with Sue Smith (Chapter 11), you will see that we mention how our experiences in therapy affirm the teaching of IFS. "It's like they've read the book," Sue says of her parts, and I recount how true to my life is the list of manager fears (Pastor & Gauvain, 2020, pp. 60–62; Schwartz & Sweezy, 2020, pp. 140–146). As I write this in November 2020, I am fortunate to have IFS therapy weekly. This is a difficult month for my system, and while I've done much therapeutic work of many kinds on what happened when I was six years old – and much of it has been successful and healing – I am now coming to realise that key protectors were left behind.

This month, my therapist and I have been working with a pair of polarised protectors who are mortal enemies. But as I befriend them, they spontaneously move beside each other, united for the first time by a common positive intention. Even though I am a certified IFS therapist, these infant protectors of mine need and want the Self-energy of my therapist to be there with and for them, and for me. The protectors share their fears: *if we didn't do this there would be nothing: a void; annihilation.* What a privilege to have my therapist hope-merchant to them. In their fear and entrapment, they hear from her the clarion call proclaiming safety, peace, and an end to the reign of terror, at the same time as they sense the Self-energy in me.

Transition reflection

"My parts appreciate having therapy with someone who is a trained psychotherapist as well as being trained in IFS." (Sandra Hailes, psychotherapist in private practice, level 3 IFS)

Therapy welcomes all parts

One of my earliest influences in embracing IFS was experiencing Voice Dialogue as a client. During my first experience of one-to-one therapy with a trainee in the model, I now see that we were doing the Voice Dialogue equivalent of parts mapping. I would become aware of a subpersonality, find its place in the room, and embody it by sitting, standing, speaking, and/or moving as it wished. This was a gentle, freeing experience and one in which I and the trainee therapist welcomed each of my subpersonalities. All were welcome and equally so – even the quietly suicidal one who sat on the floor like a tombstone, unresponsive. Ideally in therapy, especially IFS therapy, we can all experience this attitude of all parts being welcome or what I have recently begun to think of as an attitude of "multi-partiality".

In a sense, Self is multi-partial in that all parts are welcome to share their experiences, be heard, understood, appreciated, and valued. Self listens with the same attention and authentic interest to each part's own unique perspective (bias). Multi-partiality is about honouring, valuing and favouring each part equally. Self doesn't judge one part as better than another or worse. Self trusts and validates each part's realities and truths, though they differ from Self's own and from that of other parts. Self lets each part know it matters and transformation comes from parts no longer having to sacrifice themselves for the system either as protector or exile. Self is equally available to attend to the multiple identities and experiences of the system that readily present themselves, as well as to those identities and experiences that might be absent or as yet unheard from.

Letting your clients be your tor-mentors

There are various reasons to embrace the concept that clients are our tor-mentors (Redfern, 2023; Schwartz, 2021, pp. 149–157):

- a part taking us over in session/in our work, gives a potential opportunity to make a repair or apologise to the other;
- our parts being activated leads us inside to do our deeper work in therapy, with peers, or on our own;
- our parts being activated can also lead us to do inner work in supervision; and
- the activation of our parts can provide transformative information when brought to supervision and, for example, recognised as a parallel process.

Schwartz writes and often talks about how his early work with clients and the formative IFS community of therapists and trainers brought up much in him that had to be attended to in therapy. He was frequently faced with trailheads and chose to follow them and do his work (Schwartz, 2021). Schwartz encourages therapists and practitioners to permit their clients to point out when they see parts active, especially if they are impeding the therapy and the relationship. This can increase client agency, and, if the IFS professional responds appropriately (validating the client's experience, unblending from the activated part in the moment and committing to befriending the part further), it can provide a corrective or reparative relational experience[6] for the client. This de-pathologises and normalises the existence of parts in each one of us.

There are other ways to respond to such a challenge from a client that can potentially deepen the work:

Client: "You're frustrated with me."

Therapist: "What if I were frustrated with you? What would that say about you?"

Client: "It would mean I'm not doing it right?"

Therapist: "And what if you aren't doing it right?"

Client: "That means I'm not good enough."

Therapist: "Are there parts inside already feeling not good enough?"

Client: (Moved) "Yes, yes there are."

There is a therapeutic maxim that therapists cannot take clients deeper than they have gone themselves.[7] I see this regularly in supervisees who have their own sceptical parts blocking access to Self or protectors who lead the system refusing access to their exiles. This makes it hard for them to access the C qualities necessary to help their clients. Schwartz and Sweezy (2020, p. 278) explain how Self attracts Self. (Remember, if the words "therapist" and "client" don't match your circumstances, adjust the language accordingly):

> Self-energy is also contagious. When a Self-led therapist approaches a client, the Self of the client—and the Self in the client's parts— activates. Like a tuning fork, the vibrating Self of one system sets the Self in motion in all proximal systems because individual Selves are connected to the Self everywhere ... This is one reason why we prioritize accessing the Self in therapists.

Schwartz explained in a live consultation session that I had with him as part of the IFS Continuity Program (Schwartz et al., 2021, month two), that more and more he finds when he does supervision that he works with parts of the therapist or practitioner that are getting in the way. He then proceeded to help me U-turn towards my inner system so that I could begin to befriend a shame protector who had been urgently blocking my curiosity towards a supervisee and getting the opposite of what it intended for the system (i.e., shame reactions in both of us).[8]

Here is an example from my clinical practice in which a clinical psychologist, who is part-way through Level 1 training, is attempting to use IFS with a client who has severe eating distress. Our supervisory relationship is two sessions old, and this therapeutic relationship has dominated both sessions. Part of the second session features paying attention to facet five of The 8 Facets of IFS Supervision – the IFS model (Redfern, 2023, Ch. 14) and the supervisee's IFS skills. We looked at the actual nuts and bolts of IFS and helped her grasp a couple of the key concepts of IFS, which may help anchor her as she, understandably, continues to be "at sea" with the model. It is apparent that this is helpful to the supervisee, *and* it is not enough.

This client is experienced as a true tor-mentor, and we contract to have the supervisee do a U-turn. She turns towards a terrified rescuing therapist part; and once a few other protectors have agreed to make space, this part meets and trusts Self and is overwhelmed enough to instantly hand over responsibility for the therapeutic relationship. The supervisee remains inside and invites the protectors who gave space to become aware of what has happened. I ask the supervisee to extend her appreciation to them. It's beautifully moving and she reports calm and clarity, whereas before her head was "fried" both while with the client and in between sessions. Naturally, there is further work for the supervisee to do on the inside: this calm and clarity are not likely to persist indefinitely until further work takes place at a deeper level and with continued attention to the relationship with the rescuing protector.

As Schwartz and Sweezy point out (2020, p. 87): "When a client shows weakness or neediness, tells us we are dead wrong, or challenges our competence, our unhealed wounds put us at risk of not doing our job well." Therapists (and others trained in IFS therapy) can do and say things that are (p. 88) "the opposite of therapeutic. We need to be aware that our protectors are entirely capable of confusing, injuring, and defeating our clients" or whoever it is they are relating to (children, partners, colleagues, customers, patients). In a perhaps less extreme impact, our protectors can also just keep our clients stuck. This is where letting clients be our tor-mentors and reflecting on our activated parts by ourselves, or giving them space in therapy (or supervision) can be useful and allow any useful information to surface, as in the following couple of examples.

I've been working with a supervisee for eight months and she regularly brings a particular client to supervision. Much of the work so far has involved me noticing the parts blending with her and helping her notice them. It goes something like this:

> *Supervisor:* "So, a part of you believes that part of the client?"
>
> *Supervisee:* "Ah, yes, of course, it's a part saying that. ... Yes, I seem to believe that part every time ... Ah, and that's what the client does, too ..."

On another occasion:

> *Supervisor:* "I can understand why your system feels under a time pressure and I can really get how defeated you are feeling. (*Pause*) Might this indicate how the client feels?"
>
> (*A parallel process*)
>
> *Supervisee:* (*With a big exhalation*) "Yes, of course ... that feels a bit better."
>
> *Supervisor:* "It's about validating the client's defeated part while not buying into its version of reality."

Following trailheads from the certification process

Like any accreditation or qualification process that requires an external reviewer to review live or via audio or video recording a therapy session, the IFS certification process is likely to trigger parts. I remember during my initial counselling training, sharing three different audio recordings with three different people involved in assessing my performance (two tutors and my placement supervisor). This was long before I had come across IFS and, naturally, I had parts active in the process. In hindsight, it seems that my system chose recordings specifically designed to provoke negative judgment of my abilities by each evaluator. Thankfully, after "having been found wanting" twice and getting some awareness of the self-sabotaging of my system, the third recording was basically sound and good enough to get me through.

Transition reflection

"Parts really want to be validated, they really believe what they believe, AND they really want it not to be true and for me not to believe it." (Anon)

As a supervisor, I have had the privilege of using IFS therapeutically with supervisee parts provoked by the certification process and/or in response to recordings. These include:

- Talkers
- Educators
- Procrastinators
- Critics
- Perfectionists

A supervisee and I have just started working together for certification consultation/supervision. Our first session together explored the elements of the certification process as well as some case conceptualisation around a difficult client relationship. The second session was wholly taken up with insight, working with a cluster of parts activated by beginning the process of becoming certified. Initially, we worked to establish that I am different to the parent who used to monitor the client's homework and set and mark mock exams. "That is not my way," I explain, "plus the supervisee has Self inside to lead his system so I do not have to take that responsibility." Then we turn to the cluster of protectors related to the other parent:

Supervisor: "How do you feel towards all these parts?"

Supervisee: "Like I'm in the centre and they're all around and I realise they are parts."

Supervisor: "Great, let them feel the difference; You are there, and they are parts. See if they'll trust You to handle stuff – with their help."

Supervisee: "Ah, they didn't like that at first, not until you added 'with their help' …"

(*I facilitate the supervisee befriending his parts who come to see that they are on the same team, and each has a valid reason for doing what they do. The polarisations relax, with, for example, the procrastinator agreeing to lighten up and give "pause for thought" rather than freezing the system. The parts are updated and realise the father's judgment is no longer valid, and also that he was not what they thought: perfect.*)

Supervisor: "What do these parts want from you going forward?"

Supervisee: "Understanding and appreciation. (*He opens his eyes and grins broadly*) I really enjoyed that, meeting them all. … It was great to do that for real rather than just think you know how to do it."

As all but one of the supervisee's protectors said they did not protect exiles, this may have been enough to free up the system. If not, then I would expect the supervisee to take this to therapy rather than use up all his supervision time focusing on this, especially as he has a full client-load awaiting our attention.

In my experience and understanding of supervision, it needs to offer and be more than therapy (see Chapter 9). Hughes and Pengelly (1996) draw attention to what I see as a crucial difference between the two activities. Supervision focuses on three participants: client, therapist/practitioner, and supervisor and is for the benefit of the client primarily and for the practitioner/therapist secondarily.

Although I am glad that IFS can be used therapeutically in supervision and I very much enjoy working in this way with supervisees, I do not spend all our supervision time on inner work, and I consider that I have more to offer than a therapy contract which can be fulfilled elsewhere by a dedicated therapist (see also Chapter 9). If I only offer therapy or inner work in supervision, then I am wasting my additional supervision skills, passion and training and preventing the supervisee from using our time together to explore and discuss in ways that may not be available elsewhere apart perhaps from on a Level 3 training (see Chapter 11 for a transcript of a supervision session).

IFS therapists/practitioners as clients

As many of you will by now have realised, IFS therapists and practitioners can sometimes feel like tricky clients. This makes sense to me as parts in both professionals can fear exposure and feeling not good enough. My advice is to be transparent about this during contracting. If you are the therapist-client, you might like to consider giving your IFS professional explicit permission to parts-detect; if you are in the role of therapist, you might seek explicit permission to parts-detect and explain that parts who want to be Self are normal and to be expected. Professionals, attend to the parts of you that get activated interpersonally: parts who want to lead the system (see Chapter 8), Drama Triangle parts, competitive parts, I-know-best-parts or insecure They-are-bound-to-be-better-at-IFS-than-me-parts. If you have access to Self's courage, you might give your client permission to point out parts they notice in you (see above). I have had some clients who have felt able to do this and I have appreciated the opportunity to unblend further. Similarly, attend to the parts that get activated intrapersonally: rescuers, victims and persecutors such as inner critics, and the exiles they protect. The more inner healing work you can do, the more easily you will be able to access Self and help your therapist/practitioner-clients to do the same.

Also, remember that it is normal to have parts that hold bias as well as parts that want those parts/that bias to not exist (anti-bias parts). I urge all those who use IFS professionally to become familiar with the work of Kate Lingren and Percy Ballard (Schwartz et al., 2018) on Bigotry From the Outside In (BFOI) (Pastor & Gauvain, 2021; Lingren, 2023). It is possible that therapist-clients may have parts holding unconscious (and conscious) prejudice against IFS practitioners. And it works the other way too with practitioner's having parts biased or in some way antagonistic towards therapists. This makes sense as difference can be hard and scary for our parts. Belonging to a community and not belonging are emotive subjects, especially as we form our professional identities. Remember that co-creating interpersonal safety and accessing intrapersonal safety are what working with IFS is all about. It's not easy and it is a perpetual endeavour we face with each new relationship and each new part. I'm making these points in the service of shame prevention and shame and fear reduction.

Learning as a client

After 22 years of therapy (on and off), I still have exiles to free and bring home to s/Self. In addition to the transformation of my inner system, therapy is and has been useful in learning IFS. As I have made the transition to becoming an IFS therapist and supervisor/consultant, there have, inevitably, been blocks in the road. The first block to surmount was direct access. In my experience as a student and a PA on Level 1 trainings, there just does not seem to be the space, the time, or the safety(?) to practise direct access in the triad work. For me, as for my supervisees, we learn to do this "on the job" and it can be a big hurdle to overcome. I spend much time as a supervisor helping supervisees address this gap in their experience. As a client, I remember the relief when a therapist used explicit direct access with a part of my system for what felt like the first time. It felt good to the part, it felt good to the system to see/feel how someone else did it, and inside I heard *I think your therapist has had some supervision* (rightly or wrongly, I don't know, as I didn't check it out).

Having your own therapy helps depathologise the pain

Despite having parts who fear being judged as narcissistic (*She's always talking about herself, this author*), I want to share how important I believe it was to my system that my first-ever therapy experience was in-patient group psychotherapy for PTSD (post-traumatic stress disorder). It was here my highly avoidant, dissociation-dominated, intellectually driven system began to understand that human emotional and psychological pain is:

- Normal and common to all
- Healthy
- Survivable
- Impermanent
- Inevitable

Approaching the emotional/psychological pain and allowing it into existence in the presence of containing Self-energy (provided by the therapy team, although I would not have used the term Self-energy back then) was:

- A valuable source of information
- Humanising (rather than living as I was as a "productive robot" or "mobile brain")
- Enlivening
- Empowering

Here I began to learn that living in my head, avoiding my emotions, and numbing myself was injurious to my mental health (I had recently "tipped into" quantifiable PTSD in my 30s) and physical health which has become apparent since entering my 50s). Naturally, I am still in process with this, and my protective system often fights against feelings, at least initially.

Having IFS therapy and allowing yourself to go to your exiles in their painful, terrifying places and surviving, coming back from them (and with them potentially), and healing them, will help your own protective systems relax enough to let your Self be present to your client's exiles. Similarly, your protective system will be less likely to collude with client parts who avoid, numb, distract, bypass pain and so on. We all have parts at some time or other who collude with client parts who "Don't see the need to revisit the past, that's behind me" or tell you "I've dealt with that already."

Another reason I am pointing this out is because I agree with one of my supervision trainers Robin Shohet, who highlighted that society in general doesn't seem to have a conceptual framework for being with emotional/psychological pain long enough for it to transform (Shohet, 2021). I think this can be true of some IFS professionals also, who hold unconscious beliefs and biases, at least initially, about stopping people's pain or helping people cope with their pain (which is different to believing the emotional pain can transform). This is one of the reasons I choose to highlight the writing of Ecker et al., 2012 (see Chapter 6), because they believe in transformational healing. Similarly, British psychotherapist, trainer and author Peter Afford explains this well when writing about brain (i.e., nervous system) change: "The therapist needs to get the client's neuroplasticity working, which may mean pointing his attention to emotionally uncomfortable places" (2020, p. 34). He also warns about the double-edged sword of language, which "can trap us into merely 'talking about' and going nowhere meaningful. ... Rather, the talking needs to reach the deeper, more meaningful and sometimes more emotionally difficult places that they [clients] haven't spoken from before." (2020, p. 36)

Naturally, many of us will have parts who polarise around these notions. It is worth exploring within yourself regarding your own beliefs (see the third of the self-reflection exercises below) and considering how you might respond to others' beliefs around emotional/psychological pain. I also suggest you consider emotional pain from the IFS frame or lens. Do you have a sense of what this might be, or has it not come up as an idea before? Here are a few of the IFS concepts I find particularly relevant (see Schwartz & Sweezy, 2020, especially Ch. 20; page numbers in the bulleted text below are from this volume):

- Exiles carry the painful and distressing stories of the client's life.
- Although it may identify with its pain, an exile is not the pain or the burden it carries.
- Exiles seek redemption (an end to their pain or a reversal of their burdens – for example, "I am unlovable" becoming "I am lovable") which, through no fault of their own, part(s) cannot make happen without Self.
- Exiles' inner pain and distress can be unburdened and transformed through the steps of healing, and even spontaneously, in the presence of Self.
- Protectors get to set the pace of therapy.
- Protectors already have the task of exiling, denying, distracting from, or soothing emotional and psychological pain, so, it is important to get them on side when offering to go towards and be in a different way with this pain.
- It is important to gain permission from protectors for exiles to be approached.
- Backlash[9] (extreme thoughts, feelings, behaviours, responses) is possible if the pain in the system is approached too quickly, without permission or without ecological sensitivity.[10]

- Protectors may feel shame, guilt, or regret at (through no fault of their own) not being able to heal the exiles' emotional and psychological pain.
- Although protectors share the same goal of warding off emotional pain, managers and firefighters often polarise about how to achieve this.
- Parts who want to be Self[11] seem to have an aversion to and fear of emotional pain and want to "shoosh it better" and "stop all the fuss".
- IFS offers a "no-overwhelm contract", whereby exiles can be asked not to overwhelm the system with their pain and distress which helps parts let Self stay present and available; and gives protectors confidence to step aside in the first place (p. 271).
- Self does not react to exile/emotional/psychological/physical pain in the same way that parents, teachers, relatives, and society in general react, "with impatience, denial, criticism, revulsion, or distraction" (p. 32).
- The IFS paradigm teaches that everyone – wounded, wounder and wounded healer – has inner pain that can drive extremity. This brings a certain sense of equality and acceptance of the other.
- The IFS paradigm emphasises compassion or *feeling for* not *feeling with* parts in pain (see Chapter 5) (p. 117):

> When we lead with the Self, we feel connected to and deeply caring for others; and more than that, we have the clarity to see and hear their feelings without the distortions of our own projected pain; we feel calm and curious about how to help; and we have the confidence, creativity, and courage to act effectively on their behalf.[12]

Exercises

Various self-reflections

1. Take some time and reflect on your journey as an IFS client. Doing this verbally with a peer; in writing using your journal; by creating a piece of artwork or sand tray, or any other way that feels right, you

   - might want to include the exiles and protectors you have unburdened.
   - could include the before-and-after pictures/descriptions of the protectors.
   - might want to use a chronological timeline approach.

Next, reflect on how that therapy benefits you as an IFS professional. (You might use the same piece of artwork/sand tray/journal page/conversation, or start another.)

- Recall and include occasions when something clicked into place in therapy.
- Include any examples of how unburdening a particular exile/protector in your system seemed to clear the way for a client(s) or supervisee(s) to do similar work/meet similar parts.
- Include any examples of where it has felt different to learn something through experiencing it as a client compared to learning about it from a book or while attending a training course.

2. If you are not in IFS therapy, take some time to have Self host a meeting with your parts to hear parts' views on this. Have Self lead any action required. This might be to research a therapist or practitioner and go on their waiting list if they have one; find an IFS therapy group; find a peer for mutual peer-facilitated sharing; or ask your IFS supervisor if they are open to a separate IFS therapy contract for a specific length of time or piece of work.

3. Spend some time on your own, with a supervisor, peer/consultation/ therapy group, to explore the core beliefs held by your system around emotional and psychological pain.

Here are some beliefs commonly held by our parts, ranging across quite a broad spectrum (Here I am using the word "pain" as shorthand for emotional/psychological discomfort or distress as opposed to physical pain):

Pain is bad
If I let my clients feel their pain, I've failed
I have to end a session with the client feeling positive/pain free/happy/safe …
I'm frightened of it in myself/clients/children/animals/anybody …
Numbing pain is useful in the short-term but in the long-term, can lead to serious health issues
It's best to avoid all such pain and hope it goes away
I'm functioning fine, I don't need therapy
She/he/they seem fine, best not to pry/ask/reach out she/he/they will only feel worse/embarrassed/like a victim
She/he/they are holding it together; if I pry/ask, they'll fall apart and then I'll have to put them back together again
If I go to the pain, I'll not come back/survive/be able to function
Pain gives important information
I can be with my clients in their pain
I have confidence in my client's ability to heal their own pain

Catharsis feels great and is therapeutic; the more the better
Pain is good
Pain cleanses
I've only worked with protectors so far; I'm frightened of working with exiles
I don't know how to work with exiles

Consider times when clients, colleagues, family members said or alluded to any of the above. How did you respond? Reflect on how you might respond if any of your IFS clients' parts vocalised one of the above or something similar.

Notes

1 The name used in IFS for people, or more specifically their parts, who "guide us to deeper healing by activating our parts" (Schwartz & Sweezy, 2020, p. 279).
2 For details of IFS certification see: ifs-institute.com/trainings/ifs-certification
3 The term for "an emotion, image, inner voice, thought, physical sensation, or impulse that, when brought into focus and followed, will lead to a part" (Schwartz & Sweezy, 2020, p. 46). In therapy, clients usually find and follow trailheads that are "the manifestation of a part in distress".
4 I use this term to refer to Self remaining in the driver's seat of the inner psychic bus rather than a fearful part blending and taking over. I think for others the term may be a riding term regarding not being thrown from the horse's back which takes courage, balance, presence etc.
5 Therapists are humans, too, we (our parts) get scared in the face of certain clients and certain parts of clients. This is normal and not blameworthy, wrong or unprofessional. Having said that, how we respond to that fear can be unprofessional and hurtful to clients if our parts blame them for being "too much" or "punish" them in some way to manage our own inner discomfort, blind spots, or prejudices.
6 See the writings of Petrūska Clarkson (1993, 2003) which are recommended reading for trainee counsellors.
7 During IFS Continuity Program month two's live call, Schwartz (Schwartz et al., 2021) advises a consultee (Jane) to do her own exile work, so she won't be so scared of going to her client's exiles. Elsewhere, he states (Schwartz & Sweezy, p. 141), "Therapists who cannot take care of their own exiles should not work with clients' exiles."
8 I first learnt about the self-defeating nature of protector behaviour from Mike Elkin, who talks about irony being the driving force of the universe. The irony being that my part trying to avoid shame was constraining Self's presence and causing a disconnection inside of me and between me and the supervisee – which was experienced by me as shameful, and I think by him. See Schwartz & Sweezy (2020, pp. x, 60).

9 See Schwartz and Sweezy, 2020, pp. 18, 19, in which Schwartz talks of parts of clients having "horrible experiences" after therapy sessions and wondering if these "ferocious response[s] come from parts who felt endangered by me. Had I alarmed them by focusing on the client's vulnerability too fast?"

10 By "ecological sensitivity", I understand being sensitive to the patterns and balances of relationships between all the elements of an environment or system – in this case a person's inner world. (See Schwartz & Sweezy, 2020, pp. 5, 18–19, 21, 23, 24, 29, 41–42, 204.)

11 In "When a Self-Like Part Steps in for the Self" (Krause et al., 2017, pp. 23–24) the authors explain that a Self-like part seeks to help the exile feel better prematurely before they have told their story, thus silencing them.

12 This does not apply only to those working in a therapy setting: at the 2021 IFS Conference, independent management consultant Helen Telford spoke of her Self-leadership in her presentation to which I refer in Chapter 1.

11

In others' words

Introduction

There is a metaphor used in therapy circles offered as encouragement to wounded healers and their clients journeying towards health and greater wholeness. (It also seems rather odd, a bit of a stretch and ecologically unfriendly.) The idea is that a person's trauma or distressing symptoms, etc., are likened to a forest of trees that needs to be cut down to make a path to reach health on the other side. You might think every tree has to be felled in turn, but that is not necessarily so. Sometimes just the trees around the edge need to be toppled in a certain way and as they come down, they take another row/layer of trees down with them, thus making the work seem easier and faster than at first supposed. Another forest might have one big tree, which if felled would carve a path right down the middle of the forest allowing passage. Do you get the idea? As I said in the last chapter, being alone and "going it alone" used to be my preferred ways of being in the world. However, over the course of my journey with IFS, this has been shifting, making this chapter and other collaborations possible.

This chapter includes:

- an interview with one of the first therapists trained in IFS in the UK;
- an excerpt from an IFS supervision session with a colleague I have the privilege of accompanying as he transforms his professional and inner worlds

Also, see the eResource of handy hints for those transitioning from student to IFSI program assistant by Louise O'Mahony and myself. (http://www.routledge.com/9781032153094)

DOI: 10.4324/9781003243571-16

An Interview with Sue Smith

Sue's "potted history"

Sue: "I am from a working-class background in the North West of England and I'm the youngest of six children. I've not done counselling always. I worked in an office when I left school. I wanted to do art really. So, I did A levels at night-school and then a full-time year-long Foundation in Art, which I loved, but my parents thought there were no jobs in art so I trained as a graphic designer; I didn't really like it. I ended up working in newspapers, and then had the kids. What got me into counselling was having the kids really, because, um … it made me start to question how I'd been brought up. I'd never really seen that there are different ways and having my own kids I thought maybe that my upbringing wasn't always very helpful and started to wonder about that and wanting to be a better parent really.

"I ended up doing an introduction to counselling 20 years ago, and then carried on counselling training with some gaps in between – working in a women's refuge and things like that. I did person-centred counselling training, and my tutor was really involved in Hakomi and she brought in little elements of that or she told us something about it; and I was really interested in mindfulness and did my dissertation on that. I finished my diploma in 2005 and then I thought I'll do a degree - it looked like they (BACP) were going to say all psychotherapists must have a degree. I thought *I actually love learning, so I'll just carry on, this is so good*. Also, it was a bit of *what if I lose this?* And *I'll continue to learn, which is just going to help me; and I love my tutors*. So, I finished the BA in 2008 with first class honours, which I was pleased with."

Finding a fit with Hakomi, looking back from an IFS lens

Sue: "I'd already started to dabble a bit in Hakomi, attending some of the intro days and then the trainings, and I really liked it and I got loads from it. I don't know if you know much about Hakomi?

Emma: "I've read Kurtz's book (2015) but other than that I don't have personal experience of how it's done in a session or anything like that. I'd be interested in your take on it."

Sue: "So, there are key elements to it; and one is this sense of mindfulness and loving presence – your intention to be with the client in loving presence, which is basically Self-energy."

Emma: "Ah ha, yes."

Sue: "But it could be a part that's doing that, do you know what I mean? I was thinking about it later, you could still have some part kind of trying to be loving. But this is the Hakomi take on the Buddhist principle of loving presence, which was really helpful. One of the ways they help you to connect with that is finding something you appreciate in the other person so you can feel this sense of loving presence, and I really love that. It was really helpful to have this way of being, this place, which is a really important thing for me and, of course, Self-energy is one of the things I love about IFS.

"There's that, and then another element is that you're tracking – tracking present-moment experience, what's going on right now which I know is an important element of person-centred counselling. You're making contact statements, just noticing to the person that you are tracking. So, you might say to the person, "You've taken a breath" or "I see you sigh there" or something that lets them know you're there, you're present, you're with them, you're noticing."

Emma: "It's not the person-centred reflecting back and paraphrasing, it's more noticing something else."

Sue: "Something in that moment that…

Emma: "…they might not be aware of."

Sue: "They might not be aware of it and even if you aren't actually saying it, you're noticing it."

Emma: "Yeah, great. OK."

Sue: "So, you're kind of tracking all of that – which, later, I've come to understand could also be considered as parts-detecting. Also, you're tracking what they call 'indicators'; something that indicates your core beliefs. So, um, it might be that the person doesn't really make eye contact, or something about the pace, or the voice, or the speed, some kind of body movement … like I'm doing this now (pointing the index fingers of each hand and twirling her hands in relation to her head). You're noticing all these little signs, which give you an idea of burdens and beliefs of parts in the system. Another link to IFS is you just get curious about that: 'Oh, what is this thing that you're doing?' And then you would do what they'd call an 'experiment', and you might slow that movement down and they might do it slowly or you might do it so they could see you do it. And you're saying, 'So just get mindful and just maybe slow that thing down or do that thing and see what comes up'. So, from that, something would come up. Now I would understand that as a part that would come up, probably."

Emma: "Or more information from the part."

Sue: "More information yeah, or you might, once they've slowed that down, they might then discover some words that come with it or a memory. It's like a different way of getting to whatever is there, whatever is underneath this (does the hand movement again)."

Emma: "Almost like a trailhead? That (replicating Sue's hand movements) could be the trailhead to follow."

Sue: "Yeah, and then the other element is that you would get all this information but there would be certain things you would do. Like you might kind of 'take that voice over' so that they (the person in client role) could hear it and then something else might come up for them through hearing that. Something else would come up from them not having to say those words, or a polarised part answers that voice. Another element is that you then do something or offer something or see if they would like to try something that is potentially a 'nourishing experience'. In all this, there's this underlying principle of whatever you (the person in client role) are doing, the intention is to have a nourishing experience that is then like a different pathway ... maybe that you've not known. If you can't look at people, for example, the nourishing experience might be finding out what it's like to safely start to look at someone in a titrated way or however feels right for you. Maybe you've always felt alone, and you'd like to have someone come and sit beside you."

Emma: "So almost like the redo; a reparative kind of experience but in the external world?"

Sue: "Yeah, this is the theory, I guess. If you've not got that experience set up, if it's never happened, then how do you know what that's like? Or if that pathway isn't in place, sort of thing, just beginning to offer them a new experience."

Emma: "Hakomi teaching is that the therapist would need to bring in that idea of some nourishing experience, because the client wouldn't necessarily have that available from their own experience."

Sue: "They might not; but you could ask, you know, you might say 'What would feel ...?', but more often ... you might offer something."

Not making the full transition to the whole Hakomi process

Sue: "And that was one of the things that I didn't necessarily feel as comfortable with and didn't get comfortable with because in the meantime I discovered IFS. I don't think I ever really did that aspect of Hakomi, apart from at the trainings. That's one of the things I have found about transitions, it's just so easy to go back to what you know and it's a real challenge to kind of have confidence in this new way and to practise what you don't know as well."

Emma: "Yes, I hear you with that. It's like the persistence of 'This is for me, this is my goal, this is who I want to be: a Hakomi practitioner. I'm going to do these things and practise these things and become skilled at these things' almost wasn't there. (Sue makes affirmative noise) Instead, it's like 'I'll do some of those practices, but then, I'm not sure about that one, so I'll do what I know'. Or 'I'll only take it this far', or ..."

Sue: "Yeah, yeah, and it almost felt like I was really being mainly a person-centred counsellor who became more aware of loving presence and tracking. Yes, those were the things I feel like I really took with me and felt like they fit with me, absolutely fit with what I knew."

Emma: "Sure."

Falling back on what is already known and practised

Sue: "Equally, I guess, my client group at that time was young people, so it didn't feel quite right, partly because of my client group. Maybe if they'd come in and said 'I want to try Hakomi' it might have felt different and I'd have gone for it more, but they didn't and then IFS came along. Also, I'd get to a point where I'd get a bit stuck in Hakomi, like, *OK, this has come up for the client, but I don't know what to do with it*. Basically, in IFS language, an exile would be triggered. Something would be triggered and sometimes I felt a bit, *Oh, I don't know how to stay in this model and continue with the work* so then I'd go back to person-centred ... because that felt more comfortable or safe or I knew what I was doing more there, especially when I knew there was something that felt vulnerable."

Emma: "Yes, absolutely, that makes a lot of sense to me."

Sue: "I stayed with Hakomi a really long time. I helped on lots of trainings and stuff, and I enjoyed the feel of it. It felt spacious, there were lots of things that felt good about it but I just never really, completely, took it into my work."

Emma: "Yes, and I guess what I'm hearing is that the loving presence aspect really spoke to you (Sue agreeing) and you were able to do that as a practitioner and as a person. You enjoyed that as a client and therapist (Sue nods) but some of the 'protocol of Hakomi' didn't fit for you, so you didn't go through the whole protocol always."

Sue: "Yeah, and that might have been different if I'd kind of stepped into it more, maybe it would have got more comfortable, but it didn't."

Embracing Self-leadership

Emma: "Yes, and meanwhile IFS had come along."

Sue: "And that felt like *Ah, this really fits*, and I think that was the other thing because at that point I had a lot of parts who were looking to someone else to help me. In Hakomi, I still felt like I was looking out there for someone to help me."

Emma: "So, the loving presence was there but the notion of the leadership of that loving presence wasn't there?"

Sue: "It wasn't in me."

Emma: "It wasn't in you. It was out there; you were wanting that leadership from outside."

Sue: "Yeah, exactly, exactly. So, though I was in it – the world of Hakomi – for quite a while, it was IFS for me personally that really made me go OMG, *I've got this as well!* and that made such a massive difference. So, when I found IFS, even though it was a process to get into it and feeling confident in it took a long time, I knew I just really loved it. It made total sense. It was a relief; it was such a huge relief. After a lifetime of feeling unconfident and looking to other people I was able to think *Oh, there's some hope here.*"

Emma: "Yes, so that concept of Self-leadership really hit home. I remember earlier you spoke of that search when you became a mother and how important that concept is in that role, let alone as a therapist – that we have the resources inside us, and our kids have resources, too, if we can help them access them."

Sue: "Yeah, exactly, and I think perhaps when I was with other people – sometimes it's like that isn't it? … I could be there more for other people but not for these parts of me. I wasn't there for these parts of me."

Emma: "Got you, yes, so that was a big part of the transition you had to make at some point, that Hakomi in a sense hadn't got you to, nor really person-centred therapy; but something about the IFS and this idea of the U-turn of Self-to-part inside as well as Self-to-part outside really helped turn things around in some way."

Sue: "Massively, yes, because it did feel a bit like I'm here (gesticulating over to her left) just basically jumping from part to part – I'm in this part, I'm in this part. You know with Hakomi and person-centred it was just like one after the other (miming with her hands a pile building up in front of her) but not this kind of stability of Self and being able to relate from and to that. And that's what felt *Wow!* This was really wonderful news (gentle laughing) to just get even a hint of that felt really so hopeful; and, of course, when I did the training in IFS, I'd never heard of it, I'd never heard anything about it. It was only because Ginny Bennet brought it over here. She was very much in the Hakomi world, and was just such a wonderful soul, I thought, *Oh well, OK I'll sign up.* I didn't know anything; I turned up and trained with Schwartz in 2010. And it's weird now how much the internet and our use of it has changed. Apple had just brought out their phones, but it wasn't the way we use it now, I don't think."

Emma: "So, Ginny got him over here, over to Sheffield."

The challenges of learning IFS in the first UK cohort

Sue: "Yes, we were all in the church hall in Sheffield and then the next year we did the Level 1. It was just really, really good. ... One of the things that was difficult was the fact that ... there was no one else in England who knew about it. It was just the people who'd been on that training and, weirdly, the States seemed so much further away than it does now."

Emma: "Well, of course, yes."

Sue: "Like I could have found a therapist... well, I couldn't really afford it anyway."

Emma: "Yes, American pricing is different to ours."

Sue: "But I wouldn't have thought to; it just wasn't the normal thing to do to have Skype sessions or anything like that. So, basically, just trying to practise..."

Emma: "...with each other."

Sue: "Yes, but then it wasn't online or anything. I had to drive over to Sheffield and one person was there and we'd meet up to practise and just tried to practise as best we could really."

Emma: "Wow."

Sue: "And that 'red book' (Schwartz, 1995) was out. That was there, but I'm not really the best learner through reading. And then, I think, I did kind of start using it, but it was that same kind of pattern – a little bit of *Oh well, I know that other stuff*. So, I think working with IFS fitted some people. I'd try it and if it fitted, then I would stick with it, and I'd follow it through."

Emma: "OK, so you'd follow the whole protocol with some people if it fitted for them and they were open to it and able to do it yeah?"

Sue: "Yes, and then with other people if it just wasn't a fit, I'd still go back to person-centred. But also, once the IFS framework was in place ... it's just like, for me, and perhaps it's like this for everyone, I just couldn't get rid of it! That's it then, it's like this ... (Emma laughing) I've found something that works. I can't see life any other way now."

Emma: "I get that. There's something similar about my transition, partly I've got this supervision aspect and I want to do IFS in supervision, and I've got this supervisee who doesn't know IFS and at first, I thought *Aww. I've got all this stuff I can't use*. It's like I want to use IFS whenever I get the opportunity, it's kind of disappointing not to."

Sue: "Yes, I know exactly what you mean, I can't get rid of it. ... That was the other thing, I kept on going to the Hakomi trainings and helping, but then I got to the point where I felt like I can't really go anymore because I know this way now. Like I can do Hakomi up to a point, but then as soon as an exile is triggered, I can't not do this IFS. To me it feels like the most helpful thing I can do, so how can I not do it?"

Emma: "OK, so it almost felt unethical to not be with an exile in an IFS way?"

Sue: "For me. For someone who knows Hakomi really well, then I'm sure they would absolutely have that and hold that, but for me personally I started to know IFS more and feel like this is the zone for me. So, I ... stopped then."

Emma: "Yes, well that makes sense, almost like if you've got a foot in two camps, it's like *No, actually, I want to have both feet in one camp.*"

Sue: "Yeah, but I can bring these things which are so helpful with me (miming carrying things through the air from the left to the right and down in front of her)... but then I'll go back to IFS."

Emma: "Yes, so it's not like you've dropped it all, it's there as well, some aspects of it (Sue agreeing) but it's not *instead of* IFS."

Sue: "Yeah, definitely. I'm so grateful for it. The other thing it did was it kind of made me feel safer with people. That's another thing that Hakomi gave me – that there's the potential to feel safer with people than perhaps I would have done. That's because it's so relational, but then to kind of have that awareness you don't have to rely on them (i.e., rely on the other person for a sense of safety) because you've got this Self that makes me feel safe. I guess there's a potential for relationship, good relationship, healing relationship but, *I don't have to rely on you, it's OK if you don't say the exact right thing because I've got me.*"

Emma: "Great. Yes, yes."

Doing IFS in the early days

Sue: "So, let me think where we are. With IFS it was just this process of trying to stay with it in a bit of a desert really of not much, like really having to work at kind of connecting with people and practising. But I did, I really did, I persisted with it and used it and used it more. And at that point, I was working with kids and that added another layer of complexity because it's not as straightforward. I was working in a primary school and a high school and some of the high school students especially just loved it and would use the sand tray and I'd think, *I know it made a difference to them.* That is such a good feeling. Um, but then with the little ones it was kind of like, *OMG, this is so complex*, so sometimes I would just go, *OK, I'll have my parts step back and be in Self and just be with this and respond from that place. Just don't worry too much about trying to figure it all out.* I suppose it was almost a bit like heightened person-centred, but in Self."

Emma: "You really *being* Self to their system."

Sue: "Yeah, yeah, so um, so that was kind of like an added sort of trickiness working with children."

Emma: "Mm, so at some point did you start moving to working with adults?"

Sue: "That just gradually came in because ... I started to work for a national childrens' charity supporting families whose children were at risk of being taken into care because of issues in their family system. So that was working with individuals rather than with the whole system. It might be working with the kids, or with the parent, it could be anyone in the family system. So, then I started to work more with adults as well as with young people in the youth offending team. Again, that was a challenge. It was quite challenging really to get the young people there to engage and I was thinking at the time *This is so hard* – you know Maslow's triangle and the hierarchy of needs[1] – and thinking sometimes: *Is this exactly the right thing for them?*"

Emma: "Right, it was like they were at the bottom levels before they could do the psychological work?"

Sue: "Yeah, and sometimes it was really good, and I felt like I'd made a difference. And it was really helpful to have the IFS framework even if sometimes you were basically doing direct access and implicit direct access. And sometimes we'd externalise parts through drawing for instance, and you know kind of have clients get some awareness of their parts and how much space they're taking up and all of this. So, kind of bring it in as much as felt right for that person really without them running out the door; just trying to maintain the relationship was a big thing."

Emma: "I guess that's also a part of learning the model, how much you offer to a person depending on where they are at, with you, and in their circumstances. Sometimes they are ready for the whole protocol and sometimes they are not ready for the concept of Self, or they might be OK to externalise parts a bit. So, it's kind of recognising what you are comfortable with, what they might be comfortable with and seeing how it goes."

Sue: "Yeah, and really trusting that, because you know, sometimes, I could have parts that sometimes feel like *IFS is so helpful* or, offer 'we could do it this way', but it's not right for them. It's really trusting that intuition and noticing the parts that feel worried about using it too."

Emma: "In you?"

Sue: "In me and asking myself *What is this?* to see if it is a valid intuition that it probably wouldn't be right for that person in some way, or is it some part of me that makes an assumption that it wouldn't be right for that person and therefore I'm less in Self-energy?"

Emma: "Yes or is it a part of you trying to not do IFS by saying it's not right for them (the client) when actually your part doesn't want you trying it or something." (Sue agreeing)

Perspective

Emma: "Wow, this journey!"

Sue: "I know, it's quite nice to speak about it actually. At times IFS was just so helpful in that work with children and young people – to even begin to see how parts relate to each other in a family. Sometimes the child would have a terrible relationship with their parent, it had just gone off the rails. And just to help them get a bit of awareness that they have this part that comes up in them and that triggers that part in the mum and then the mum does this and da da da, and underneath there's still love."

Emma: "Yes, really helping the kids almost know that mum's got parts, too, that are triggered and that gives potential for 'And there's more to mum than just her parts'.

Sue: "Yeah, and sometimes having a conversation, you know saying, 'Do you want me to speak to them (the parent) and try to explain some of this a little bit?'"

Emma: "OK, so you would educate the parents sometimes as well (Sue agrees). Great. And that brings hope to the systems."

Sue: "Yeah, and just to get that understanding that underneath all of that there is something they have in common which is that they actually do really care about each other or there's something there that is connecting in some way."

Emma: "And by that, do you mean Self, and the positive intention of the parts or …?"

Sue: "Both, … the parent is getting angry but underneath that they are worried, or they want you to stay on the rails because of whatever, they don't want you to be hurt."

Emma: "Yeah, absolutely."

Sue: "So, kind of this capacity to see it in different ways, to reflect on it with a different perspective. So, then I just started to have a private practice and started to see more adults. I still see some kids, but mainly adults."

(After some discussion regarding Sue having gained a Master's Degree in Dance and Somatic Wellbeing, the discussion moves on to explore the role of supervision in Sue's IFS journey.)

Learning, supervision, and loneliness

Emma: "I'm thinking about you being a learner. You love learning, and also, by the sounds of it, you like reflecting, learning through reflecting. I wonder about the role of supervision in your journey. I don't know if you've got any thoughts on that about where you are now or where you've been in IFS or Hakomi or person-centred or ..."

Sue: "Yes, that's a really good question. I think it's been at times a bit tricky because I do have some IFS supervision, but I also have my 'normal', that is, person-centred supervision and my supervisors who've been ongoing throughout. I have to have this regular monthly supervision and I've always kept that as person-centred and it's not because I think it should be person-centred but just because there wasn't anyone that was here and a supervisor, so it's just been like that. So, I've felt a bit like in my supervision, I've always been translating for them my thinking or having to do something to explain it. But I've had really wonderful supervisors, too, who kind of hold that and are just very relational and really good at getting me to reflect and stuff but it would have been perfect, to have someone who was person-centred and had done IFS. That would have been just a dream, and if they'd had some experience working with children. But I couldn't get all of those elements, so I went for someone who was person-centred and had the experience with children."

Emma: "Yes, tricky."

Sue: "At times, it's felt like a little bit lonely. This could be my parts; well, it will be my parts, because there's not been ... as I'm describing this whole journey I'm thinking, *You're on your own doing that, you're on your own knowing that, no one else in the room knows anything about that – how you are seeing the world ... and what you know.*"

Emma: "So really pioneering in a sense. And that brings some loneliness because you didn't have people who knew what you were doing or trained with you; or a supervisor to supervise you. ...I guess partly this is why I'm writing this book, because of the loneliness. I also have experienced some loneliness in some aspects of my work. I wondered *And how does IFS fit with EMDR? And how does it fit in supervision?* All these questions I've been kind of dealing with in my own head mostly, not with anybody else and I kind of want this book to be like a companion, so somebody doesn't feel so alone. And, thankfully, now people do have more access to IFS supervision, or they might have an IFS supervision group that somebody in the States, a lead trainer, runs for them or ... It's not going to be as lonely as your journey but even so, there is quite a bit of aloneness. I guess there is in learning anything, but there is particularly in learning something that is not yet mainstream."

Sue: Exactly, I totally agree with you, Emma; and I really relate to that constant kind of tussle in my mind of *Does this fit with that? And how does this fit with that?"* And then that shift of, *OK, if I was doing that model, I'd be doing this but I'm trying to step into this model so what response is then called for?* It's a real ..."

Emma: "... It's quite a big ask."

Sue: "It is, isn't it? I'm really glad you're writing this."

Emma: "Well, I'm delighted that I've had this time to talk to you because this is so what I was hoping for. Hearing about your journey has really brought to life all these different aspects of transitions, of learning something new and then learning something new again and what do you maintain all the way across or what do you drop. It's a big, big thing. And it's something that happens outside the training room as well. You know, you're with your young offenders or you're with your child client who comes with a parent and that's where you kind of learn it. And then in your own head when you try and work out *What happened, what went wrong, what did I do there, and what was OK?* It's like the training room fills in just a little piece of the jigsaw, maybe a bit of blue sky and the other stuff we kind of gather for ourselves from other places or bring it in from a different jigsaw (miming creating a jigsaw from pieces in the air). 'Yeah, that fits there!'" (laughing)

Sue: "It takes so much courage – and those times when it goes wrong, when you don't make the right call and it's so painful, too, and how that then lands on our parts."

Emma: "Or the shame and the fear, I used to get so angry when I was first learning IFS. In my Level 1 training I had two very different trainers/therapists and I was(moving her head looking from side to side and speaking in an exaggerated voice) *They're not doing the same thing! And it doesn't relate to what's on my page!* (Sue laughing) It nearly fried my brain. Parts would get so angry and tussle with *I don't know what's going on.* Yes, so there's so much to work through."

Working with our parts

Sue: "It's such a massively courageous thing. We're kind of talking about this other layer we're asked to do as IFS therapists which is to work with our own parts, *Oh, I've just discovered this part and now I need to work with this part,* or *Now I see this part needs some attention.* It's huge really, isn't it?"

Emma: "Yes, and I guess, all the things we've been talking about in terms of the transition, dropping things, taking things forward, you do that if you learn anything like if you went from person-centred to EMDR. But the additional extra that you are now raising is this U-turn aspect of working with our Self-to-part relationships and that's a whole other thing to hold and deal with."

Sue: "It totally is, and that journey which initially for me was faltering, to say the least – partly because of the fact that we were just working with each other because that was all that felt available and affordable. That commitment to really working with your parts and the parts that stop that and the parts that make you forget (Emma laughing) like Jeez, those mysterious parts that somehow are just 'murkying' things… you know what I mean?"

Emma: "Those 'parts that we can't quite spot as parts'. That makes me think of us having our own therapy. We can work with our own parts but it's helpful to have other people who can help us all the way through the protocol or whatever. That's a whole new area of learning as well for me. Because even though I know IFS, my parts don't. If I've got a protector that's been active since I was six, they're not going to have the answers that the parts who've studied IFS are going to have. So, I'm going to have to go through that whole hope-merchanting thing afresh with each protector potentially and it's lovely when my therapist can just do all that for me, hope-merchant to my parts. It's great."

Sue: "Even though you know the model, when someone's doing that with you and they're kind of saying the words that we need to hear of the protocol, parts are like, they genuinely come back with things … as if they've read the book of IFS: 'But if I don't do that what will happen?' It's like they've read the book, but they so *haven't* read the book!"

Emma: "I so get what you say, it's like those six or seven protector fears[2] or (however many), it's like they've read that page and they pick number five. But it's not, that's truly what they believe."

Sue: "Yes, and … it's news to them that they could be helped or that the system won't be overwhelmed. They're genuinely like 'really? OK, I'll give it a try'."

Emma: "Yes, and I guess that speaks to me of how amazingly this whole therapy has kind of been fine-tuned and comes from people's real experience (Sue agrees), which gives me more confidence or gives me confidence as well as my Self's confidence which is kind of nice. Although I've still got to put the work in, exiles that still need healing, and their protectors aren't giving up what they're doing, not until they're sure."

Sue: "It's a big commitment, isn't it?"

Emma: "Yes, it's a life-long commitment and a lifestyle commitment, I guess, for me, and it sounds like for you."

Sue: "Sometimes they just go and do their thing these parts, like those political parts I have."

Emma: "Yes, who feel so strongly about stuff."

Sue: "Yes, I'm always curious about those ones. It takes time to get to those ones."

Emma: "Yes, it does, there's a real wisdom in the timing of things, I find."

Sue: "And the fact that they're not just carrying your stuff, they're carrying ..."

Emma: "Yes, so almost like if something in the outside world isn't ready, things on the inside aren't ready either or vice versa ..."

Sue: "Yeah, and just this kind of like the complexity and the weight of cultural and legacy and ancestral burdens; sometimes they also feel like important pieces of information."

Emma: "Yes, absolutely. Wow!"

Sue: "Does that seem OK or is there anything else you want to ask, does that cover the main things?"

Emma: "It feels kind of complete somehow."

Sue: "I feel the same."

[Over the past decade and more, Sue Smith has been part of the IFS UK team of Nicola Hollings and Olivia Lester, Krissy Tingle and Liz Calvert. She currently assists on IFSI training programs and runs IFS workshops.

This discussion took place in November 2020 and since the interview Sue has continued to enjoy integrating dance, movement, somatics, Hakomi and creativity with IFS.]

An excerpt from a supervision session with Paul Khosla (December 2020)

Paul is working with me with a view to gaining his individual consultation hours to become an IFS certified practitioner. He has come to IFS therapy after a career as a multi-skilled bodyworker and now specialises in Craniosacral therapy, Chinese Herbal Medicine, and IFS, either separately or integrated together to suit each client.

We have had four supervision sessions over three months and Paul is in individual IFS therapy. With Paul's permission I am sharing below an excerpt from our most recent supervision session. I include this in the book because, for me, it is a great example of the type of work/exploration/attention that needs to take place in transitioning to a new modality – in this case IFS.

Paul: "Is it OK if this session I bring some 'themes'?"

Emma: "Absolutely if that's what your system needs."

Paul: "One of the things I'm noticing is I struggle to manage the continuity of the work from session to session. I don't know how much to refer back to the previous session or even the original agreement or contract for what to focus on, and how much just to work with whatever is present in the system at the time."

Emma: "OK, I guess from here, I'd say that's a pretty common thing for a therapist to struggle with at this stage and I'm wondering how to respond. (*After taking some time to go inside, I decide to be curious rather than to teach*) I'm realising that this might be familiar to you from your bodywork – how much to go with what the client presents in the moment and how much to check on what brought them in the first place or both or ...*"

Paul: (*Closing his eyes and being inside for a moment or two and emerging with a wry smile*) "Well, I'm realising there's the acupuncture style of working: 'I know what's wrong. I'm the expert. I'll fix it, that's my job.' There's also the cranial style of working: 'Let's see what's present in the system to work with while gently bearing in mind the original presenting issue.' (*More time inside with eyes closed*) Then there's a part who when the going gets tough kind of moans: 'Why are you doing this? Why do you put yourself through this? It's too hard, it will all go wrong, and you'll feel like a failure.'"

Emma: "You might feel shamed?"

Paul: "Yes. And, I'm just realising, these parts are easily swayed by the client. Where the client stands in terms of the therapist being the 'expert' or the 'follower' affects how I am in sessions."

Emma: "That makes sense to me. And I guess to you? (*he nods*) And you are aware that underneath polarities and triangles of parts like these will lie exiles[3]? (*see Figure 11.1 which depicts a common polarity between a part wanting to be the expert, polarised with another part wanting to have the client be the sole expert and a third part trying to resolve the dilemma by giving up.*[4]) That these parts protect exiles? (*Paul signals yes*) Are you in therapy and have somewhere to take this?"

Paul: "Yes, yes, I am. I'm wondering if perhaps the client and I have become diverted or lost focus? There's also a part who judges the client or an element in the parts I've mentioned of judging the clients for expecting me to be the expert. So that's fairly normal ... to have these inner conflicts?"

Emma: "Yes, absolutely and I appreciate you bringing them here like this. The more you work with your protectors and heal the exiles, the more conscious choice you will have to be clear about what to work with and when. There's one thing I wanted to mention: bear in mind also that the client's protective system is set up to keep you away from exiles. Get curious about whether the client's preferences are to do with avoiding doing the work and perhaps respond to that in some way that feels right to you."

Paul: "That's helpful. The next 'theme' I want to bring is my system's perceived lack of a scientific explanation for the IFS process. A part is really frustrated with that. I know Ecker's Therapeutic Reconsolidation Process (TRP) (Ecker et al., 2012) but would you be able to speak to that?"

Emma: "Sure (*Stopping to take a pause to consider what to share and where to begin*). I guess the first thing I want to share is the example of the lemon. I mean that when we suck a real lemon and when we imagine sucking a lemon the same places in our brains will be activated or 'light up' (Hamilton, 2014). I'm not sure the body and mind distinguish between what is real and what is imagined and that seems relevant to the IFS processes in the inner world."

Paul: (*Seeming relieved*) "Yes, I see, that's helpful."

Emma: "Also, I'm aware of the different types of memory. That there is implicit body memory and how in therapy as an adult we follow the body back with curiosity, and images, words and thoughts come that were not necessarily there in the first place when we began with the body. So, are they created by the body or by the imagination or were they there already and we discovered them? I don't know in my own head[5] whether these come forth from the work or are 'added into it' and I guess, if I'm in Self and the client is in Self when we're moving through the steps of healing, I believe I don't need to know the answers to those questions.

"I also want to say, that I can appreciate your part's frustration, and I don't have a similar frustration myself. I have a part who likes some idea of how things work – like with EMDR, there are several different theories for how it works, and they are just that *theories*."

Paul: "This part gets frustrated that no one knows who or what Self is … you know, which part of the brain relates to what. Polyvagal theory is popular and everyone talks about it as if the vagus nerve is one thing when there are 12 cranial nerves and the one everyone is talking about is the 10th cranial nerve."

Emma: "Ah, this part of you really likes to know the details. I get that, and unfortunately, as far as I know that sort of detail for IFS isn't available yet. I believe it's being worked towards, and I think Dick had his brainwaves measured while doing a therapy session or something to try and find answers to these questions. I guess maybe the pandemic might have interfered with completing that work. Again, I can really get that part's frustration and (with a grin and feeling playful) I'm just wondering if this part has met Self yet?"

Paul: "Hmm. Well, I hope it was OK having an 'odd session' like this. It's really great to have the space I can bring this to."

Be the expert   **Follow the client**

It's too hard – give up

Figure 11.1 Triangle of conflicted protectors

> *Emma:* "Absolutely, this is great work. Conversations like this need to happen alongside your learning and practising the model. Facing what is triggering you and deconstructing and reconstructing who you are as a professional and exploring what you believe and don't believe is really important. I appreciate being part of this."

Notes

1 Maslow's Hierarchy of Needs is represented as a pyramid of ascending needs, beginning with more basic practical needs at the bottom rising to self-actualisation at the top. See *Motivation and Personality* (1997).

2 The Online Circle month 4, 4.1, (Schwartz et al., 2016) teaches about 7 protector fears. In the Level 1 Manual (2020), Pastor and Gauvain have extended the number of protector fears (pp. 60–61).

3 The Online Circle month 7, 7.2 (Schwartz et al., 2016) teaches that there are three functions of polarisations: attempting to bring balance in the system; the protection of exiles; distracting from getting to the exiles and doing deeper work.

4 The IFS Online Circle month 7, 7.2 (Schwartz et al., 2016 teaches that when two protectors are in conflict (in this case, Be the expert vs Follow the client), there is often a third protector trying to resolve or mediate the conflict (in this case, Give up, it's too hard).

5 This conversation took place more than two years ago and further to exploring some of Peter Afford's work (2012, 2020), I believe I would now frame a somewhat different reply.

References

Afford, P. (2012). Engaging the body changes the brain. *Irish Journal of Counselling and Psychotherapy*, 21(2), 8–12.

Afford, P. (2020). *Therapy in the Age of Neuroscience*. Routledge.

Alison, E. & Alison, L. (2020). *Rapport: The Four Ways to Read People*. Vermillion.

ALLEN, i. & Anderson, A. (2020, November). Overcoming depression and anxiety online summit: Interview with Richard C. Schwartz.

Anderson, F. (2021). *Transcending Trauma: Healing Complex PTSD with Internal Family Systems Therapy*. PESI Publishing & Media.

Anderson, F., Sweezy, M. & Schwartz, R.C. (2017). *Internal Family Systems Skills Training Manual: Trauma-Informed Treatment for Anxiety, Depression, PTSD & Substance Abuse*. PESI.

BACP (British Association for Counselling and Psychotherapy). (2018). *Ethical Framework for the Counselling Professions*.

Booth, F. (2023). IFS consultation: Fostering the Self-led therapist. In E. E. Redfern (Ed.) *Internal Family Systems Therapy: Supervision and Consultation* (pp. 193–208). Routledge.

Broadwell, M. M. (1969) Teaching for learning. *The Gospel Guardian*. 20(41): 1–3.

Burris, C. & Schwartz, R. C. (2022). The art of negotiation in IFS sessions – challenging protectors and workable agreements (Online Course). IFS Institute.

Catanzaro, J. (2023). Trusting Self to heal: Removing constraints to therapists' Self-energy transforms their treatment of eating disordered clients. In E. E. Redfern (Ed.) *Internal Family Systems Therapy: Supervision and Consultation* (pp. 94–108). Routledge.

Chesner, A. & Zografou, L. (2014). *Creative Supervision Across Modalities*. Jessica Kingsley Publishers.

Clarkson, P. (1993). *On Psychotherapy*. Whurr Publishers.

Clarkson, P. (2003). *The Therapeutic Relationship* (2nd ed.). Whurr Publishers.

Collins, S. (2020). *The Ballad of Songbirds and Snakes (a Hunger Games Novel)*. Scholastic.

CSTD (Centre for Supervision and Team Development) (2009). Advanced Supervision Resource Book. CSTD.

Cooper, S. & Corey, K. (2023). Serving those who served: Providing IFS-informed supervision and consultation to clinicians treating military veterans. In E. E. Redfern (Ed.) *Internal Family Systems Therapy: Supervision and Consultation* (pp. 159–175). Routledge.

Drouilhet, A. (2023). Consultation for the IFIO Therapist. In E. E. Redfern (Ed.) *Internal Family Systems Therapy: Supervision and Consultation* (pp. 64–77). Routledge.

Earley, J. ((2012). *Self-Therapy* (2nd ed.). Pattern System Books.

Ecker, T., Ticic, R. & Hulley, L. (2012). *Unlocking the Emotional Brain*. Routledge.

Erskine, R. G., Moursund, J. P. & Trautmann, R. L. (1999). *Beyond Empathy: A Therapy of Contact-in-Relationship*. Routledge.

Fisher, J. (2017). *Healing the Fragmented Selves of Trauma Survivors: Overcoming Internal Self-Alienation*. Routledge.

Floyd, T. (2023). Creating access to IFS training and consultation for BIPOC therapists – Black Therapists Rock leads the way. In E. E. Redfern (Ed.) *Internal Family Systems Therapy: Supervision and Consultation* (pp.78–93). Routledge.

Goulding, R.A. & Schwartz, R.C. (2002). *The Mosaic Mind: Empowering the Tormented Selves of Child Abuse Survivors*. Trailheads Publications.

Hamilton, D. R. (2014, October 30). Does your brain distinguish real from imaginary? https://drdavidhamilton.com/does-your-brain-distinguish-real-from-imaginary/

Hawkins, P. & Shohet, R. (2012). *Supervision in the Helping Professions*. Open University Press.

Henriques, A. & Shull, T. (Hosts). (2021, February 26). The therapeutic dose of empathy in IFS with Alexia Rothman [Audio podcast episode]. In *IFS Talks*. https://podcasts.apple.com/gb/podcast/the-therapeutic-dose-of-empathy-in-ifs-with-alexia-rothman/id1481000501?i=1000510894440

Hughes, D. (2021, January 30). The nature of transformational therapeutic change with traumatised children and young people: What needs to happen? [Webinar]. The Centre for Child Mental Health (Wellminds UK Ltd).

Hughes, L. & Pengelly, P. (1996). *Staff Supervision in a Turbulent Environment*. Jessica Kingsley Publishers.

Johnson, D. R. (1999). *Essays on the Creative Arts Therapies*. Charles C. Thomas.

Karpman, S. (1968). Fairy tales and script drama analysis. *Transactional Analysis Bulletin*, 7(26), 39–43.

Krause, P. K. (2013). IFS with children and adolescents. In M. Sweezy, & E. L. Ziskind (Eds.), *Internal Family Systems Therapy: New Dimensions* (pp. 35–54). Routledge.

Krause, P.K. (2023). Parts detecting across multiple systems: The application of IFS in consultation to therapists of children and adolescents. In E. E. Redfern (Ed.) *Internal Family Systems Therapy: Supervision and Consultation* (pp. 49–63). Routledge.

Krause, P. K., Rosenberg, L. G. & Sweezy, M. (2017). Getting unstuck. In M. Sweezy, & E. L. Ziskind (Eds.), *Innovations and Elaborations in Internal Family Systems Therapy* (pp. 10–28). Routledge.

Kurtz, R. (2015). *Body-Centered Psychotherapy: The Hakomi Method* (updated ed.). LifeRhythm.

Lingren, K. (2023). Bias: How IFS consultation can increase awareness and reduce harm. In E. E. Redfern (Ed.) *Internal Family Systems Therapy: Supervision and Consultation* (pp. 124–138). Routledge.

Malmud Smith, J. (2017). Introduction. In M. Sweezy, & E. L. Ziskind (Eds.), *Innovations and Elaborations in Internal Family Systems Therapy* (pp. 1–9). Routledge.

Martins, L. (2023). Facilitating flow: Developing a framework for integrating IFS and supervision in private practice in the UK. In E. E. Redfern (Ed.) *Internal Family Systems Therapy: Supervision and Consultation* (pp. 33-48). Routledge.

Maslow, A.H. (1997). *Motivation and Personality* (3rd ed.). Pearson.

Maslow, A.H. (1998). *Toward a Psychology of Being*. Sublime Books.

McConnell, S. (2020). *Somatic Internal Family Systems Therapy*. North Atlantic Books.

Mitchell, S. (2021, June 6). IFS and the window of tolerance with Richard Schwartz and Michelle Glass [Video]. YouTube. https://www.youtube.com/watch?v=2s3E QrrA8qc

Omin, R. (2023). Consultation with therapists who have a serious illness. In E. E. Redfern (Ed.) *Internal Family Systems Therapy: Supervision and Consultation* (pp. 176–192). Routledge.

Pastor, M. & Gauvain, J. (2020). *Internal Family Systems Institute Level 1 Training Manual*. Trailhead Publications.

Redfern, E. E. (2021). The drama triangle and healthy triangle in supervision, *Irish Journal of Counselling and Psychotherapy*, 21(1), 4–8.

Redfern, E. E. (2023). In search of Self. In E. E. Redfern (Ed.) *Internal Family Systems Therapy: Supervision and Consultation* (pp. 209–235). Routledge.

Reed, D.A. (2019). Internal family systems informed supervision: A grounded theory inquiry *Theses & Dissertations*. 27. https://commons.stmarytx.edu/dissertations/27

Reed, D. & Wooten, R. (2023). A model of IFS-informed supervision and consultation: Unblending from struggle into Self-led clarity. In E. E. Redfern (Ed.) *Internal Family Systems Therapy: Supervision and Consultation* (pp. 14–32). Routledge.

Riemersma, J. (2020). *Altogether You*. Pivotal Press.

Rogers, C. R. (1957). The necessary and sufficient conditions of therapeutic personality change, *Journal of Consulting Psychology*, 21(2), 95–103. doi:10.1037/h0045357

Rotter, J. B (1966). Generalized expectancies for internal versus external control of reinforcement. *Psychological Monographs: General and Applied*. 80(1): 1–28.

Rowan, J. & Jacobs, M. (2002). *The Therapist's Use of Self*. Open University Press.

Schwartz, R.C. (1995). *Internal Family Systems Therapy* (1st ed.). The Guilford Press.

Schwartz, R. C. (2013). The therapist–client relationship and the transformative power of Self. In M. Sweezy, & E. L. Ziskind (Eds.), *Internal Family Systems Therapy New Dimensions*. (pp.1–23). Routledge.

Schwartz, R. C. (2021). *No Bad Parts: Healing Trauma & Restoring Wholeness with the Internal Family Systems Model*. Sounds True.

Schwartz, R.C. & Redfern, E. E. (2023). An interview with Richard C. Schwartz. In E. E. Redfern (Ed.) *Internal Family Systems Therapy: Supervision and Consultation* (pp. 5–13). Routledge.

Schwartz, R. C. & Rich, P. (2020). Self-led sexuality: An IFS based model for healing, pleasure, and empowerment. [Webinars September to December]. IFS Institute.

Schwartz, R.C. & Sweezy, M. (2020). *Internal Family Systems Therapy* (2nd ed.). The Guilford Press.

Schwartz, R.C. & Young, D. (2020). Healing cultural trauma with Internal Family Systems. [Webinars May to August]. IFS Institute.

Schwartz, R. C., Herbine-Blank, T., & Krause, P. K. (2016). IFS Online Circle: Foundations of the IFS Model (online course). IFS Institute.

Schwartz, R. C., Lingren, K. & Ballard, P. (2018). Internal Family Systems (IFS) & diversity and inclusion (online course) [Webinars January to April]. IFS Institute.

Schwartz, R.C., Sykes, C. & Anderson, F. (2021). Internal family systems (IFS): A compassionate approach to trauma and addictive processes (online course) [Webinars January to April]. IFS Institute.

Shadick, N.A., Sowell, N. F., Frits, M.L., Hoffman, S.M., Hartz, S.A., Booth, F.D., Sweezy, M., Rogers, P.R., Dubin, R.L., Atkinson, J.C., Friedman, A.L., Augusto, F., Iannaccone, C.K., Fossel, A.H., Quinn, G., Cui, J., Losina, E. & Schwartz, R.C. (2013). A randomized controlled trial of an internal family systems-based psychotherapeutic intervention on outcomes in rheumatoid arthritis: A proof-of-concept study. *Journal of Rheumatology*, 40(11), 1831–1841. doi:10.3899/jrheum.121465

Shohet, R. (2021). The supervisory relationship: Difficulties and delights [Webinar January 30]. Stanton Psychological Services.

Shohet, R. & Shohet, J. (2020). *In Love with Supervision: Creating Transformative Conversations*. PCCS Books.

Steege, M. (2010). *The Spirit-Led Life: Christianity and the Internal Family System*. Create Space Independent Publishing Platform.

Steege, M. (2023). Keeping the faith with IFS: Religious and spiritual parts of an internal system. In E. E. Redfern (Ed.) *Internal Family Systems Therapy: Supervision and Consultation* (pp. 139–158). Routledge.

Stone, H. & Stone, S. (1989). *Embracing Our Selves: The Voice Dialogue Manual*. Nataraj Publishing.

Syed, M. (2015). *Black Box Thinking: Marginal Gains and the Secrets of High Performance*. John Murray.

Sykes, C. (2017). An IFS lens on addiction: Compassion for extreme parts. In M. Sweezy & E. L. Ziskind (Eds.), *Innovations and Elaborations in Internal Family Systems Therapy* (pp. 29-48). Routledge.

Taibbi, R. (2021). The four stages of supervision: Establishing a lasting relationship with your supervisee, *Psychotherapy Networker*, Nov/Dec 45(6), 26–27.

Telford, H. (2021, October 14–16). The transformative power of IFS: Bringing more Self-energy into the room and to our communities [Conference session]. 2021 IFS Annual Conference: Restoring wholeness through collective transformation, Online.

Twombly, J. H. (2013). Integrating IFS with phase-oriented treatment of clients with dissociative disorder. In M. Sweezy & E. L. Ziskind (Eds.) *Internal Family Systems Therapy: New Dimensions* (pp. 72–89). Routledge.

Winter, M. (2021). The new supervision: Are we meeting the needs of today's therapists? *Psychotherapy Networker*, Nov/Dec 45(6), pp. 21–26, 64.

Wonder, N. (2013). Treating pornography addiction with IFS. In M. Sweezy and E. L. Ziskind (Eds.) *Internal Family Systems Therapy: New Dimensions* (pp. 159–165). Routledge.

Wonder, N. (2023). Making the unconscious conscious in IFS consultation of sexual abuse, sexual offending, and sexual compulsivity cases. In E. E. Redfern (Ed.) *Internal Family Systems Therapy: Supervision and Consultation* (pp. 109–123). Routledge.

Yalom, I. D. (2001). *The Gift of Therapy*. Piatkus Books.

Appendix I
Competencies for self-assessment

A: *Foundational IFS Competencies*
- Reliable access to Self-energy
- Listening to presenting problem and identifying key parts involved
- Assessing client's external constraints
- Introducing the model, if applicable
- Getting client buy-in for IFS therapy or coaching, etc
- Contracting to work on target part(s)
- Using the 6 Fs appropriately
- Addressing manager fears and/or negotiating with firefighters
- Helping clients unblend
- Working with polarised parts
- Direct access (implicit and explicit)
- Hope-merchanting to individual parts
- Co-creating a therapeutic relationship

Foundational IFS Competencies contd
- Helping client extend/increase Self-energy to target part
- Contracting with exiles to not overwhelm (if needed)
- Able to complete all steps of healing (witnessing, unburdening, etc)
- Facilitating/aiding client redo and retrieval
- Inviting positive qualities
- Facilitating IFS-style integration
- Switching to new target part
- Facilitating expression of appreciation to parts from Self
- Parts-detecting (self and other)
- Using IFS supervision fully
- Using IFS therapy well

B: *Additional Therapeutic Competencies*
- Knowing how to position yourself accurately and transparently in your marketplace
- Being boundaried and attending to practicalities (breaks, endings, referring on)
- Taking a history and client intake
- Contracting and gaining informed consent; attending to diversity, equity and inclusion
- Holding confidentiality

B: *Additional Therapeutic Competencies (Contd.)*
- Taking notes
- Working ethically
- Being a reflective professional
- Relational skills (e.g., recognising ruptures and making repairs, appropriate use of self-disclosure)

C: *Additional Competencies for* Your *IFS Context*

Appendix II
Reflecting on previous training and existing practice

Exploring role and relationship

a) In your core training or previous experience, what were you taught, or what did you learn and embrace about the nature of the therapist/ healer/professional role[1] and the therapeutic/healing/supervisory relationship?[2]

Below are phrases to prime your thinking as you reflect. Endnotes provide and signpost you to key IFS information on therapeutic concepts and practices.

- Being the good enough mother
- Congruence, empathy[3], and unconditional positive regard heal
- Contact outside sessions is solely for scheduling purposes[4]
- I act as a midwife
- I am a secure attachment figure for the client to earn secure attachment.
- I am an active listener
- I am the expert[5]
- I follow the client, I don't play the expert
- I give clients homework
- I grandparent the next generation of therapists
- I hold coaching clients accountable
- I identify as a wounded healer
- I interpret[6]
- I let the client lead
- I make up for client deficits[7]
- I motivate the other
- I offer a reparative relationship[8]
- I'm a change agent
- I'm a gatekeeper to the profession
- Therapist neutrality is key

Reflecting on healing and change

b) In your core training or previous profession, what were you taught, or what did you learn and embrace about the nature of healing[9] and change?[10]

Below are phrases to prime your thinking as you reflect. Endnotes provide and signpost you to key IFS information on therapeutic concepts and practices.

- BLS kick starts the AIP
- Catharsis heals[11]
- Challenging cognitive distortions[12] needs sustained application
- Diagnoses help treat symptoms
- Humans have healing/change inbuilt; I hold the space for that to happen
- Integration[13] is the goal
- It's my job to heal the other/make the pain go away/stop
- Medication treats chemical imbalances
- Mentalising is healing
- New behaviours need rehearsing
- People are both wounded and well
- Psycho-education and homework are important
- Separating the past from the present heals
- Supervisory conversations cause transformative ripples
- Symptom management because healing often isn't possible
- The client will need to be dependant for a while
- The relationship is the mechanism for change
- The Therapeutic Reconsolidation Process (TRP) heals
- The therapeutic relationship heals
- Unpacking the vulnerability/ trauma reduces its impact
- Working with the transference is crucial[14]
- Working with the unconscious is key[15]

Attending to psychological pain and trauma

c) In your core training and/or postgraduate supervision training, what were you taught, or what did you learn, embrace, or keep to yourself about the nature of psychological damage and psychological pain?[16]

Below are phrases to prime your thinking as you reflect. Endnotes provide and signpost you to key IFS information on therapeutic concepts and practices.

- A person-centred approach heals anything given time
- Coaches steer clear of the past/pain
- I've failed as a therapist if my client hurts/cries/doesn't cry
- Pain must be avoided at all costs
- Permanent healing is impossible
- Protocols depersonalise
- Some clients are so damaged, I must reparent them through the developmental stages
- Supervision and therapy are separate; supervisors rarely work directly with supervisee's vulnerability
- Trauma treatment involves specialist knowledge and training

d) In your previous training and studying, what were you taught, or what did you learn about working with trauma?[17]

- Boundaries are important; I don't get sucked in[18]
- I can't do trauma work as I don't know how to work with the body
- It's easy to re-traumatise clients
- Resourcing the client is essential before approaching the trauma
- Titration is key and a phased approach is key
- Trauma is a response not an event
- Work within the window of tolerance[19]

Multiplicity

e) In your core training, or previous experience what were you taught, or what did you learn about multiplicity? How do you understand multiplicity[20] now?

Below are phrases to prime your thinking as you reflect. Endnotes provide and signpost you to key IFS information on therapeutic concepts and practices.

- Complexes
- Archetypes
- Critics[21] are internalised others
- God is multiple, it makes sense humans are too
- Parts aren't real, they are purely metaphorical[22]
- Multiplicity signifies fragmentation

- Drama Triangle roles
- I'm the same towards all my clients
- Id, ego, superego
- Introjects[23] need special handling
- None
- Parent, Adult, Child
- I treat the person in front of me

Notes

1 Ch. 6 The Role of the Therapist in IFS (Schwartz & Sweezy, 2020).
2 See Module 5 pp. 131–150 of the Level 1 training manual (Pastor & Gauvain, 2020).
3 Compassion is preferable in IFS to empathy as explained in the following: "When we empathize, our exiles identify with the client's exiles, which is a threat to our protectors who fear being overwhelmed. When we feel compassion, even if our exiles identify with the client's exiles, our protectors don't mobilize because the Self is unafraid of being overwhelmed (Schwartz, personal communication, March 17, 2014)." From Getting Unstuck, p. 23, by Pamela K. Krause, Lawrence G. Rosenberg and Martha Sweezy. In *Innovations and Elaborations in Internal Family System Therapy* edited by Martha Sweezy and Ellen L. Ziskind, copyright 2017 by Taylor & Francis. Reproduced by permission of Taylor & Francis Group.
4 In IFS Continuity Program month two's live call (Schwartz, 2021) Schwartz fields a question/judgment about caretaking parts of a therapist taking a middle-of-the-night call from a client. He speaks from his experience working with clients' extreme protectors when he would not restrict contact to scheduled appointments. Coming from Self rather than from a caretaking part, he might be flexible regarding contact as clients heavily into working with exiles may need more access than at other times. This will also depend on the level of need of the client.
5 See Schwartz & Sweezy, 2020 p. 42.
6 See Schwartz & Sweezy, 2020, pp. 19, 52.
7 "The resource of Self is innate and does not have to be provided by the environment through good-enough parenting, and/or long-term attachment-style individual therapy" (Schwartz and Sweezy, 2020, p. 17). "Self knows how to love and help parts and does not need to be coached nor developed." (ibid, p. 48). IFS is not an additive model (Schwartz and Sweezy, 2020, p. 106).
8 An IFS therapist's relationship with a client is very important and, in some ways, corrective or reparative. See Schwartz and Sweezy, 2020, p. 20 and p.22.
9 Schwartz and Sweezy, 2020, pp. 48 & 50-51, for example.
10 The Self of the client is the healing agent, or as Schwartz and Sweezy (2020, p. 84) put it "the primary attachment figure for the client is the client's Self". See also Ch. 3 The Self in Schwartz and Sweezy, 2020.

11 McConnell (2020, p. 106) writes: "IFS is not a catharsis model. The point is not to purge emotions but to restore voice to the silenced, exiled parts and have them be heard by Self."

12 IFS is a constraint-releasing model in which beliefs are burdens and can be let go of (Schwartz & Sweezy, 2020, p 106) rather than countered.

13 The concept of integration has a particular meaning in IFS, Schwartz and Sweezy (2020, p. 39), write "… when we are in a Self-led state, we have a sense of continuity and integration. We feel more unified—because we are."

14 In IFS when transference and countertransference emerge, they can be worked with in terms of parts of the client and parts of the therapist (Schwartz & Sweezy 2020, p. 20).

15 Schwartz writes, "For years I did not want to accept that psychodynamic therapists were absolutely right on certain topics … people are driven by unconscious phenomena … the perspective of IFS provides a different understanding of—and way of working with—these traditionally psychoanalytic observations. We can enter the unconscious and interact with it directly, asking questions …" (Schwartz & Sweezy 2020, p. 19).

16 See Ch 10 for my understanding of IFS teaching regarding emotional and psychological pain.

17 In the IFS Continuity Program month 2, live call Schwartz (Schwartz & Rich, 2020) suggests that IFS professionals working with clients with high levels of trauma show they care about them and reciprocate their love in ways that the clients can trust and recognise. Though, obviously, how "boundaried" one is depends on one's training, experience, choice, context and so on.

18 In the same consultation as mentioned in Endnote 4 above, Schwartz reveals an interesting take on the therapist being available for the call by suggesting that the therapist's guides or the client's may have had a hand in the therapist being awake at that time.

19 Schwartz is clear and vocal that therapists proficient in and confident in using IFS do not need to teach grounding or affect-regulation skills and that Self has a "huge window of tolerance" (Schwartz & Sweezy 2020, pp. 270–271).

20 See Schwartz and Sweezy, 2020, pp. 24–42, Ch. 2 Individuals as Systems.

21 Inner critics are not just internalised others (Schwartz & Sweezy 2020, p. 55).

22 Schwartz teaches very clearly that parts are inner beings with complete personalities, they are not metaphors (see Schwartz & Sweezy 2020, p. 266, Ch. 20 "The Laws of Inner Physics").

23 Introjects and introjection, (Schwartz & Sweezy 2020, p. 22) and "Phenomena such as 'internalisation' and 'introjection' are viewed in IFS as burdens that can be released rather than as qualities of a part" (pp. 38–39).

Index

Note: Page numbers in *italics* refer to figures, page numbers in **bold** refer to tables. The letter "n" indicates an Endnote.

The term therapist includes practitioner. The terms supervision, supervisor and supervisee include consultation, consultant and consultee.

Exercises have generally not been included in the index.

9781032153094